D0909970

PATRICIA MONK is a member of the Department of English at Dalhousie University.

The concepts of the Jungian theory of personality have long held considerable interest for Robertson Davies, both outside his fiction and as the explicit subject of *The Manticore*.

This interpretive study discusses Davies' use of Jungian psychology as both a structural and a thematic device and touches on related themes of illusion and the nature of reality.

Drawing extensively on early reviews and articles, Monk sketches the background to Davies' preoccupation with psychology, revealing its influence on his early writings, including the effect of the Jungian concept of the persona on *Shakespeare's Boy Actors* and the concept of the shadow on the Samuel Marchbanks material. She also notes the introduction of the important themes of illusion, as a mask for reality, and ambivalence which are extended in the Salterton trilogy, *Fifth Business*, and *The Manticore*.

Monk concludes that *World of Wonders* reveals an apparent but unsuccessful attempt on Davies' part to get away from Jungian psychology, and an exploration of alternative myths of human identity: the romance myth of the hero and the Spenglerian myth of the Magian soul.

PATRICIA MONK

The Smaller Infinity:

The Jungian Self in the Novels of Robertson Davies

UNIVERSITY OF TORONTO PRESS

Toronto Buffalo London

© University of Toronto Press 1982
Toronto Buffalo London
Printed in Canada

ISBN 0-8020-5544-3

Canadian Cataloguing in Publication Data

Monk, Patricia, 1938–
    The smaller infinity

    Includes index.
    ISBN 0-8020-5544-3
    1. Davies, Robertson, 1913–   – Criticism and
    interpretation. 2. Davies, Robertson, 1913–
    – Knowledge – Psychology.   3. Jung, C.G. (Carl
    Gustav), 1875–1961.   I. Title.
    PS8507.A95Z75   c813'.54   c81-095145-2
    PR9199.3.D3Z75

D2568zm

To

my mother and my sister

and

in memory of my father

9-28-63

Contents

Acknowledgments / ix

Prologue: The Smaller Infinity / 3

1   The History of an Affinity / 5

2   Towards Ambivalence / 22

3   A Choice of Worlds / 43

4   Interface / 74

5   A Country and Its Foreigners / 105

6   The Naked Magician / 147

Epilogue: Untreadable Ground / 182

Notes / 185

Index / 207

Acknowledgments

Without the help of a considerable number of people this book would never have been published. In particular I would like to thank Robertson Davies himself for his interest in and generous encouragement of my work; Professor D.O. Spettigue of Queen's University for equally generous encouragement as well as helpful and provocative criticism; and Professor R.L. McDougall of Carleton University who began the whole affair by lending me a copy of *Fifth Business*. I would also like to thank those of my friends who cheerfully answered innumerable questions in their specialities.

Parts of the book have appeared in articles in *Studies in Canadian Literature, English Studies in Canada,* and *The Dalhousie Review.* I would like to acknowledge the courtesy of the editors concerned in allowing the material to reappear here.

This book has been published with the help of a grant from the Canadian Federation for the Humanities, using funds provided by the Social Sciences and Humanities Research Council of Canada, and a grant to the University of Toronto Press from the Andrew W. Mellon Foundation.

The Smaller Infinity:
The Jungian Self in the Novels of Robertson Davies

We must always bear in mind that,

despite the most beautiful coincidence

between the facts and our ideas,

our explanatory principles are none the less

only points of view.

C.G. Jung

Prologue: The Smaller Infinity

The Jungian element in the fiction of Robertson Davies has become increasingly well known and discussed since the publication of *The Manticore*. But *The Manticore* is only the obvious manifestation of a much larger Jungianism (to borrow Davies' own word for the body of Jung's theory and ideas of human personality) which can, I believe, be shown to inform all his work from the earliest journalism to the latest novel and collection of talks. All of it (even the plays, which, for various reasons including lack of space, I do not discuss) can be shown to relate in an important and integral way to his knowledge and understanding of Jung. Furthermore, Davies has explicitly expressed his interest in and admiration for Jung in interviews, talks, and lectures, and, with all due respect to the proponents of the 'intentional fallacy,' what a writer as articulate as Davies considers personally important demands attention.

Jung, however, is a large subject. His *Collected Works* comprise twenty thick volumes, and there are two volumes of letters as well as his share of *The Freud/Jung Letters*; his topics range from modern psychiatry to medieval alchemy. But, as Frey-Rohn points out, 'whether the question was one of knowledge or abnormal psychic phenomena, it was always the mystery of the human personality that fascinated Jung and challenged his thinking.'[1] Only in the intensely personal and poetic 'Seven Sermons to the Dead,' however, does Jung attempt to define the human personality: 'Man is a gateway, through which from the outer world of gods, daemons, and souls ye pass into the inner world; out of the greater into the smaller world. Small and transitory is man. Already is he behind you, and once again ye find yourselves in endless space, in the smaller or innermost infinity.'[2] Here 'man' is seen as a microcosm of the universe, and, just as the outer universe is infinite, so is the inner universe of the human personality: it is 'the smaller ... infinity.' In his clinical and general writings, Jung resolves the mystery of the human personality in the concept of the self – a human being developed to the fullest potential of that inner infinity – as part of a complex theory of the nature of consciousness and the unconscious in the individual and in the group which also includes the concept of the archetypes of the unconscious. It is on this massively structured, complex theory that Davies draws, but within the whole sweep of Jung's ideas and theories Davies' own interest is quite specific. He concentrates on the 'mystery of human personality,' and is fascinated by what, ultimately, we mean by the term 'human.'

There is, however, one slight complication concerning Davies' Jungianism. Because Jung's ideas are so extensive, complicated, and littered with pitfalls for the unwary, Davies' preoccupation with them (as I show in some detail in my first chapter) is also long and complex – although it contains, perhaps, fewer pitfalls. His Jungianism is implicitly present in his early journalism as well as in his extended writings of that period, but it is in the novels of the Salterton and Deptford trilogies, which are the works of his full maturity as a writer, that Jung's theories can be seen most clearly as the shaping power in the stuff of his fiction. Moreover, in the course of his long involvement with Jung, Davies' response to the man and to his theories is constantly changing and developing, and there is no reason to suppose that, however finally Davies seems to have dealt with them in *World of Wonders*, he has in fact completely finished with them.

Such a relationship is more than the simple involvement or preoccupation that I have been calling it so far. Yet to call it an obsession would do Davies a serious injustice. The appropriate term, I believe, is 'affinity' as defined by the *Shorter Oxford English Dictionary*: 'relationship by inclination ... spiritual attraction,' for this definition gives full weight to the tone and importance of the relationship. Consequently I have chosen to begin my discussion of Davies' Jungianism with the history of an affinity.

1 / The History of an Affinity

The history of such an elusive thing as an affinity is not an easy one to trace, although there is at least a clearly defined starting-point in Davies' work itself. Moreover, because this affinity is deep-rooted and at the same time qualified, any discussion of its manifestations in individual works must be preceded not only by a general outline of those manifestations, but also by an examination of how (in general terms) the Jungian material is assimilated or transmuted into Davies' fiction. For the former we must look at Davies' many and varied discussions of literature and psychology; for the latter we must turn to Jung because, not surprisingly, it is in terms of Jung's discussion of the creative process that Davies may best be understood.

The extent of Davies' fascination with Jung's theories is articulated in a conversation with Donald Cameron.[1] At that time Davies was working on *The Manticore,* and the conversation makes clear not only how indirectly and slowly he approached Jung, but also that his approach was made only after a great deal of other study. Davies began with an interest in psychology in general, he reveals, even before he was introduced to it as a formal discipline: 'I had been interested in the notion that this line of thought existed even when I was a schoolboy.' The formal introduction, he goes on to explain, was made at Queen's University where 'there was a remarkable professor of psychology ... Dr George Humphrey ... [who] talked a great deal about Freud, about whom he knew a lot, and so I was led to read some Freud.' It is perhaps not surprising, then, that Freud should have taken precedence in his thought and reading. In Davies' recollection Freud 'enchanted' him because he was 'saying explicitly things which I had vaguely apprehended as possibilities,' and he was encouraged to continue, developing an 'enormous enthusiasm' for Freud and reading through the whole of his collected works.

His reading, of Freud in particular and of psychology in general, is evident in his earliest published writing where it finds considerable practical application. His Oxford thesis on Shakespeare's boy actors is primarily a study of a particular theatrical convention – that of the boy actor in female roles. Above and beyond this general interest in the relationship of the boy actor to the audience, there is also a marked and informed interest in the mental processes of the people involved, both actors and audience. The choice of this particular convention (now largely obsolete, although not wholly extinct) as his topic suggests a more particular interest, and his attempt to explain something so alien, generally speaking, to our modern experience develops into an interesting practical application of the psychology of dramatic illusion.

A more extended practical application of psychology to the subject under discussion begins with his earliest book reviews for *Saturday Night* which appeared when, as literary editor (from November 1940 to February 1942), he was writing the weekly feature 'The Bookshelf.' In reviewing *Hoaxes* by Curtis McDougall, for example, which deals with what Davies describes as 'ugly and malignant swindles,' he reflects on the psychological effect of reading about trickery and cheating:

The immediate effect of this book upon the reader is to make him mistrust everyone and everything he meets, for it is a merciless exposure of gullibility. After some reflection, however, he is even more impressed by the slenderness of those ties which hold us to the body of faith and assumption which we agree to call Truth; how very easy it would be to break those ties and launch us all upon a sea of completely logical falsehood; then comes the disquieting reflection: Is that what has happened? Are we all living as victims of a gigantic, immensely complicated hoax?[2]

Not all his psychological allusions, however, are as solemn as this. He discusses the script of Gershwin and Hart's *Lady in the Dark* more lightly: 'To settle her difficulties she [the heroine] goes to a psycho-analyst, who fixes things for her. The handling of psycho-analysis in this play is enough to make Sigmund Freud whirl in his grave like a teetotum, but it is good drama.'[3] The casual humour of this, his first specific reference to Freud, might seem to indicate no more than a fashionable nodding acquaintance with the more obvious aspects of Freudianism, but elsewhere he provides clear evidence that his knowledge of Freud is much more than casual. In another review he describes Theodor Reik's *Masochism in Modern Man* with a clarity which derives from a considerable knowledge of the subject:

Freud regarded masochism primarily as a sexual perversion. Subsequent investigators, like Dr. Karen Horney, have accepted the masochist as a person content to take a subordinate part in life, as he does in sexual matters. Dr. Reik advances the theory that masochism is actually a concealed form of aggression, and that it is present, to some extent, in great numbers of men and women and even in whole races. It can become a tremendous social force, and its method is that of Victory Through Defeat.[4]

More than just information about Freud's theories is revealed in this particular review: Davies also acknowledges his very considerable respect and admiration for Freud in the opening paragraph in which he describes Freud as 'perhaps the greatest of all social critics.'

His admiration for Freud and his work does not preclude a knowledge of and tolerance for other practitioners of psychology. In particular, a review of Virginia Case's *Your Personality: Introvert or Extravert?* indicates Davies' familiarity not only with Freud, but also with Adler and Jung: 'It is difficult to swallow Jung's psychology whole and to anyone who knows anything about the quarrels of the various psychological schools, Miss Case's criticism of Freud as too extravert, and Adler as too introvert, is highly amusing. But this book is an admirable exposition of one aspect of psychological truth, and as such I am prepared to recommend it warmly.'[5] It is interesting that this brief remark is the only reference to Jung during this early period of reviewing. Its isolation and its offhand tone certainly support his statement that 'it is difficult to swallow Jung's psychology whole,' although he must have digested enough of it to be able to review the book.

A definite change in Davies' attitude to Jung is, however, evident during his second period of reviewing for *Saturday Night* which lasted from January 1953 until March 1959. Nevertheless, it was not an immediate change. It was preceded by considerable discussion of Freud, for Davies reviewed at length each of the three volumes of Ernest Jones' standard biography of Freud: volume 1 was reviewed on 20 February 1954, volume 2 on 21 January 1956, and volume 3 on 15 February 1958.[6] In these reviews the tone of respect and admiration for Freud is maintained, and extensive reading in his work is mentioned: 'Although I think that I may say that I have read all of Freud's principal works, and many comments upon them, I have never read anything before Dr. Jones' book which suggested how great his early struggles had been.'[7] In the last there is also a tone of considerable impatience with writers who work from only a slight acquaintance with Freud's theories: 'The trouble with too many authors is that they will not read Freud, and ponder his work, nor will they let him alone; they are content with a shallow and erroneous impression of his work, and what they produce is, in consequence, a muddled romanticism.'[8] Davies' admiration of Freud, therefore, appears unchallenged during the period spanned by these reviews – a period in which Davies makes no mention of Jung except to compare him unfavourably to Freud in the review of volume 2. The comparison is made in discussing Ernest Jones' qualities as a biographer: 'He has Urbanity, as his treatment of the defection of Jung and Adler from the Freudian school of psychoanalysis shows; he is generous to a fault. Compare what he writes with Jung's cranky, self-justifying account of his break with Freud, and we soon see which is the greater man.'[9] Soon after the appearance of the review of volume 3 in 1958, Jung's *The Undiscovered Self* was published,[10] and a change of attitude in favour of Jung becomes dramatically apparent. Davies took the opportunity not only to review it appreciatively and at some length, but also to recommend Violet de Laszlo's selection from Jung's writings, *Psyche and Symbol*, as well as P.W. Martin's *Experiment in Depth*, and Herbert Read's essay on Jung in *The Tenth Muse*.[11] The tone of the review is generous to both Freud and Jung:

Though there are few educated people today who would disclaim any knowledge of the theories of Sigmund Freud, there are thousands who cheerfully admit that they know nothing about the work of C.G. Jung. The probable reason is that there is still a somewhat scandalous murk hovering above the head of Freud, whereas the murk which surrounds Jung is of a mystical character, and mysticism is out of fashion. When a century has passed it may well appear that Jung's ideas about man and his problems are more generally applicable and more practically helpful than those of Freud ... Jung's beliefs have made ... slow headway in the world. He talks about souls, and thus he offends the soured intellectuals who prefer to call their immortal part a psyche; he rebukes the bustle and strenuosity of the churches, and thereby he alienates them, for it is much easier to be busy than to be holy. Nevertheless, Jung's ideas make a slow headway, and as a therapeutic method his form of depth-psychology seems to be both safer and more lastingly effective than Freud's.[12]

The new warmth of his praise for Jung is striking, and it is clear that he has come to prefer him to Freud. He gives as his reason a dissatisfaction with Freud's 'reductive train of thought, which is very welcome to the young mind but becomes ... less welcome to the older mind' – reductive, that is, in its 'tendency to feel that the sexual etiology of neurosis explains everything.'[13] Freud's view of religion as essentially an illusion also never fully satisfied Davies, who admits to having even then the curiosity about the nature of religion which has steadily become more and more apparent as a theme in his novels. The older Davies ('after forty' he points out, and indeed when his preference for Jung first became apparent in print in 1958 he was forty-five) began to find Freud less attractive.

At this time he began 'reading and re-reading and reading again the collected works of C.G. Jung.' Here he found the same kind of intellectual excitement that he had previously found in Freud: '[Jung] had had the intellect and the ability to go into very deeply, and to talk about superbly, things which I had dimly apprehended, and so I was eager to follow.' But there was also Jung's less reductive attitude – his refusal to reduce everything to a sexual etiology – which Davies sees in part as the result of a childhood similar to his own, 'going to country schools, living with country children, knowing country things, being quite accustomed to animals and the sort of rough and rather sexually oriented – but in an ordinary, daily way – life of the country person.'[14] Furthermore, there was 'a much more ... satisfying attitude towards religion' in the 'Jungian feeling that things tend to run into one another,' which made 'enormous sense' to him. It was this satisfaction with the 'enormous sense' of Jung which determined the nature and extent of his subsequent response to psychology.

Davies himself seems to regard his change of preference as slow and inevitable. Certainly it should not have surprised the careful reader of his work at that time. Until he reviewed *The Undiscovered Self* in 1958 Davies' explicit remarks about psychology reveal his preference for Freud, but there are a number of points in the material (the book reviews up to 1958) which suggest a natural affinity with Jung. It might be said of him at this time that, although his conscious preference is for Freud, his soul is naturally Jungian.

The affinity with Jung manifests itself in Davies' preoccupations with subjects bordering on psychology but not included in it, which are products of what may roughly be termed the 'spirit' in humankind. In his discussions of folklore, myth, literature, magic, and romance, Davies can repeatedly be found in agreement with Jung and in disagreement with Freud. To begin with, Davies is profoundly serious about the need to keep in touch with our primitive roots through folklore: 'But no Canadian who hopes to understand the literature or the life of his own country or any other can do so without at least a passing glance at some of the important books on folklore which have been written since the beginning of the twentieth century; to have completely missed "The Golden Bough" is as serious as to have completely missed psycho-analysis.'[15] This view is clearly in agreement with Jung's emphasis on the value of folklore for the modern mind: 'We shall therefore turn to folklore ... In myths and fairytales, as in dreams, the psyche tells its own story, and the interplay of the archetypes is revealed in its natural setting as "formation, transformation/the eternal Mind's eternal recreation."'[16] For Jung, folklore has the specific value that the movements of the psyche can be understood as general human processes more easily in it than in individual case histories. For Davies it has more general value as an extension of our understanding of ourselves as human beings. Both agree, however, that folklore has value because it extends humanity's self-knowledge. In their agreement, both differ greatly from Freud who, referring to 'the popular treasure-house of myths, legends and fairy tales,' comments: 'The study of constructions of folk-psychology is far from being complete, but it is extremely probable that myths, for instance, are distorted vestiges of the wishful phantasies of whole nations, the secular dreams of youthful humanity.'[17] His judgment that it can offer only 'distorted vestiges' of 'wishful phantasies' is in sharp contrast to Jung's opinion that it contains the essence of psychic movement undistorted by individual variation. Equally clearly, Freud demonstrates a somewhat reductive attitude to the primitive past, similar to his reductive approach to sex, an approach which Davies already was finding unsatisfactory.

In his discussion of the value of literature, Davies can also be seen to be more in agreement with Jung. For both of them, the value lies in the immediacy and truth of literature in relation to human experience. Immediacy, for Davies, is the ability to affect the reader, and the importance he attaches to doing so can be seen in his review of John Cowper Powys' *Owen Glendower*:

The Welsh, more than other western peoples, unite the past and the present in their everyday thought; there is an Eastern quality about the Welsh which makes them so synthesize their history that events which would appear to be of purely historic interest have for them a topicality as great as that of the latest newscast. This quality accounts in a large measure for the immediacy of John Cowper Powys' latest book. It might have been an historical novel if it had not been written by a Welshman; as it is, the book is as direct in its appeal as any work of pure imagination.[18]

Literature also in Davies' view derives value from its truth, but not, he insists, necessarily from literal truth: 'there is a widespread tendency to believe that the more poetic a thing is the less likely it is to be true. For myself, I must say that I have come to assume that if something is genuinely poetic – poetic in the great sense – it is certainly rooted in some great truth.'[19] Poetic truth, however, is a mystery – in the original sense of the word, something occult – which defies explanation, just as, finally, does the creativity which produces literature: 'is even the art of the actor so resistant to analysis and description as the art of the writer?'[20] Jung also suggests that the value of literature derives from its immediacy and truth, although he attributes this immediacy and truth to the presence of archetypes:

The impact of an archetype, whether it takes the form of immediate experience or is expressed through the spoken word, stirs us because it summons up a voice that is stronger than our own. Whoever speaks in primordial images speaks with a thousand voices; he enthrals and overpowers, while at the same time he lifts the idea he is seeking to express out of the occasional and the transitory into the realm of the ever-enduring. He transmutes our personal destiny into the destiny of mankind, and evokes in us all those beneficent forces that ever and anon have enabled humanity to find a refuge from every peril and to outlive the longest night.[21]

This view is in sharp opposition to Freud's view that art is an instrument of 'mental hygiene' rather than of spiritual health, as a succinct passage in his *Autobiographical Note* demonstrates:

The realm of imagination was evidently a 'sanctuary' made during the painful transition from the pleasure principle to the reality principle in order to provide a substitute for the gratification of instincts which had to be given up in real life. The artist, like the neurotic, had withdrawn from an unsatisfying reality into this world of imagination; but, unlike the neurotic, he knew how to find a way back from it and once more to get a firm foothold in reality. His creations, works of art, were the imaginary gratifications of unconscious wishes, just as dreams are.[22]

Thus Freud leaves art only a utility value inasmuch as it is clinically therapeutic for the individual as well as for the race. In contrast, Davies by his recognition that literature is 'rooted in some great truth,' and Jung by his description of it as lifted 'out of the occasional and the transitory into the realm of the ever-enduring' attribute to literature a transcendent value, a value which has a part in the full realization of the individual self of each human being.[23]

A similar parallel between Davies' and Jung's views is evident in their remarks about magic. Davies suggests that not only is 'magical power' required to elucidate the poet's mystery,[24] but magic is still a factor in the human experience today: 'even a more than ordinarily intelligent person may believe that an author's genius can be borrowed by borrowing his idiosyncrasies. This is, of course, belief in magic, and we all believe in magic when it suits us.'[25] This view of the operation of magic in the twentieth century is clearly in accord with Jung:

Civilized man contemptuously looks down on primitive superstitions, which is about as sensible as turning up one's nose at the pikes and halberds, the fortresses and tall-spired cathedrals of the Middle Ages. Primitive methods are just as effective under primitive conditions as machine guns or the radio are under modern conditions. Our religions and political ideologies are methods of salvation and propitiation which can be compared with primitive ideas of magic, and where such 'collective representations' are lacking their place is immediately taken by all sorts of private idiocies and idiosyncrasies, manias, phobias, and daemonisms whose primitivity leaves nothing to be desired, not to speak of the psychic epidemics of our time before which the witch-hunts of the sixteenth century pale by comparison.[26]

For Freud, on the other hand, magic is simply the appearance of unrecognized repressions, a failure to connect properly with reality:

there is a vast range of what are called superstitious beliefs from which few people are completely free ... Freud showed convincingly in the section on Superstition in his *Psychopathology of Everyday Life* that such beliefs come about through the projection into the outer world of thoughts, fears, and wishes which have undergone repression; not recognizing their presence in his unconscious, and yet feeling signs of their presence, the subject concludes that they are operative in the outer world ... Such beliefs operate in the most primitive level of the mind, that of animistic magic and belief in the omnipotence of thoughts. There is everywhere plentiful evidence of this level of pre-scientific mental functioning. It is a level of the mind the strength of which is hard to overestimate, and with only the rarest of people has it been completely superseded by a more objective contact with reality.[27]

It is not the existence of the primitive in the psyche of modern humanity which is at issue here but the refusal to recognize any intrinsic value in the primitive. It is this refusal which separates Freud from Jung on this point. It is also clear that Davies shares Jung's fundamental point of view that the primitive element in our psychic make-up is valuable and that, although the magic that worked for archaic man does not work for us, we have our own magics which are effective.

Furthermore, there is for Davies more to magic than simply a common form of human belief: magic is also a component of romance. It is a desirable element of life, as he notes in one review: 'The author almost succeeds in making us seem a romantic and fascinating people, and if we shared her belief Canada might develop some of the dashing adventurous spirit which she so badly needs.'[28] 'To fascinate' originally signified 'to charm by witchcraft' (or 'black' magic – by *goetia* rather *magia*).[29] Whether the magic were black or white, we would be a magic people possessing those qualities of romance which go with magic. Davies insists, however, on a specific definition of romance in which he separates its true nature, as he sees it, from the debased popular conception. In one of his occasional pieces of theatre criticism for *Saturday Night* he is explicit: 'Only ballet permits us those flights into Romance from which we return strengthened, cleansed and with a livelier appreciation of beauty. For Romance is not weakness, as some people appear to think; it is a source of strength and inspiration; it is a necessity to anyone who is not either a stoic philosopher or a clod untroubled by a spark.'[30] What Davies says here clearly identifies romance with Jung's discussion of modes of experience where the impact of the archetypes 'enthrals and overpowers' the reader or audience (CW 15:129:82). Romance therefore becomes a psychic mode of truth – and like all psychic truths, it has 'a double face ... It is ambivalent and therefore symbolic, like all living reality.'[31]

One face, the constructive, 'light' face, Davies has already identified in his remarks on the cleansing and strengthening powers of ballet and the presentation of beauty found in it. But there is also a dark and destructive obverse. Davies identifies this side of romance as it appears in Dylan Thomas: 'The romantic impulse, when it is strong, is desperately dangerous to those whom it possesses. The romantic attitude toward life – if such demoniacal possession may be called an attitude – is one in which feeling always takes precedence over reason or reflection. The poet of popular fancy – the man of weak nature pursuing pretty fancies and communicating them in verse – is the caricature: the reality is what Dylan Thomas was, a man shaken and destroyed by a bardic fury.'[32] This possession of the artist by the creative power within him, which Davies describes as demonic, is a

thoroughly Jungian concept which Jung describes in some detail: 'We
would do well, therefore, to think of the creative process as a living
thing implanted in the human psyche. In the language of analytical
psychology this living thing is an *autonomous complex* [Jung's italics]. It
is a split-off portion of the psyche, which leads a life of its own outside
the hierarchy of consciousness. Depending on its energy charge, it
may appear either as a mere disturbance of conscious activities or as a
supraordinate authority which can harness the ego to its purpose'
(cw 15:115:75). Freud, on the other hand, sees the creative impulse only
as a prolongation into adult life of infantile fantasizing by the conscious ego, made acceptable to others by 'the essential *ars poetica* [which]
lies in the technique of overcoming the feeling of repulsion ... between
each single ego and the others,' and concludes that: 'In my opinion ...
our actual enjoyment of an imaginative work proceeds from a liberation
of tensions in our minds.'[33] The reductive attitude evident in this account of the creative process was clearly antipathetic to Davies' developing inclination towards the transcendental element in human nature
which Jung expresses so forthrightly.[34]

From these early writings, then, Davies' affinity with Jung emerges.
Myth, magic, and romance are all closely linked with both psychology
and art as they relate to the shaping of the universe by the human mind.
The evidence of the literary reviews up to 1958 reveals the strength of
the affinity, as well as the fact that towards the end of this period what
had previously been in Davies an almost unconscious affinity with
Jung gradually becomes a conscious preference. The preference
surfaces in the review of *The Undiscovered Self*. From here on Davies'
references to Jung become favourable, and his assimilation of Jung's
theory deepens to the point where it can provide, in *The Manticore*, not
only the infrastructure but also the superstructure.

This assimilation does not necessarily mean that Davies draws on
Jung deliberately and consciously for the stuff of his fiction, as if continuously consulting a file of index cards to see what his characters should
be doing (or not doing) in order to be acting in a manner consistent
with Jungian theory. For one thing, Davies himself has said that he does
not work with Jung very much in mind and that he was surprised to
discover how close the connection was.[35] For another, as Northrop Frye
points out, 'scholars ... are apt to think of an influence transmitted
from A to B as a large body of consciously held ideas. This is hardly the
way that influence exerts itself among poets ... the derivation is mainly
an unconscious derivation of phrases, even words.'[36] Jung's ideas inform
(or form from within) the whole of Davies' fiction in this way, without

Davies' conscious choice and with additional force because his view of human nature coincides so closely with Jung's. Ultimately, the patterns in Davies' fiction conform to patterns described by Jung as the archetypal figures of the human unconscious psyche.[37] Because the word 'patterns' implies a conscious activity on Davies' part, however emphatically I may state the contrary, perhaps a closer look at the nature of the patterns and at the informing process is necessary.

The term 'archetype' is not Jung's own. It was borrowed by him from other writers to refer to what he at first called 'primordial images' and 'dominants of the collective unconscious,' each of which 'represents or personifies certain instinctive data of the dark, primitive psyche, the real but invisible roots of consciousness' (cw 9(i):271:160). Indeed, as Jacobi points out, Jung found it necessary as late as 1946 to distinguish

between the 'archetype per se' that is, the nonperceptible archetype which is present only potentially in every psychic structure, and the actualized archetype which has become perceptible and already entered into the field of consciousness. This actualized archetype appears as an archetypal image, representation, or process, and its form may change continuously according to the constellation in which it occurs. Of course there are also archetypal modes of action and reaction and archetypal processes, such as the development of the ego or the progress from one phase of age and experience to another; there are archetypal attitudes, ideas, ways of assimilating experience, which, set in motion under certain circumstances, emerge from their hitherto unconscious state and become visible, as it were.[38]

This definition suggests an enormous number of potential and actualized archetypes. Yet only a limited number of the actualized archetypes (which I shall simply call archetypes) and archetypal processes are commonly encountered in the lives and dreams of individuals and in the myths (and consequently the literature) of groups. These are, so to speak, primary archetypes, and the most important are the shadow (the dark, other self), the anima/animus (the contrasexual image: female for a man, male for a woman), the magus (the old wise man), the sybil (commonly called the old wise woman), and the self (the total integrated personality, conscious and unconscious). The most important archetypal process is the process of maturation or development into the self – a process which Jung came to call 'individuation.' In their relationship to each other and in their parts in the development of the self, the archetypes move in what might be called figures (as in the figures of a dance). It is with these primary archetypes (in their Jungian definition) and this archetypal process of individuation that I am chiefly (though not exclusively) concerned in my discussion of Davies' fiction.

It is at first not easy to see how archetypes of the unconscious can be used as part of those shaping techniques of fiction which involve conscious patterning by the writer. An explanation which would apply to Davies is provided by Jung himself in his essay, 'The Relation of Analytical Psychology to Poetry,' where he draws a clear distinction between two types of creative activity. A writer of the first type 'is wholly at one with the creative process, no matter whether he has deliberately made himself its spearhead, as it were, or whether it has made him its instrument so completely that he has lost all consciousness of this fact. In either case, the artist is so identified with his work that his intentions and his faculties are indistinguishable from the act of creation itself' (CW 15:109:72). A writer of the second type, however, 'is not identical with the process of creation; he is aware that he is subordinate to his work or stands outside it, as though he were a second person; or as though a person other than himself had fallen within the magic circle of an alien will' (CW 15:110:73). Jung explains this in terms of the poet's ability to yield to the thrust of the creative autonomous complex: 'Accordingly, the poet who identifies with the creative processs would be one who acquiesces from the start when the unconscious imperative begins to function. But the other poet, who feels the creative force as something alien, is one who for various reasons cannot acquiesce and is thus caught unawares' (CW 15:115:75). In the writer of the first type, then, the shaping techniques available to the conscious mind will not distort or hamper but facilitate the transmutation of the unconscious content into verbal form because, during composition, the conscious and unconscious levels of the psyche are completely integrated. Furthermore, in the transmutation by the shaping techniques, the unconscious content will lose nothing of its energy. In my opinion, Davies belongs to the first type; he is 'at one with the creative process,' and in the production of his fiction we see this integrated psyche at work. Immersed in Jung's theory and thoroughly in sympathy with it, Davies by conscious choice allied to unconscious instinct transmutes it creatively into the stuff of his fiction.

Jung's account of the ends and aims of the creative element also illuminates Davies as a writer. In both types of creative personality the creative element is, Jung maintains, autonomous; elsewhere he compares it to a child growing in the womb or a plant growing in soil (CW 15:122:78). Although it is autonomous, however, it is not without purpose for, even though the conscious ego may have little to say in the choice of direction, the creative process is nevertheless directed to a particular end (*telos*). For Davies, as for Jung on a much larger scale, that *telos* is an understanding of the nature of human identity.

For both men, the starting point in the search for this understanding is the concept of self-recognition. One of the most important things for each individual to recognize in the universe is him or her self. Each must be able to answer the question, 'What is that "I," that Identity, or id-entity, which I know to be myself?' In one way the distinction between I and not-I is simple and is made by a baby in the first months of life: the distinction in terms of physical boundary.[39] But a further distinction has to be made, as Jung indicates when he speaks of the primitive who sees the world around him as an extension of himself: the distinction in terms of psychic boundary.[40] Moreover, the individual must not only decide how much of what he or she perceives is self and how much not-self, but also make sure that he or she identifies it correctly, or accurately, including only the appropriate data and making the right judgments. This identification is obtained by feedback or reflection from the environment (as though it were a mirror).

Lichtenberg has said that works of art 'are mirrors: when a monkey peers into them, no Apostle can be seen looking out.'[41] But the average human ape peering into any mirror, whether work of art or environment, is more likely to see an apostle than to recognize the ape reflection for what it is. The 'apostle' reflection is an illusion, representing a non-congruence between the observer's perception of the universe (appearance) and its factual substance (reality), and arising from a bias in structuring the information received from the universe . In the monkey-apostle the bias is unconscious, and what is produced is a delusion. But sometimes the bias can be incorporated consciously to produce a fantasy (such as day-dreaming, play-acting, story-telling). The individual's task, however, is always the same: to learn to see what is reflected in the mirror of art or environment without distortion and so to learn his or her true identity.

Davies, whose *telos* I have already suggested to be an understanding of the nature of human identity, therefore proceeds by a continuing exploration of the area of non-congruence between actuality and appearance – the area of what we call illusion. This is his superstructure; concealed within it, and fed by his increasing knowledge of and affinity for Jung, is an infrastructure which may be described in terms of the archetypes and archetypal processes. The process of exploration is already visible (and open to interpretation in Jungian terms) in his earliest writing, and the complete process is divided into several stages which may be traced clearly through the chronology of his published fiction.

It is necessary first for the individual to wake up to the problem involved. The beginnings of this process may be buried in childhood (Jung gives an account of his own experience in the early chapters of *Memories, Dreams, Reflections*), but in Davies' published work this stage is illustrated in *Shakespeare's Boy Actors*.[42] Here, the consideration of a purely dramatic convention leads him to consider also (although only in passing) the psychological effect on and parallels in the minds of the people involved, and the relationship of illusion to the individual's idea of his or her identity. In Jungian terms, the archetypal figure involved here is the persona.[43]

The next stage is the development of the idea of fantasy in role-playing. This development is illustrated in Davies' creation of Samuel Marchbanks and in the exploitation of that personality in the extended corpus of the work of Samuel Marchbanks. Davies also gives an imaginative exposition of the relationship between himself and his creation in 'The Double Life of Robertson Davies' where he plays with the creation of a figure in whom we can see clearly the Jungian archetype of the shadow.[44]

The plays written up to 1956, subsequent to the thesis and contemporaneously with the literary reviews and with the Marchbanks material, are rather exploitations of the possibilities of dramatic illusion than explorations of its nature. Although there are allusions to the themes of illusion and of identity in many of the plays, they are given extended consideration only in his first play, *Eros at Breakfast* (1945), in *General Confession* (1956), and in *Question Time* (1975).[45]

In succeeding stages the development of these themes becomes much more elaborate. In the three Salterton novels Davies explores the theme of illusion in the forms of fantasy, delusion, and insanity.[46] All three concern the individual's attempt to discriminate between actuality and appearance externally, and illusion is considered negatively as deception. This has to be an early process in individual development because the more accurately we view the external world, the more likely we are to be able to perceive ourselves correctly. Simultaneously, Davies explores the theme of identity in the working out, in the lives of his central characters (Solly, Veronica, and Monica), of the ego's encounters with the primary archetypes (shadow, anima and animus, sybil, and magus). He offers, furthermore, in the third book of the trilogy, a glimpse of the development of an autonomous human personality analogous to the Jungian self.

Up to this point in his fiction, the theme of illusion is developed elaborately (in some degree, perhaps, overshadowing the Jungian elements), but it is not thoroughly integrated with the theme of archetypal identity (identity revealed in the encounters with the archetypes). Moreover, his interpretation of 'illusion' in these earlier novels, although it is susceptible to Jungian interpretation and consistent with the Jungian theme, is not defined in quite the same way as it is in the later trilogy, where it is not only conceived in much more Jungian terms, but is also integrated much more closely with the theme of archetypal identity. Consequently, although the concept of illusion in the two trilogies is similar, it is not identical, and I make a corresponding shift in the nature of my discussion of it in the Deptford trilogy.

In *Fifth Business* the idea of illusion as religious faith is examined.[47] But paradoxically, in religious faith the appearance is all the actuality that it is within our capacity to realize; hence there is a sudden twist in the concept of illusion: it becomes a form not of deception, but of perception, and therefore positive. Within the same novel, Davies applies this positive concept of illusion to the internal non-congruence between the individual's self (actuality) and his mask (appearance), and demonstrates that recognition of this illusion reveals to us our role in life (as Dunstan Ramsay discovers his role as 'fifth business'). But, since the complexities of illusion can be resolved only in paradox, *Fifth Business* also explores at length the possibility of defining human identity in Jungian terms as the Jungian self: the transcendent, ambivalent personality born from the clash of the opposites in the human psyche. This novel, appearing after a twelve-year silence, marks an important transition in the pursuit of a definition of human identity. In it Jung's name is mentioned only once as 'that old fantastical duke of dark corners.'[48] Like the tip of an iceberg, however, this single reference hints at the massive infrastructure of Jungian ideas below the surface of the novel.

This Jungian infrastructure becomes visible superstructure in *The Manticore*, where the themes of illusion and of identity are explored in terms of the Jungian archetypal process of individuation.[49] In addition to discovering *what* he is (role), the individual must also discover *who* he is (identity). In Jungian terms role is the equivalent of the persona, and for Dunstan Ramsay the discovery of his persona is sufficient. For David Staunton, however, it is not: the persona is only one element of his identity, and he must recognize, accept, and synthesize all the separate archetypal elements before he can discover who he is. David Staunton's story introduces a further paradoxical twist in Davies' exploration of the nature of illusion: all these archetypes are illusions because they are simply the appearance in us of psychic energies (whose appearance is the only thing we can recognize about them), so that the unity we recognize and accept as our identity (our self) is also an illusion. But, although Davies uses Jungian theory and analytic framework as super-structure and visible *mythos* of the novel, he ends in a finely balanced ambivalence towards the possibility that Jungian theory can provide an approach to defining human identity. To some extent, his ambiva-lence is inevitable. Jung himself was aware that his archetypes are 'specific illusions.'[50] His discussion of the unconscious and the self in 'Psychology and Religion' also suggests the nature and inevitability of Davies' predicament at the end of *The Manticore*, for Jung points out that the nature of the unconscious is such that 'there is bound to be an illimitable and indefinable addition to every personality.'[51] Davies is con-fronted with the fact that he has gone as far as psychology (which must necessarily limit and define) will take him, and that what lies beyond is no longer psychological but spiritual.

In *World of Wonders*, the investigation of the themes of illusion and of identity is continued, and they are examined in wide-ranging discus-sions of truth and illusion, reality and falsehood, good and evil, God and the devil, using metaphors of identity and identification drawn chiefly from that home of illusion, the theatre (and its scion, film), and implying that identity must be defined in spiritual as well as psycholog-ical terms.[52] It is significant to note that, according to Davies, the job of theatre (and therefore also, we may legitimately infer, of illusion) is to illuminate the spirit.[53] Davies goes beyond mere ambivalence in *World of Wonders*, however, for in it he presents his story through alternative myths of human identity, the myth of the hero (as found in fairy-tale and folklore) and the myth of the Magian soul (as articulated by Speng-ler), in a fictional matrix from which Davies says he has deliberately tried to exclude 'Jungian trappings' as far as possible.[54] Consequently, the novel is interpretable in Jungian terms, but the Jungian *mythos* or superstructure of *The Manticore* is reduced to its original function as infrastructure. Davies seems to be trying here to reduce Jungianism to the status of one alternative myth among several available as frames of reference for the discussion of what it is to be human, but he is not wholly successful.

In conclusion I would suggest that, although the Jungian *mythos* is important to Davies, it is not important only *per se*. It is not only an end in itself, but also the means to an end: the discovery of the nature of human identity. In his discussion of literary influence, Frye says that 'Every creative person has an interconnected body of images and ideas underneath his consciousness which it is his creative work to fish up in bits and pieces. Sometimes a phrase or a word comes to him as a kind of hook or bait with which to catch something he knows is down there.'[55] For Davies the hook or bait which enables him to fish up in bits and pieces his understanding of human identity is his affinity with Jung. Rather than merely the word or phrase which Frye suggests as the means by which influence is transmitted among poets, it is Davies' empathetic response to the totality of Jung's thought and work which gives him access to the 'something he knows is down there.'

The history of Davies' affinity for Jung is a complex one because both Jung's ideas and Davies' development as a creative writer are themselves complex. I propose now to examine in detail the works which form the separate stages of Davies' development in order to illuminate some of the complexities.

2 / Towards Ambivalence

Samuel Marchbanks tells us that Robertson Davies appeared on the stage very early in life: 'He first appeared in public at the age of three in the Ferguson Opera House, Thamesville, as an Israelite child in an opera called *Queen Esther*; he was one of a chorus of children in bathrobes and turbans who hailed the victorious Mordecai in a spirited number in which the words "We triumph, we triumph" were repeated with typical operatic persistence.'[1] His enthusiasm for the stage proved permanent, and it was not surprising that after he had begun to study psychology the two interests should have become linked. A symbol of that link may be found in the word *persona*, which is both a dramatic term and a term in Jungian psychology, and which in Davies' earliest writing provides an important key to the themes of illusion and identity. *Persona* originally designated a player's mask; Jung uses it to designate 'the form of an individual's general psychic attitude towards the outside world.'[2] To Davies the connection between the two must have seemed both obvious and yet also worth further investigation, for in *Shakespeare's Boy Actors* he explores one of the aspects of Elizabethan theatre involving the concept of the persona in a very striking way.

In the ancient theatre the player's masks were actual physical masks, but in the English Elizabethan theatre masks were no longer worn. They had been replaced by certain conventions of delivery, movement, make-up, and costume which were designed to contribute to the overall convention of dramatic illusion which Davies defines, necessarily in elementary terms, in *Shakespeare for Young Players*: 'in writing plays we must always consider an element which we will call the Convention of Dramatic Illusion. A convention is something which everyone agrees to believe, whether it is true or not, and there are many conventions in the theatre.'[3] Among them, in the Elizabethan theatre, was the convention that women's roles were always played by boys or young men. It is this convention Davies makes the subject of his thesis and examines in some detail.

The production of dramatic illusion in the Elizabethan theatre was, Davies suggests, largely achieved by two complementary factors: imagination and technique. Imagination was needed not only by the audience, but also by the players: 'It needs imagination to play a fairy or a witch in broad daylight, and the Elizabethan theatre must have been a great breeder of imagination, for nothing daunted it, and not merely Oberon and Titania, but Caliban, Puck, and Ariel walked its enchanted stage' (SBA 170–1). So the boys would, in a very real sense, have collaborated with the audience in the use of imagination to produce the dramatic illusion of their femininity.

Technique, however, would reinforce the players' imagination, and the boys would be thoroughly trained in a variety of skills which would also contribute to the production of dramatic illusion. From Davies' discussion of the boys' training it becomes clear that part of the assistance would come from the very simplicity of the technique involved:

The boy actor would also be required to spend some time in learning the management of his dress, for the clothes of an Elizabethan lady were always heavy, and the dresses of the players were celebrated for their richness ... A boy, when dressed for his part, would seem much taller and more impressive than ordinarily he would, and there can be no doubt that this would form a striking contrast with his appearance of fragility when he was forced by the circumstances of the play to change into his doublet and hose ... Make-up, too, would do much to create the illusion of beauty. (SBA 32–3)

For the audience, the illusion would be further reinforced by what may be called the 'stock response' in Elizabethan dramatic writing. According to Davies: 'The tendency of Elizabethan dramatic technique, and particularly in the plays of Shakespeare, is to take great pains to present the boy actor as a woman, and not to disturb that illusion when it has been established. This was rendered much easier by the existence in the minds of Elizabethan audiences of well-defined types of the heroine, the hero, and the villain' (SBA 57).

The method behind this and other techniques was, he suggests, mixed, and in this mixture lay its strength: 'The Elizabethan stage does not adhere either to the formalism which its limited resources seemed to impose upon it nor does it make a determined effort toward naturalism, but wavers between the two and employs each in turn and both together as the whim of the dramatist dictates. It is extremely likely, however, that this eclectic method of presentation was a strength and not a weakness, and provided a very adaptable medium with which to work' (SBA 38). The effect of the over-all dramatic illusion was, Davies indicates, a greater objectivity, a great distancing between the stage reality and audience's reality, which allows sudden reversals of attitude involving the boy/woman: 'It was the greater objectivity of the Elizabethan stage illusion which made possible such scenes as that in *All's Well that Ends Well*, where Helena, immediately after a soliloquy in which she confesses her love for Bertram, is used merely as a foil for Parolles, feeding him with questions as he gives a harangue about virginity' (SBA 175). Davies' point seems to be that because these two scenes are within a play the audience would not regard Helena's behaviour as inconsistent, as they probably would if they encountered a similar change in a woman in real life. What this discussion of objectivity and the production of the boy/woman illusion emphasizes is that the audience was not apparently in any danger of confusing the actor with his female role. What was seen on the stage was a representation of a woman, not a real woman, and the audience was no more likely to confuse one with the other than we would be to confuse a store dummy with a real human being.

The boys had to be trained, however, to understand that they were producing an illusion, for any confusion about reality and pretence (any feeling, for example, that the audience would regard them as women rather than as boys playing women) would produce embarrassment, especially in scenes requiring physical love-making on the stage; to overcome it they would have had to be taught to eliminate self-consciousness: 'the first duty of an actor is to overcome his self-consciousness and to do anything that is demanded of him without embarrassment, an emotion which rapidly spreads to the audience and ruins dramatic illusion. Embarassment would be natural in an untrained boy, and his response would probably be ridiculous, but the rigorous training ... would soon fit the boy for this part of his task' (SBA 184). In fact, a boy's natural embarrassment in playing a female role, however rigorously it might be suppressed by his training for purposes of performance, was probably his greatest safeguard against becoming confused between himself and his role. The distinction between his male self and his female role would operate unconsciously.

For the actresses of the eighteenth, nineteenth, and twentieth centuries who played in Shakespeare, however, no such safeguard existed. The result, as Davies points out, was confusion not only between identity and role, but also between real and fictional people:

The autobiographies of the actresses themselves are filled with raptures about their Shakespearian roles, and during the nineteenth century the transports become almost comic, so intensely do the ladies identify themselves with their favourites among Shakespeare's heroines. It was during this period that Helen Faucit wrote feelingly and self-revealingly of her experiences as an actress in Shakespeare, some of her roles evoking experiences almost mystical in character, and Mary Cowden-Clarke was so possessed by the reality of Shakespeare's women that she wrote *The Girlhood of Shakespeare's Heroines* ... in which each one is equipped with the background of an entertaining childhood and such sweet traits as the ruder-minded Shakespeare had neglected to include in the plays. (SBA 1–2)

In modern cinema and theatre, Davies points out, the confusion has spread to the audience and is evident in

the response of an audience at any sort of entertainment in which men and women are equally concerned. The personality and beauty of a leading actress are certain to beget in the male half of the audience a concern for her which is partially directed at the character whom she represents and partially at her as a popular favourite. This duality of personality is shown with admirable clarity by the more unsophisticated members of a cinema audience who, when describing the plot of a film, very frequently speak of the heroine by her own name rather than that of the character whom she represented. This personal interest is almost equally strong, although less readily confessed, among the members of the audience at a play. (SBA 178)

Today television audiences confuse the fictional characters and the actors to an even greater extent.

The relationship between a player's identity and his or her role on stage has a parallel in the psychological make-up of the individual: in Jungian terms it is the relationship between the ego and the persona. The persona (the role) is an adjustment between the ego and the outside world: 'The persona is thus a functional complex which comes into existence for reasons of adaptation or personal convenience, but is by no means identical with the individuality. The persona is exclusively concerned with the relation to objects.'[4] It further resembles a theatrical role or mask in that it is a convention: 'the persona ... is a compromise between individual and society as to what a man should appear to be.'[5] In the structure of the psyche the persona lies between the ego and the outside world in the conscious mind. It is protective as well as adaptive; but it is also susceptible to malfunction and can damage the ego it is designed to protect: 'In an individual well adjusted to his environment and his own inner life, the persona is merely a supple protective coating that makes for easy, natural relations with the outside world. But under certain circumstances it becomes too convenient to hide one's real nature behind the covering; the persona becomes mechanical. This has its dangers, the mask freezes and behind it the individual wastes away.'[6] In this malfunction of the personality in which the ego is overwhelmed by the persona, there is a clear parallel with the confusion of identity and role by the Shakespearian actresses Davies describes and by cinema, theatre, and television audiences as well.

In both cases – the confusion of identity and role in the theatre and the confusion of ego and persona in the psyche – the problem stems from the inability to distinguish between reality and illusion. *Shakespeare's Boy Actors*, therefore, can be seen in Jungian terms as an encounter with the idea of the persona, the distinction of which is a first step in the analysis of human identity. The discussion in the thesis, by exploring the importance of separating player from role, ego from persona, and, consequently, reality from illusion, can therefore be distinguished as the first step in Davies' development of the concept of human identity within a frame of reference which is clearly familiar to him and thus well understood.

The next step in this development was the gradual emergence of a fictional second self, Samuel Marchbanks. In what may be called for convenience the Marchbanks material (the newspaper columns which appeared under this pseudonym and the essay, 'The Double Life of Robertson Davies') it is possible to examine Davies' concept of the second self. Because Samuel Marchbanks did not emerge at once as a full-fledged diarist, and did not restrict himself to the diary alone, the Marchbanks material is not homogeneous in form, content, or tone.[7] Furthermore, Marchbanks is the creation of a busy, harassed newspaper editor, and thus rather haphazardly developed. We must nevertheless give him some attention as a part of his creator's exploration of human identity.

The nature and purpose of the original column were set out by Davies in the first instalment. Taking the title, 'Cap and Bells,' as his starting-point, he writes:

Why Cap and Bells? For several excellent reasons. A column must have a name of some kind, and it is preferable that the name should give a clue to its nature, should be, as it were, a brief table of contents ... But the ordinary common or garden columnist who must combine the tasks of roving reporter, book reviewer, art, music and drama critic, trained snoop and funny man all in one must choose his title with care, so that it may cover all of his many aspects. Hence, Cap and Bells ... The object of this column is to amuse and entertain. That has always been the job of the man who wears the cap and bells. But to amuse and entertain is not always to be funny; no one is more dreary than the man who is always funny.[8]

Although this introduction suggested that the column would cover a wide variety of subjects, 'Cap and Bells' and its successors rapidly became primarily book-review columns. Other topics, such as 'Why Not a Canadian Drama?' 'How Literate Are Canadians?' and 'Swinging Gilbert and Sullivan,' are included, but discussion of these wider issues is usually suggested by a book.[9]

Perhaps inevitably, and certainly appropriately in view of the utilitarian function of the column, Davies does not project Samuel Marchbanks as a personality in his own right in these reviews and discussions. In them, Samuel Marchbanks is merely a label for the reviewer – a pseudonym.[10] The name seems to have been chosen without reference to the creation of a second self; when Davies did first experiment with that, his creation was Dr Amyas Pilgarlic, whom he introduced in *Saturday Night* in December 1940:

We have been most fortunate in securing the services of Dr. Amyas Pilgarlic (a D. Litt. both of Padua and Leyden) to review our children's Christmas Books. Dr. Pilgarlic, born in 1842, was an intimate friend of Matthew Arnold and Carlyle, and first dazzled the world of learning in 1865 with his proof that the phrase, All my eye and Betty Martin, was a corruption of a medieval Latin prayer to St. Martin, beginning, Ah mihi, beata Martin. Since then he has been engaged in a conclusive study of the Ethic Dative in the Cornish Tongue, which he has graciously interrupted in order to write the present article. When approached in the matter, Dr. Pilgarlic said, with a dry laugh: I think I can do it, for after all I'm in my second childhood myself.[11]

Dr Pilgarlic made another appearance the following Christmas, but it was his last.[12] His portrait is overdrawn – Dr Pilgarlic is a mere grotesque, a caricature, suggesting that Davies was not yet deeply involved with the creation of a second self, and that Dr Pilgarlic is not really a significant figure.

The creation of a second self, however, was the next step Davies had to take in dealing with the problem of identity. And it had to be taken as soon as he became more deeply involved with the problem and felt it more urgently (although it may not have presented itself to his conscious mind as a problem). When this point was reached, Dr Amyas Pilgarlic had to be discarded as unsuitable – everything about him, including his name, gave him away as a fiction. He was, therefore, too unequivocal to serve Davies' purpose, which required a figure about whose reality or unreality no decision could be made with certainty. By the time Davies reached this point, however, he had in Samuel March-banks a figure with all the necessary ambivalence. Samuel Marchbanks had been writing book-review columns for about two years, but in these reviews there was no element of personal identity to confirm or deny his reality. He was, therefore, close enough to the border be-tween fact and fantasy to provide a suitable medium for exploring it.

The flexibility of the diary made it an obvious choice as the form of his presentation. As editor of the daily *Peterborough Examiner*, Davies may have had such practical considerations as keeping readers interested and saving time (because diary entries could, at least to a certain extent, be written up ahead when time offered). In addition, Eleanor Roose-velt's diary *My Day* and George and Weedon Grossmith's fictional *Diary of a Nobody* served as examples of the diary as an expository form:[13]

Sunday, Oct. 24th: I decided today that this column sticks too rigidly to book-reviews and expository articles, and is in imminent danger of becoming pon-derous; would it not be a good idea to keep a diary in it? After all, Mrs. Roosevelt has countless readers for "My Day"; but then, she travels about so much, and meets so many interesting people, whereas I never stir from my office and rarely speak to anyone. Still, one of the best diaries ever written was called "The Diary of a Nobody"; if one nobody can write a diary, another nobody can at-tempt it. It seems to me that most of the diaries I have read have been written with a possible reader in mind; only Pepys wanted to be completely secret, and was consequently indiscreet in his revelations; indiscretions make the best reading of all. But Mrs. Roosevelt and I are never indiscreet – at least, if we are, we have no intention of telling several thousand people about it; let them commit their own indiscretions, if they want something to gossip about.[14]

Furthermore, on the artistic level, the same flexibility produces a med-ium extremely well suited for 'experimental' writing. The diary offers the writer a loose or open form – one which is free of structural de-mands (such as plot) and of topic restrictions (such as a book-review column), but which has an intrinsic continuity in the identity of the diarist.

The diary also has an intrinsic ambivalence, even if the writer does not have publication in mind. Nobody can produce a truly objective record of the facts of his or her own life, and yet, in spite of this, some people (as Davies makes clear in discussing three published diaries) still try:

[The diary] is a form of confession. Is that the clue to these three books, all of which are of unusual interest and value? Are they in our hands because the writers were driven by an urge which they may not have understood and could not control, to confess as much as they knew of themselves – to get down on paper all of the truth that they could command? And to whom were they confessing? None of these books has been written or published in hope of gain or fame. Are these written confessions a bid for an existence after death, a perpetuation of personality?[15]

Each diary contains not the whole truth, but only so much of it as the writer can command, and consequently, as a partial truth, the diary must always lie in the middle ground between fact and fiction. It is this intrinsic and therefore relatively stable ambivalence in the form which supports the precarious ambivalence Davies is trying to achieve in creating Samuel Marchbanks as a second self. Samuel Marchbanks must be carefully balanced between a purely and obviously fantastic creation (such as the discarded Dr Amyas Pilgarlic) and the purely factual (a label for the real personality of Davies himself).

The ambivalence is further supported by the choice of material proper to the diary. Marchbanks' diary is neither a chronicle of his adventures (like that of Pepys) nor a vehicle for speculation and reflection (like the early journals of André Gide). The entries balance material from both the inner and the outer life of the diarist, sometimes within a single entry: 'My dentist told me last week that modern man eats too much soft food, which weakens his bite and loosens his teeth. But this afternoon I bit my tongue with such vigour that I nearly bit it off. I do not understand how anyone could possibly have a stronger or more destructive bite than I have. Probably I am the only writer and critic in Canada of whom it can be truthfully said that his bite is worse than his bark' (9 April 1949). That events in Marchbanks' life closely parallel events in Robertson Davies' life is revealed in Gordon Roper's Introduction to *Samuel Marchbanks' Almanack*:

Early one June evening, now twenty-two years ago, after a dinner spiced with Marchbanks tabletalk, my hosts and I talked for awhile on the verandah of Marchbanks Towers before I went on my way to see my wife and new son in the Peterborough Civic Hospital. The following Saturday evening I did what many Peterborough people did in those days – opened the *Peterborough Examiner* at the editorial page to read 'The Diary of Samuel Marchbanks.' The Tuesday entry ran: 'Was chatting today with a man who had just had a baby; that is to say, his wife actually had the baby ...'[16]

Roper also suggests that events in their inner lives show similar parallels: 'Marchbanks' feelings and opinions are those of Robertson Davies – selected, transmuted, and dramatized as a verbal performance.'

The same entry demonstrates yet another kind of ambivalence in its shifts between the mundane and the fantastic. Taking off from a neatly phrased statement of mundane fact the entry rapidly soars into the realm of the fantastic with its proposal of a book on *Radiant Fatherhood.* Samuel Marchbanks plainly exists in a mundane world: 'Persuaded some other members of my household to do a little preliminary work in the garden, and then I prowled round with a camera taking pictures of them as they slaved ... Let others do the world's work; my job is to write about what they are doing' (26 April 1947). Marchbanks has a house (Marchbanks Towers), a household, and a job, but we know very little about them. They are sketched in as background, or used almost like stage props which are suggestive imitations rather than real things. In this everyday world Marchbanks wrestles with problems created by snowstorms, poor train-service, hay fever, and committee meetings. At times the treatment is completely prosaic in keeping with the subject, but more often than not the prosaic in his everyday world suddenly acquires a fantastic dimension. The Marchbanks relatives provoke this transmutation most frequently, either collectively or individually: 'The only time I ever got a real thrill out of one of Mrs. Bond's ditties was when my brother Fairchild came home from my Great-Uncle Hengist's funeral, and sat down at the piano and burst into "The End of a Perfect Day" in a loud plangent tenor ... Always a tactless fellow, Fairchild' (11 January 1947). His furnace is another source of inspiration to fantasy of the most varied sorts, culminating in an entry which also incorporates one of Davies' major preoccupations:

I am having my furnace psycho-analysed. For years I have put up with its ugly temper, its unaccountable fits of melancholy, and its occasional flights into stark, raving madness. Now I have a specialist in the cellar who is taking it all to pieces, cleaning it, fitting it together again, and giving it a new heart and a new soul. Inevitably, the furnace resents such treatment, but the specialist is used to that; all psycho-analysts know this symptom. As a usual thing he treats it with kindly firmness, but I heard him hit it a belt with a hammer this afternoon,

and I assumed that the ugly creature had bitten him, and had to be subdued
by violence ... I feel a certain sadness about the step I have taken. I pretended for
years that my furnace was sane, and excused its moodiness as mere nerves,
but the time came when I had to throw aside the sham and admit that the thing
was crazy – a lunatic of the most dangerous kind. That was when I called in
the specialist; and when he said the psycho-analysis would be needed, I felt the
relief which comes from knowing the worst. (10 August 1946)

But not everything which provokes this fantasizing has to be as close
to him as his family or domestic problems. Casual observation almost
everywhere can provoke similar flights.

The shifts between mundane and fantastic in the background and
between inner and outer events in the choice of material create an
uncertainty of expectation or response in the reader which Davies needs
in order to induce the acceptance of a protagonist who shifts between
clown and critic. Samuel Marchbanks is enough of a clown to be consistently entertaining; he is also enough of a critic to cause acute discomfort.

On the one hand there are a number of entries in which Samuel
Marchbanks' humour is turned on himself. As part of the clown image,
he is presented as somewhat clumsy: 'I crept off to the bathroom and
cut myself with a razor I have used for years; I have a fear of new-
fangled contrivances' (22 December 1945). He is deficient in good
citizenship: 'Attended a committee meeting tonight, to decide certain
matters bearing upon the public weal, and tried to look serious for
three hours and a half. As I am incapable of concentrating on any single
theme for more than an hour at a time, this was a strain on my his-
trionic powers. My imagination wandered ... It is useless to put me on
committees; I have an incorrigibly frivolous and vacillating mind' (25
January 1947). Shortly after, he reveals a similar deficiency in taste: 'But
then, I am a coarse fellow who has never really appreciated the genius
of Wagner; probably it is above me' (1 February 1947). Furthermore, 'I
live,' he informs us, 'a non-mathematical life, full of uncertainty, unreason, and delicious surmise' (24 January 1948).

On the other hand, in his criticism, interwoven with the lighter
pieces, he sounds a more serious note; he is fierce in his attack, for
example, on the herd-mind or mob-thinking: 'How I loathe people
whose fetish is modernity! Do they really imagine that they are the ultimate product of evolution and that nothing worthwhile will follow
them? If so, they will find Eternity an intensely humiliating experience'
(8 January 1944). But his fury is even more aroused by vulgarity ('we

live in an age unsurpassed in all history for the grossness and vulgarity of its emotion' [15 January 1944]), stupidity ('there was a time when the superstition and fearfulness of the ignorant masses was thought to be the great danger to civilization, but now it looks as though the superstition and anxiety of the learned were even more dangerous' [2 February 1946]), and complacency ('We are apt to forget that the people who burned witches were the sober scientific citizens of the day, and could prove they were right in a hundred perfectly satisfactory ways' [15 April 1944]). The antidote, he is convinced, is common sense: 'Freud was a great scientist and a magnificent thinker, but he was even more distinguished for his common sense; what a pity more psychologists do not possess that quality' (15 March 1944). The criticism fits into the pattern of the diary, and the critic blends smoothly into the comedian.

As I have suggested already, it is the form, background, and material of the diary which have prepared the reader for the ambivalence in the protagonist. This preparation is thorough enough even to accommodate such apparent polarities in the character of Samuel Marchbanks as his attitude to duplicity. His condemnation of sham is evident in an entry discussing a visit to the opera: '"The Medium" was particularly good, evoking in sound as well as to the sight all the sordidness and intellectual squalor of a phony spiritualist's den, and the peculiar plight of the unhappy people who resorted to it' (23 August 1947). At the same time, he cheerfully acquiesces in some of the subterfuges involved in his own life, as his response to a request for 'a list of the best books I have read in 1950' makes clear:

I can never remember what I have read for more than a week after I have finished it, but I suppose I can fake as impressive a list as anybody else. The main thing about such a list is that it should suggest that you never read anything but the best and that you pay attention to what you read. If possible, the list should contain at least two books that other people will not have heard of. Personally, I often read for twenty pages at a stretch without taking in a thing; I am thinking about something else. But I am a great hand at reading books which other people have never heard of ... I never read anything any more but I am an old hand at preparing lists of the ten best books. (3 February 1951)

The diary is clearly the work of a man of literary taste: "Went to bed early and read about Dr. Johnson" (27 January 1945); but he is not afraid to let us know about his blind spots: 'This evening heard some gramophone records which recited most of T.S. Eliot's play "The Cocktail Party." Reflected that if they had just drunk a great deal more at that party, none of the painful events in the play would probably have happened.' (17 February 1951). The accumulated effect of the ambivalence is that the reader is able to accept from Samuel Marchbanks the paradoxical idea that a thing can be both terrible and funny: 'personally I like being a man, and I can face with stoicism the possibility of being a woman, but I dread the intermediate period, during which I should be an It, tossed hither and thither on the turbulent seas of irreconcilable ambitions' (7 August 1948).[17] And if the humour can be accepted, so can the terror: we laugh not nervously but sympathetically.

So far I have argued that in Samuel Marchbanks Davies created a second self, choosing Marchbanks because of his ambivalent status between a real person (Davies himself under a pen-name) and a fictitious character.[18] Ambivalence is also the dominant feature of the character of Samuel Marchbanks himself, as well as of the form, material, and setting of the diary. The dominance of the concept marks its importance to Davies, suggesting that ambivalence is the key both to the nature of the relationship between Davies and his second-self figure, and, when this figure is considered in Jungian terms, to the place of the Marchbanks material within Davies' treatment of the theme of human identity.

A discussion of the nature of the relationship between the two selves (when it is discussed at all) usually employs the more obvious terms double or Doppelgänger, although the two are not perfectly synonymous, and alter ego.[19] Samuel Marchbanks, however, cannot be squeezed into any of these categories, and in refusing to categorize him specifically as a Doppelgänger, a Freudian double, or even loosely as an alter ego, I am making more than a terminological distinction.[20] For, although Samuel Marchbanks is not a demon figure of the occult as is the Coppelius/Coppola figure in Hoffmann's 'The Sandman,'[21] and although he cannot be explained in Freudian terms as 'a dysfunctional attempt to cope with mental conflict,'[22] he does share with the Doppelgänger an association with the dark side of human personality, and he does have, like the double, an explanation in psychological terms. Furthermore, it is through consideration of his darker qualities that he can be categorized.

The most engaging characteristic of Samuel Marchbanks, which if not strictly dark is at least somewhat suspect in Canada, is his exuberance: he enjoys his pleasures and suffers his miseries vigorously and uninhibitedly. A wedding is one of the occasions for this exuberance: 'I like weddings, too ... my instinct is to laugh uproariously, and to en-

courage the bride and groom with merry whoops' (29 November 1947).
From this exuberance springs also the energetic Leacockian parody of
the Canadian spy trials of 1946 in 'Diary of a Foreign Agent': 'Was
roused before seven this morning by a telegraph boy with a message.
It read, "Am sending crocheted pillow shams today stop Auntie." I
blanched, and the paper fell to the floor from my nerveless fingers, for of
course this was a code, and it meant, "All discovered stop prepare to
fly at once stop" and it was from my spy-master, Serge Pantz' (2 March
1946). As a natural corollary of his exuberance, Marchbanks cannot
tolerate those who lack it, considering them small of soul: 'I am beginning to have a violent dislike for the phrase "good taste." So often it
means whatever is inoffensive , meagre, drab, half-dead and inconsider-
able ... "Good taste" is socialism in aesthetics – a scheme to establish a
norm to which everyone can do lip service, and to outlaw or discom-
mode those who have tastes which are real, individual, and valid' (19
March 1949). This fierce impatience can verge on savagery: 'Canada
can ill spare the firm grip which Dafoe had on national and international
affairs. It was absolutely impossible to bamboozle him; his technique
in dealing with a meretricious idea was comparable to that which Jack
the Ripper employed in dealing with meretricious persons' (22 January 1944). Such exaggeration may explain why some of his humour was
alleged to be crude.[23] Crude in another sense is Marchbanks' passion
for puns, as in 'meretricious persons,' and his liking for practical jokes:
'The time I gave my Aunt Lettice the turtle nicely wrapped and in a
jeweller's box, she fainted dead away; if I had just hung the turtle on the
tree unwrapped it wouldn't have been the same thing at all' (29 December 1945).

There is, however, a more subtle mischief in his discussion of conversation: 'I prefer talking to women. For many years I talked to men by
preference, and at least I found out that very few of them have anything of interest to say. Now I talk to women by preference, to see if they
are any better. I don't think they are, but they display a greater fanci-
fulness in their errors than men do' (12 August 1944). In this he manages to cut both ways simultaneously. There is a similar element of
mischief in his aphorisms on mother-love, 'Every mother thinks her goof
a swan' (21 June 1947), and the longing for an adventurous life; 'it
seems to me that most of us get all the adventure we are capable of
digesting' (6 January 1945).

His attacks on hypocrisy, however, demonstrate more than mischief.
In a vigorous and forthright entry directed at the proponents of *de
mortuis nil nisi bonum*, he writes:

Heard of the death of an enemy of mine today – a contumacious, pygmy-minded fellow who has always wished me ill and done me harm whenever he could. Naturally, I was cheered by the news that he was out of the way for good, and said so. I have never taken any stock in that ridiculous cant that one should say nothing but good of the dead; if a man was nasty in life, he is just as nasty in death ... I grieve when my friends die, and, when an enemy dies, I am glad; if he dies a violent or dishonourable death I am downright delighted. (29 March 1947)

There is, of course, an element of common sense in this strictly rational approach to a subject hedged about with irrational tabus. Moreover, because the state of one's soul is an equally irrational tabu, Marchbanks' commonsense approach equally thoroughly satirizes the subject as presented in religious propaganda:

Somebody sent me a tract through the mail today. I have a taste for tracts, and read this one with relish. It seems that I am a lost soul. I pondered on this and decided that it was nonsense. Though normally sinful, I am far from being a great sinner; I haven't the time or the necessary vitality and imagination for a life of sin. High-grade sin is uncommon; apathy is the real problem of the world. I don't suppose there are more than a million really distinguished sinners on earth, but I dare not guess at the number of spineless, the disgruntled, the inert and the boors. They are the ones who get in the way when anything important has to be done. (26 February 1944)

The same approach disperses most of the aura surrounding 'etiquette': 'Became involved in a discussion about etiquette tonight, a subject which I detest ... I have the highest respect for good manners, but I doubt if they can be learned from a book; mere conformity to rules cannot create an illusion of good breeding or fine feeling ... Surely the secret of good manners is social easiness, and I am never so easy as when mopping, dunking, talking with my mouth full, and shouting and laughing. Perhaps I am a Noble Savage; perhaps not even noble' (15 January 1949). Exuberant, arrogant, intolerant, mischievous, and iconoclastic, Marchbanks may be; nevertheless, he is expending his energy in the pursuit of 'good breeding' and 'fine feeling.'

These aims, however, play a minor role in the diary itself and hardly carry enough weight to counterbalance the force of the characteristics deployed in the pursuit. There is, however, some measure of ambivalence in our response, because the qualities which we see in Samuel Marchbanks are all qualities which both outrage and attract us. They

outrage us because they violate our system of social interaction as a
human group: Samuel Marchbanks does not conform to convention;
he breaks the agreed rules of acceptable behaviour. But at the same time
these qualities attract us because they are qualities which we as individual
human beings share with him: they appeal to the 'savage' in each of us
which has had to be suppressed in the process of learning the rules
and conforming to group standards. But, however thoroughly the savage is suppressed, he can never be entirely eliminated from our psyche,
and his reappearance is always possible if convention breaks down.

   This suppressed savage is, in Jungian terms, the shadow – one of the
major archetypes of the unconscious psyche. Because of its general
similarity to the more familiar Freudian concept of the id, the shadow is
probably the most easily understood of the archetypes. Jung regards
the shadow's presence and characteristics in rather less condemnatory
terms than Freud regards the id: 'Everyone carries a shadow, and the
less it is embodied in the individual's conscious life, the blacker and
denser it is ... If the repressed tendencies, the shadow as I call them,
were obviously evil, there would be no problem whatever. But the
shadow is merely somewhat inferior, primitive, unadapted, and awkward; not wholly bad. It even contains childish or primitive qualities
which would in a way vitalize and embellish human existence' (CW
11:131, 134:76–8). Jacobi describes the development of the shadow
within an individual as an ongoing process complementing the development of the ego:

The development of the shadow runs parallel to that of the ego; qualities
which the ego does not need or cannot make use of are set aside or repressed,
and thus they play little or no part in the conscious life of the individual ...
And because in the course of our lives we are constantly having to inhibit or
repress one quality or another, the shadow can never be fully raised to consciousness. Nevertheless it is important that at least its most salient traits should
be made conscious and correlated with the ego, which thereby gains in strength
and vigour and comes to feel more firmly anchored in our nature.[24]

It is important in relating the Jungian concept of the shadow to the
Davies/ Marchbanks duality to note that the shadow is a part of the
unconscious psyche and therefore lies behind the ego as it faces the
objective world outside. In purely psychological terms Samuel Marchbanks is not a persona, for the Jungian persona lies between the ego and
the objective world in the conscious psyche. And because, as Jacobi
points out, the persona can be raised only partially to consciousness and

correlated with the ego, the shadow and the persona are quite separate elements of the psyche. In creating Samuel Marchbanks, Davies is not putting on a mask by creating a persona but stripping away his acquired persona.

Samuel Marchbanks is not only raised to consciousness, but also externalized in a way in which the shadow in a non-creative personality is not. It is this, perhaps, which marks the difference between the writer and other people: the writer can manifest the figures of his subjective inner world in the outer objective world consciously and for a purpose. Jacobi points out that every individual can manifest inner figures outwardly, but unconsciously and in a limited way: 'The shadow may be manifested in an inward, symbolic figure or in a concrete figure from the outside world. In the first case it is embodied in the material of the unconscious, perhaps as a dream figure personifying one or more of the dreamer's psychic qualities; in the second case, we project one or more of our latent unconscious traits upon someone in our environment who is suited to this role by certain structural qualities.'[25] The writer, however, apparently does not need an outside figure on which to project his unconscious shadow – he has the ability to maintain an external manifestation of an inner figure without any extrinsic support.[26] As Davies' first major fictional character, Samuel Marchbanks demonstrates his early command of this ability.

The importance of this difference between the unconscious mental processes of the writer and of the non-writer should not be underrated. In both the material is the same: the partial contents of the unconscious psyche. In the non-writer these contents are largely ignored by the conscious mind (unless they erupt into a neurosis), but in the writer they come under continuous, careful, conscious scrutiny and are put to professional use. It is clear, therefore, that some distinction must be recognized between the psychotherapeutic approach to the unconscious contents and the 'creative' or non-psychotherapeutic approach.

For Jung, analytical psychology was a *Heilsweg*, 'a way of healing and a way of salvation,'[27] and the unconscious contents revealed in the neurosis constitute both the symptoms and the suggested treatment;[28] for the creative artist however, the unconscious contents provide the raw material with which he works at whatever level of the psyche (conscious or unconscious) the creative process operates in him personally. The distinction is that the psychotherapeutic approach will be directed to the healing of the 'traumatized' psyche and the establishment of the healthy personality, possibly as a first step towards individuation. The creative approach, on the other hand, will be concerned only with the shaping of the material into a formal aesthetic structure – a work of art. The former approach is personal, the latter impersonal.

There is, however, one important similarity between the two approaches: both use the material instead of ignoring or dismissing it. Jung himself points out that, 'mere suppression of the shadow is as little of a remedy as beheading would be for a headache' (CW 11:133:77). The material has to be raised to consciousness, examined, and controlled by the ego: 'If an inferiority is conscious, one always has a chance to correct it. Furthermore, it is constantly in contact with other interests, so that it is continually subjected to modifications. But if it is repressed and isolated from consciousness, it never gets corrected' (CW 11:131:76). The shadow should be 'correlated with the ego,' that is, set in a relationship with the ego, as a result of the psychotherapeutic process.[29]

The artist also sets the shadow in a relationship with his conscious personality. But he does so by giving the shadow a formal, autonomous existence within a verbal structure. Jacobi points out the frequency with which the shadow appears as a figure in works of literature:

The shadow figure is ... a frequent theme in art. For in his creative activity and choice of themes the artist draws very largely on the depths of his unconscious; with his creations he in turn stirs the unconscious of his audience, and this is the ultimate secret of his effectiveness. The images and figures of the unconscious rise up in him and carry their powerful message to other men, although these do not know the source of their 'rapture.' Shakespeare's Caliban, Mrs. Shelley's *Frankenstein*, Oscar Wilde's *The Fisherman and His Soul*, Stevenson's *Mr. Hyde*, Chamisso's *Peter Schlemihl*, Herman Hesse's *Steppenwolf*, Aldous Huxley's *Grey Eminence*, not to mention Mephisto, Faust's dark tempter, are examples of the artistic use of this motif.[30]

The powerful message of literary manifestations of the shadow has a counterpart in what Jung describes as the 'emotional nature' of the shadow's non-literary manifestations: 'Closer examination of the dark characteristics – that is, the inferiorities constituting the shadow – reveals that they have an *emotional* nature, a kind of autonomy, and accordingly an obsessive or, better, possessive quality.'[31] Equally important is Jung's observation that the shadow has a 'kind of autonomy,' for this provides for the 'autonomy' of Samuel Marchbanks, even before Davies begins to draw on the resources of literary technique for the diary. The energy and autonomy of the shadow, therefore, form a psychologically true foundation for the ambivalence which is one of

Davies' major concerns in developing Samuel Marchbanks and the diary.

There is even an ambivalence about the shadow itself which contributes in a minor way to Davies' general structure of ambivalence. For, as Jacobi makes clear: 'paradoxical as it may seem at first sight, the shadow ... may also be represented by a positive figure, for example, when the individual whose "other side" it personifies is living "below his level," failing to fulfil his potentialities, for then it is his positive qualities that lead a dark shadow existence.'[32] According to Barbara Hannah: 'Jung even said in a seminar once that it was possible to find up to eighty per cent gold in the shadow.'[33] The 'gold' in Samuel Marchbanks consists of the vigour, exuberance, and honesty which Davies had to suppress, as Roper points out, in order to accommodate himself to Peterborough life: 'Davies developed the "Diary" partly to entertain his *Examiner* readers, and partly to blow off steam. Daily newspaper work required him to hold in his strong dramatic instinct and exuberant imagination; moreover after Oxford, London, the Old Vic, and the *Saturday Night* editorial room, some of the pieties of a provincial Ontario town were galling.'[34] A review of the volume of selections from the diary, however, suggests that Davies' 'carefully cultivated bizarre appearance'[35] offered at least a token defiance of these pieties, which, wherever they may be held, have little in common with the gold in Samuel Marchbanks.

It is important to notice that the ego must always exercise final control of the shadow. In the diary, wit and style clearly demonstrate the presence of the controlling ego. Roper's suggestion is that the shadow's energy is merely allowed to release itself through the diary. It is clear from the content of the diary itself, however, that the energy of the shadow is directed to the pursuit of ego-selected, highly civilized aims which for Davies/Marchbanks include good breeding or fine feeling and artistic excellence. The effect of ego-control is to produce a state of tension: there is a continual opposition between the thrusting energy of the shadow and the resistance of the ego as it restricts this energy to selected levels and to the pursuit of selected aims. The balance is extremely delicate, but Davies maintains it even when Samuel Marchbanks appears at his fiercest. Because the energy of the shadow is allowed so much free play within the diary, however, and because his effectiveness is partly on an unconscious level, Samuel Marchbanks becomes disturbingly powerful. He seems, in fact, more powerful than his creator: 'It is the general belief in Peterborough ... that Samuel Marchbanks is a disembodied entity – of the most dubious ancestry –

which (or who) has gradually obtained more and more complete possession of the body of our once beloved colleague ... and it seems practically inevitable that Davies will ultimately disappear and be entirely subsumed by Marchbanks.'[36] The discrepancy was appreciated by Davies and is exploited in 'The Double Life of Robertson Davies,' where Davies introduces himself as the butt of the forthright humour and contempt of Marchbanks. According to Marchbanks, Davies is

fawningly courteous; I am forthright. He is mangled by self-doubt and self-criticism; I am untouched by these ridiculous ailments. He has a conscience as big as a grand piano; I have no more sense of obligation than a tomcat. He makes excuses for everybody and tries to be charitable ; I know a boob or a phony when I see one and I see a great many. He is inclined to be moderate in pretty nearly everything; I regard moderation as a sign of physical or intellectual weakness. He is just about everything which I detest; I am everything which he fears and seeks to avoid.[37]

The essay exploits with wit and humour the encounter between the ego and the shadow. But the encounter itself extends throughout the duration of the diary, and the essay acts merely as a summary of or coda to it.

The importance of recognizing Samuel Marchbanks as a shadow figure must not be underestimated. There is a striking parallel between this recognition and the first stage in the effort of clinical analysis, the resolution of the shadow: 'This effort must lead into the unconscious part of the psyche, into everything that has been left behind in our efforts to adapt to the world. As a rule the first "figure" we encounter there is the so-called *shadow*.'[38] The resolution of the shadow in analysis is needed so that the analysis can proceed to deal with the other elements of the unconscious psyche: 'For only when we have learned to distinguish ourselves from our shadow by recognizing its reality as a part of our nature, and only if we keep this insight persistently in mind, can our confrontation with the other pairs of psychic opposites be successful. For this is the beginning of the objective attitude toward our own personality without which no progress can be made along the path of wholeness.'[39] This throws considerable light on the development of the theme of illusion and identity at this point in Davies' development. For as clinical resolution of the shadow leads towards an objective view of one's personality, so the exploitation of a literary manifestation of the shadow marks a step forward in the definition of human identity.

The concepts involved in this step are those of twinning, inversion of qualities, and ambivalence of response. Twinning demonstrates that a personality is not a monolithic structure but contains separate though related elements, just as twins can be identical but remain different individuals (and as Samuel Marchbanks is separate from Davies yet integrally related). Here the Jungian idea of the shadow as 'the dark brother' is introduced.[40] Inversion of qualities, demonstrated in the characterization of Samuel Marchbanks, introduces the idea that the whole must contain both of any given pair of psychic opposites. This agrees with Jung's fundamental principle that all psychic life is governed by a necessary opposition because 'there is no balance, no system of self-regulation, without opposition' and 'the psyche is ... a self-regulating system.'[41] The third factor is ambivalence, and we have seen how carefully Davies develops the structure of ambivalence to the point where the reader accepts the paradoxes he presents. Paradoxical thinking, the capacity to assimilate opposites, is necessary because of the presence of the opposites within the psyche, opposites which are not reconcilable but must be held in tension as opposites. The point, Jung says, 'is not conversion into the opposite but conservation of previous values together with recognition of their opposites' (cw 7:116:76) .

The suggestion common to all three factors is that, like the self of Jungian psychology, human identity will be formed by the synthesis of separate parts into a whole. This suggestion initiates but does not complete the definition of that identity. Synthesis is, as it were, merely the construction principle; the elements on which that principle is to work are not yet defined. Davies has still to put forward the pairs of opposites which are to be synthesized. Just as the initial encounter with the persona in *Shakespeare's Boy Actors* contains a suggestion of the return to the discussion of role-playing in *The Manticore*, so the initial encounter with the shadow in the Marchbanks material contains a suggestion of a return to the discussion of the shadow in *Fifth Business*.

The element common to both discussions of the shadow is the connection of the shadow with the problem of good and evil. 'The shadow' Jung says 'is a moral problem that challenges the whole ego-personality, for no one can become conscious of the shadow without considerable moral effort. To become conscious of it involves recognizing the dark aspects of the personality as present and real. This act is the essential condition for any kind of self-knowledge' (cw 9(ii):14:8). The opposition of good and evil is an opposition which psychology must take into account: 'Thanks to the doctrine of the *privatio boni*, wholeness seemed guaranteed in the figure of Christ. One must, however, take evil rather more substantially when one meets it on the plane of empirical psychology. There it is simply the opposite of good' (cw 9 (ii):75:41). It is also an opposition which each individual must try to resolve by recognizing the shadow: 'If you imagine someone who is brave enough to withdraw all these projections, then you get an individual who is conscious of a pretty thick shadow. Such a man has saddled himself with new problems and conflicts. He has become a serious problem to himself, as he is now unable to say that *they* do this or that, *they* are wrong, and *they* must be fought against ... Such a man knows that whatever is wrong in the world is in himself, and if he only learns to deal with his own shadow he has done something real for the world' (cw 11:140:83). But, as Jacobi points out, '*all* the projections can never be made conscious and withdrawn,'[42] and the shadow must therefore always be present to some degree in the individual psyche.

Although there is little overt consideration of good and evil in the Marchbanks material, the continuous presence of the shadow, Samuel Marchbanks, in the psyche of his creator is suggested at the end of 'The Double Life of Robertson Davies': 'It appears that we shall go on together for quite a while, whether he likes it or not. I shall certainly last as long as he does.'[43] This remark offers a covert hint that the question of good and evil is one which has to be taken into account throughout the whole process of defining human identity. It also reminds us that, although we should not take this casual creation of a busy man too seriously, neither should we entirely discount it.

It is obvious, then, on the basis of this discussion of *Shakespeare's Boy Actors* and of the Marchbanks material, that a Jungian interpretation of Davies' work can be a productive interpretation. Both the initial encounter with the persona in *Shakespeare's Boy Actors* and the initial encounter with the shadow in the Marchbanks material are important stages in Davies' development of a concept of human identity, and both contain ideas which are expanded in the later work. His understanding of Jung deepens and increases in complexity during the period in which they were written, and, although his initial response to Jung may not have been entirely sympathetic, he was by nature so in tune with Jung that to apply Jungian concepts to his work in no way distorts it. With this point established, a consideration of the novels in Jungian terms may confidently be undertaken.

3 / A Choice of Worlds

The successive stages in Davies' attempt to define human identity overlap in time, so that *Tempest-Tost*, the first of the Salterton trilogy (which
Leaven of Malice and *A Mixture of Frailties* complete), was published in
1951, three years before Samuel Marchbanks' final appearance in 'The
Double Life of Robertson Davies.' Davies first plays with the idea of
illusion, almost parenthetically, in *Shakespeare's Boy Actors*, but in the
Marchbanks material he presents a development of this idea of illusion
in a thesis of ambivalence: the proposition that a psychic whole must
contain both of any given pair of opposites and that the construction of
such a whole must be governed by the principle of synthesis. The
Salterton trilogy takes this thesis a step further by presenting a series of
linked dualities which have to be synthesized, but, because synthesis
must work on clearly separate elements, part of the discussion in the
trilogy is the analysis of the elements into their respective dualities.
Within each novel, therefore, Davies explores both the nature of the
duality involved, through the development of the theme of illusion,
and also the resolution of that duality as a mode of psychic identity,
through a Jungian psychologem of the archetypes and the self.[1] To
execute this he creates an intricate pattern of images, themes, and structures on the topics of illusion and identity.

Illusion, as it is presented in the Salterton trilogy, is an appearance
which masks reality, much as it is in *Shakespeare's Boy Actors*. It is,
however, both more complex and (in terms of the deception involved)
more dangerous than it is shown to be in the earlier work. Consequently, for the purposes of examining the pattern Davies sets up in the
trilogy, I have categorized illusion informally under three headings in
order to accommodate both the increased complexity and the increased
negativity of the concept. The categories are defined by two criteria:

whether the illusion is voluntary or involuntary, and whether it is corrigible or incorrigible. Those forms of illusion which are voluntary and corrigible (daydreaming, acting) may be grouped under the general heading of *fantasy*; those which are involuntary and corrigible (misunderstanding, hallucination) may be described as *delusion*; those which are involuntary and incorrigible are various forms of *insanity*.[2] Each of the categories of illusion is introduced in a number of examples, of which the more important can be studied in detail and the less important at least glanced at. The more important examples comprise the large structural events of the novels, such as the production of *The Tempest* in *Tempest-Tost*, or the libel case in *Leaven of Malice*; the less important include such things as the characters' daydreaming.

The Jungian psychologem presented in the trilogy is that of the development of the self, which in Jung's terminology is called *individuation*. In the course of individuation the ego is confronted with the archetypes of the unconscious as they are manifest in his or her own life, and must recognize and learn how to cope with them. In each novel in the trilogy, Davies shows a character or characters going through various stages of this confrontation: Hector Mackilwraith in *Tempest-Tost*, Solly Bridgetower and Pearl Vambrace in *Leaven of Malice*, and Monica Gall in *A Mixture of Frailties*. The complexity of Davies' handling of characters in the process of individuation increases considerably as the trilogy progresses (Hector's individuation is barely started by the end of the novel, whereas Monica's is traced from beginning to end), and this increase in complexity may be attributed, at least in part, to Davies' increasing interest in Jung during the intervening years.

These two themes, the theme of illusion and the theme of identity through Jungian individuation, are developed in parallel in each novel. They are, however, not totally independent: the theme of illusion is used to reveal, through the stripping away of illusion and the revelation of the underlying actuality, the nature of the mundane state and, by contrast, the nature of the transcendental state which is also the natural state of the individuated self. Admittedly, at this stage in Davies' development of the ideas, the connections between the themes are not made as firmly as they are in *Fifth Business*, for example. Nevertheless, the themes are connected, and in each novel the appropriate approach to the theme of identity is through the theme of illusion.

Tempest-Tost, published in 1951, is the first of the trilogy and the simplest in thematic and structural pattern. The theme of illusion is explored as fantasy (in the Salterton Little Theatre's summer production of Shakespeare's *The Tempest*), and as delusion (in Hector Mackilwraith's infatuation with Griselda). The theme of psychic identity is incorporated in the same deluded infatuation for, in Jungian terms, it represents Hector's confrontation with one of the archetypes of the unconscious, the anima. The narrative of the novel, following the production of the play from the decision to play *The Tempest* to the close of the more-or-less triumphant first night, charts not only the course of a delusion but also the first stage of individuation.

The Salterton Little Theatre chooses *The Tempest*, according to Nellie Forrester, to spite other little theatre groups: 'They'll be jealous, you see. They've never done a pastoral. They've never attempted Shakespeare' (TT 38). Davies seems to have chosen it because *The Tempest* is intrinsically a play of fantasy. In a discussion of dramatic fantasy he describes *A Midsummer Night's Dream* as 'the greatest fantasy in our language, and perhaps in any language; its only near rival is *The Tempest*.'[3] The implications for the Salterton Little Theatre production become apparent in view of the definition of fantasy which immediately follows this remark: 'Like *beauty*, the word *fantasy* has been claimed too often by weak or wounded people as a description of the products of their own insufficiencies. But fantasy means, literally, a showing or revelation, and beauty can be alarming as well as transporting.' The Salterton Little Theatre has, by choosing *The Tempest*, laid itself open to the approach of a revelation and so to the possibility of revolution (in the sense of change or mutation) which in matters of the psyche is apt to follow a revelation.[4] In fact, the production of *The Tempest* effects a dual revelation. It reveals not only the mundane reality (in the lives and personalities of the Salterton Little Theatre Company), but also the transcendental reality (symbolized and invoked by the play itself).

The first part of the revelation, that of the mundane reality, is essentially a revelation of human spiritual inadequacy. This inadequacy is demonstrated in the company's delusion about the nature of what they have chosen to recreate. Certainly they all understand that they are setting about creating a fantasy, for Solly points out that Hector 'wants to be one of the gaudy folk of the theatre, weaving a tissue of enchantment for Mrs Caesar Augustus Conquergood' (TT 81). There is no delusion involved in this, however, because all the players, Hector included, understand that they are playing parts. In co-operating in the production of *The Tempest* they are participating in the creation of a fantasy (a voluntary and corrigible illusion) and as long as they understand it to be a fantasy, it is harmless.

Nevertheless, because no one (except the producer, Valentine Rich, an outsider) understands the true nature of fantasy (as Davies defines it), all of them are deluded about what is actually going on in the play. Their delusion is nowhere more obvious than in the business of casting the play, the result being what Hugo McPherson has called the 'chilling ironies' of the discrepancies between the players and the roles they play.[5] In most cases, the delusion produces the ironies simply by the failure of the company to recognize the true nature in some cases of the role, in other cases of the player. In the case of Roger Tasset's Ferdinand, the irony is, as McPherson suggests, one of simple discrepancy between the shabby libertine and the noble and honourable prince whom he plays; here the delusion is due to the failure of the other players to recognize Tasset for what he is. Conversely, in the casting of Juno, the delusion results from a failure to recognize Juno for what she is: not simply 'a classic countenance' as Professor Vambrace would have her in the person of Miss Wildfang, but 'an awful one for the boys' as Valentine Rich maintains in defending her choice of Bonnie-Susan ('The Torso') Tompkins for the part. Miss Wildfang's unsuitability for the part of Juno is a demonstration of ironic discrepancy similar to that between Tasset and Ferdinand; Bonnie-Susan's suitability, however, is a demonstration of ironic parallelism, which is further repeated in the casting of the stodgy Hector Mackilwraith as the equally stodgy Gonzalo and the outsider Georgie Shortreed as the monster Caliban. Up to this point the ironies produced by delusion, however chilling, are simply dramatic ironies of a very common literary sort.

In the casting of Professor Vambrace as Prospero, however, the irony is more complex. Without doubt Davies does intend the straightforward ironic discrepancy, which McPherson notes, between Prospero, the 'learned nobleman and loving father,' and Vambrace, the 'cloistered and egotistical pedant.' But Davies also suggests, in a form of double irony, that a similarity exists between player and character: both are power-wielders and manipulators. Because of this similarity, a curious relationship exists between their differences: where Prospero is loving, Vambrace is possessive; where Prospero is learned, Vambrace is pedantic; where Propero is generous, Vambrace is spiteful; and where Prospero is a king, Vambrace is merely a bully. The relationship in each case is one of inversion, so that Vambrace in the end becomes the negative image of Prospero.

The extent of the discrepancy between Vambrace and his role as Prospero is a forcible illustration of his spiritual inadequacy. Moreover, because Professor Vambrace might be supposed to be among the more enlightened members of the community, the depth of his spiritual inadequacy clearly reflects the generally low spiritual state of the whole community. Mean and meagre-spirited, its members are sunk in the mundane reality and barely touched even by their close contact with the transcendental vision of the play which reveals them for what they are.

This revelation of the transcendental reality – the world of the archetypal figures, and of magic, order, and harmony – is the second part of the dual revelation. For the most part the nature of this reality is left to the reader's own imagination and understanding of the play. But it is unmistakably a reality of great beauty, and beauty, in special circumstances, can evoke a response from the most mundane:

Sated with food, the actors showed no signs of going home. Cobbler and his wife and children were sitting on the lawn, singing for a large audience. The treble voices and the one bass were sweet upon the moonlit air.

Come again,
Sweet love doth now invite –

they sang, and other voices were stilled to hear them. (TT 333)

Even the mean and meagre-spirited members of the Salterton Little Theatre company, Davies implies, are not altogether beyond a response to beauty.

The beauty of *The Tempest*, however, does not merely reveal the transcendent reality, but looses its powers upon the mundane world, which is why, as Davies points out, beauty is dangerous. There are characters in *Tempest-Tost*, namely Valentine Rich and Humphrey Cobbler, who have already made their accommodation with the transcendent powers, and for them the loosing of the powers is harmless, as it is for those who are still too young to have reached the stage of such a confrontation, Pearl Vambrace and Solly Bridgetower (although these two are not far away from it). But for Hector Mackilwraith, who has reached the stage when he must confront the transcendent powers, the loosing of them in the mundane world is a real danger. As the vision of *The Tempest* is recreated by the production of the play, so the power envisioned in it is unleashed against the unsuspecting player of Gonzalo.

Hector's confrontation with the transcendental powers is worked out in terms of the Jungian psychologem of individuation, and specifically in terms of that part of it which takes the form of an encounter with the anima. As the encounter progresses, it becomes obvious to other characters in the novel, as well as to the reader, that Hector is going through some kind of inner upheaval, for several of them comment on his plight; Humphrey Cobbler, for example, crudely diagnoses Hector's problem as 'the male climacteric' (TT 370). P.W. Martin, describing the same syndrome in Jungian terms, first quotes Dante, 'In the midway of this our mortal life, I found me in a gloomy wood, astray/Gone from the path direct,' and then comments: 'This is typical. It is around "the midway of this our mortal life," about thirty-five or forty years of age, when a man passes the meridian, that the individuation process normally starts.'[6] Davies emphasizes the timing of this crisis in Hector's life not only by Solly Bridgetower's offhand comment that Hector is 'stage-struck ... at his age' (TT 81), but also by an authorial comment: 'He was forty when he decided that he would like to act, and planned and exercised his common sense to secure for himself the part of Gonzalo' (TT 123). Hector, in this particular summer, has reached the crucial meridian of his inner life, as well as the turning point in his career (indicated by the letter from his friend in the Department of Education), and the equivalent in his life of Dante's 'gloomy wood' is his infatuation with Griselda.

The reference to 'planning and common sense' is more than merely an ironic hint that these are the very qualities which Hector uses to lever himself into a psychological crisis where they will be of absolutely no use to him and where he will lose most of his belief in their value. It is a reference to the fact that the meridian crisis always involves the 'opposition of functions and of conscious and unconscious attitudes.'[7] Jung's theory of functions postulates four modes of apprehension (functions): thinking, feeling, sensation, and intuition; these are grouped in two pairs of opposites (thinking/feeling, intuition/sensation); the individual's selected mode (dominant function) lies in the conscious mind and its opposite lies in the unconscious.[8] In Hector's meridian crisis, the general upheaval is presented as a series of three specific psychological reversals, of which a reversal of the function-type is the first.

Through Hector's reliance on planning and common sense Davies indicates the function-type to which he belongs. In Hector's inner struggles as an adolescent 'he was lucky enough to find the god which suited him in mathematics, represented in his schooling by algebra and geometry. In these studies, it seemed to him, planning and common sense were deified. There was no problem which would not yield to application and calm consideration' (TT 114). Hector's superior or dominant function is clearly *thinking*, in the Jungian definition of the term as 'the psychological function which, following its own laws, brings

the contents of ideation into conceptual connection with one another'
(CW 6:830:481). Moreover, because of the way the psyche is structured,
the opposite function to thinking is *feeling*, defined in Jungian terms
as 'a process that takes place between the *ego* and a given content ... that
imparts to the content a definite *value* in the sense of acceptance or
rejection ("like" or "dislike")' (CW 6:724:434). In addition, it must be
noted that, 'as determinants of behaviour, these two basic attitudes are
mutually exclusive at any given time; either the one or the other
predominates.'[9] Consequently, because of the dominance of his thinking
function, Hector is necessarily deficient in feeling.

The reversal in the function-type which forms a part of Hector's meridian crisis is, therefore, the activation of this dormant function of feeling. Because Hector has suppressed it for so long, it has remained
'undifferentiated and wholly embedded in the unconscious,' and so 'has
an infantile, primitive, instinctive, archaic character.'[10] Once activated
and finding an outlet in his relationship with Griselda, his capacity for
feeling overwhelms him: 'He loved Griselda, and it seemed to him
that in that love there was no room for thought of himself. His longing
for her was a pain which filled his whole body' (TT 342). The sheer
intensity of his released feeling confronts him, finally, with the inadequacy of his way of life and threatens his sanity.

The second reversal, somewhat subordinate to this upsetting of the
functional-type balance, is the reversal of Hector's attitudinal habitus –
the extraversion/introversion balance of the psyche. Hector is clearly
an introverted personality: he is 'solemn and silent,' and the major
events of his life (his decision to become a teacher, his decision to obtain
a degree, his passion for Griselda) are worked through in the secrecy
and isolation of the introvert. But after he has met and fallen in love
with Griselda, 'for the first time in his life Hector discovered that it was
possible for someone to be more important to him than himself' (TT
203). His longing for Griselda has set in motion the process of turning
his vision outward, rendering him a little more extraverted.

The third reversal in Hector's meridian crisis is the reversal of his
attitude to the feminine, and this involves a confrontation with one of
the feminine archetypes of the unconscious. (He must, in the normal
course of events, confront all of the archetypes, but Davies' story does
not take him this far.) The specific archetype which erupts into activity at
this point in is life is his anima – his soul-image:

The soul-image is a specific *image* ... among those produced by the unconscious.
Just as the *persona*, or outer attitude, is represented in dreams by images of

definite persons who possess the outstanding qualities of the persona in especially marked form, so in a man the soul, i.e. anima, or inner attitude, is represented in the unconscious by definite persons with the corresponding qualities. Such an image is called a 'soul-image.' Sometimes these images are of quite unknown or mythological figures. With men the anima is usually personified by the unconscious as a woman; with women the animus is personified by a man. (CW 6:808:470)

In his description of Hector's student days at Waverley University Davies emphasizes that Hector had to work his way through his year on campus and that the working student 'has not time to be young, or to invite his soul' (TT 121). But if the anima is not invited, she will come unasked and choose her own time to do so.

In line with Jung's own first experience of the anima (MDR 185–6), Hector's first encounter with her is aural not visual: 'it was as though another voice, a clear, insistent voice, spoke to him' (TT 155). It happens immediately after Griselda congratulates him on getting the part of Gonzalo, so that it is clear that this has been the stimulus. Davies has already indicated the lack of feminine influence in Hector's life: 'And it was a fact, though it was of interest to no one but Hector, that he had never known any intimacy – no, not the slightest – with a woman' (TT 122). This fact is echoed in Hector's own thoughts at this point. In his dream the same night the anima figure emerges from the unconscious: 'Recurrently during the years his dreams had been plagued by the phantasmata, the hideous succubi, which visit the celibate male. This night, for the first time in his life he dreamed that a beautiful woman, lightly clad, leaned toward him tenderly and spoke his name; her smile was the smile which he had seen the night before. He woke in the night to the knowledge that for the second time in his life he was in love' (TT 156). The dream suggests, from a Jungian point of view, the presence of the psychic forces of the unconscious, just as the 'succubi' of his earlier dreams represent in Jungian terms warning appearances of the anima in her negative aspect while he has been repressing this element. In his dream the anima is still unidentified: she is merely 'a beautiful woman,' and he recognizes only the smile; it is his conscious mind which on waking makes the identification with Griselda. Unable to recognize consciously the feminine element within himself as part of himself, yet forced to do something by its autonomous incursion into his consciousness, Hector projects it onto Griselda as the most suitable 'bearer.'

That Hector's encounter with the anima should take the form of a projection (the embodiment of the archetype in an actual person in the individual's life) is perfectly normal. In discussing the nature of projection, Martin points out that:

in actual life a man normally encounters the anima first in the form of a projection. There is a sudden overwhelming 'falling in love' and for a while nothing else in the world matters ... From her he expects everything. She knows the Great Secret, she holds the key to life. The thought of separation is impossible; existence would be meaningless without her ... A special light pervades the whole landscape, illumining especially the woman on whom this projection from the unconscious has fallen. Clods who have never attempted any such thing before take to writing verse. So long as the projection lasts, the man is held by a completely irrational attachment. His thoughts and his footsteps lead persistently in her direction – and inevitably so, for she has upon her an essential part of his inmost being.[11]

Hector's infatuation follows this pattern closely. His sudden realization of being in love, his unreal expectations of Griselda, and his inability to stay away from her conform to the model Martin outlines.

The ending of Hector's infatuation, with the withdrawal of the projection from its bearer, also conforms to Martin's description of the nature of projection. When Valentine Rich rescues Hector from the mess he makes of trying to hang himself (because he thinks Roger Tasset has seduced Griselda), Davies comments that 'her comfort had started him back on the road to self-possession ... His spirit was returning' (TT 362). The last phrase is more than metaphor: his anima, his soul or spirit, has been projected onto Griselda, and unless it is withdrawn his psyche must remain incomplete. When this withdrawal takes place, Griselda loses the numinous aura with which she, as the bearer of such a projection, has been surrounded, and Hector is then able to see her as she really is: 'Now, mysteriously, he was no longer afraid of her ... For the first time Hector saw that she was not much more than a child' (TT 374–5). Hector's return to a more stable psychological state completes this confrontation with the anima, yet he will never be quite the same again because he has taken one step to psychic maturation, or individuation. And with this return, Davies' exploration of the theme of identity through the psychologem of the encounter with the anima is drawn to a close.

The links between the theme of psychic identity, as explored in the Jungian psychologem, and the theme of illusion, as set out in the Salterton Little Theatre Company's production of The Tempest, are made through Hector Mackilwraith. He is involved in illusion as a result of his participation in the fantasy involved in the production of *The Tempest*, and the ironic similarity between Hector and Gonzalo illustrates not only the delusion of the Salterton Little Theatre Company, but also the over-all discrepancy between the mundane reality and the transcendental reality. Specifically, it is in Hector's mind and life that the duality of the mundane and the transcendental is distinguished and examined. It is the fantasy of *The Tempest* which activates the emergence of the anima into his life and wakens his dormant, undeveloped feeling: 'He ran over a few speeches in his mind. Poetry – even such poetry as Shakespeare has given to Gonzalo – is like wine; it is not for unseasoned heads. The rhythm and the unaccustomed richness of the words worked powerfully upon Hector's sensibilities, which had until this time been teetotallers in the matter of poetry. He was in a melting mood' (TT 153). Finally, his infatuation with Griselda is delusional, not only as illusion, but also as a Jungian projection. Because Griselda in this sense is a projection of his anima, Hector can be said to be in love not with Griselda, but with the image of his own soul as he sees it overlaying Griselda's true identity. This delusional quality is reason for the disastrous outcome of most loves based on projection, even mutual projection, and Hector's delusion is emphasized by the fact that he sees his love progressing in a series of daydreams (themselves forms of illusion) – 'his little mental drama' (TT 203) – and is repeatedly humiliated by his inability to translate them into physical reality. In Hector's achievement of a relative serenity of spirit at the close of the novel both themes are brought to a satisfactory narrative close, although Davies' dealings with them have hardly begun.

In *Leaven of Malice* (1954) the pattern of the themes of illusion and identity is less clear-cut, for the book is more complicated in its plot and does not rely on a single structural framework such as the production of the play provides for *Tempest-Tost*. Nor does the underlying psychologem emerge quite so obviously from the pattern of illusion, because the illusion here is that involved in identity. The analysis of the duality involved in illusion and its resolution in terms of a psychologem of the Jungian archetypes are, however, unmistakable.

The theme of illusion in *Leaven of Malice* is much darker in tone than in *Tempest-Tost*. There are three contributory factors. To begin with, the discussion of the duality of the transcendent and mundane realities here is unrelieved by the presence of any sustained vision of the transcendental world such as is implied by the presence of *The Tempest* in *Tempest-Tost*. (In fact, no structure of fantasy is present, although

Solly's and Pearl's pretence of an engagement, forced upon them by the false engagement notice, might qualify as a perverted fantasy.) The theme of illusion is worked out almost entirely in terms of delusion. Delusion is dangerous even in *Tempest-Tost*, where Hector's delusion almost costs him his sanity and his life. But the delusion of Bevill Higgin in *Leaven of Malice* (that Pearl Vambrace is the woman who refuses him library privileges at Waverley University) has consequences more far-reaching than Hector's, for it affects other people and in incalculable ways. Finally, Davies introduces two examples of insanity (the third, involuntary and incorrigible, form of illusion): the first is Professor Vambrace's almost paranoid reaction to the false engagement announcement and the second is the catatonic schizophrenia of Gloster Ridley's wife. Both fulfil minor structural functions in addition to their thematic function of intensifying the sombreness of the illusion.

The link between these separate elements is the concept of personal identity as distinct from the concept of psychic identity in the transcendent world. Personal identity is the individual's identity as an individual within the mundane reality and specifically within a social group. It is explored through a number of related examples, each touched on in a different part of the narrative and each in some way involving the way in which the individual is recognized in the group.

The working out of the concept of personal identity largely concerns Gloster Ridley. The concept is introduced in the first part of the novel, which shows Ridley at his work of editing *The Bellman*, where it takes the form of multiple hints throughout the narrative: Ridley meditates on his hoped-for doctorate which will be 'a symbol of security and success' (LM 4), and which can also be seen as an identifying social symbol; he is 'determined to do nothing which might appear two-faced' in his dealings with Mr Shillito (LM 7), which provides a hint about the possibility of manipulating identity; the letters to the editor on his desk include two anonymous letters and one under a false name, which together suggest the possibility of applying a true/false distinction to the concept of identity; the complexity of the nature of identity is suggested in the joke concerning the visitor who is 'about like' the Boss himself (LM 16–17); and Ridley's own 'trick of having private and usually inadmissible names for people' (LM 33) suggests the presence of a subjective element in the identification of the objective reality of somebody else's identity. But in addition to this pattern of multiple suggestion, there are three major questions about personal identity, all of which also concern Ridley.

The first question is raised by the insanity of Ridley's wife. She has been schizophrenically withdrawn for fifteen years, as Ridley explains to Mrs Fielding: 'She hasn't recognized me once in the past fifteen years, and now I don't even see her ... She lies there all day, curled up on a mattress in a corner, with a blanket pulled over her head' (LM 262). An entity can be identified only by reference to something outside itself and, in the case of a human identity, by awareness of identity as a human being separate from other human beings yet part of the human group. The problem raised here, therefore, is whether Mrs Ridley, neither communicating with nor (so far as can be ascertained) aware either of herself or of her fellow human beings, has an identity.

The second question is how far the external distinguishing marks of the individual determine identity. This question is examined through Ridley's anxious desire to be 'Doctor Ridley.' Ridley reveals to Mrs Fielding his own belief that such externals as a doctorate of laws with its 'red gown' also distinguish him internally as a different individual, as 'a person who couldn't possibly have created that accident, who couldn't possibly have done that murder' (LM 264). Whereas Ridley gives predominance to the exterior distinguishing marks in the determination of personal identity, Mrs Fielding introduces the contrasting idea of self-awareness as a determinant: 'a red gown can't change your own opinion of yourself. The man you live with ... doesn't wear a red gown. He's the man that counts' (LM 265).[12] Both inner self-awareness and exterior distinguishing marks are necessary for an individual's personal identity.

The third question is which external features are reliable indicators of personal identity and which are not. Ridley's concept of 'making' himself into a person 'who couldn't possibly have created that accident' implies that personal identity is under conscious control. If so, it becomes a variable in the human equation instead of a constant, and consequently people cannot be taken at 'face' value. Davies illustrates this question with three cases of mistaken identity. The first, on which the plot of the book largely depends, is Higgin's confusing of Tessie Forgie with Pearl Vambrace; Higgin makes this mistake because he fails to realize that a desk with a nameplate on it is not a reliable indication of the identity of the person seated behind the desk; the error here is in the assumption that the name and the person are the same. The second case is the general mistake of believing Humphrey Cobbler responsible for the false engagement announcement; the people who make this mistake do so because they find Cobbler strange: 'He looked like a gypsy. His appearance was of the sort which causes housewives to lock up their spoons and their daughters' (LM 72); the error here is in the assumption that appearance is a reliable indicator of identity. The third mistake is that made by Mrs Bridgetower and her friends in welcoming Higgin into their social circle; they make this mistake because they believe that the gentility of his 'manners,' because it is like their own, means that he is the same kind of person as they themselves are; the error here is in the assumption that 'manners' are a reliable indicator of personal identity, for manners are a group not an individual characteristic, and therefore cannot indicate personal identity. In each case something irrelevant 'masks' the true 'face' of the individual whose identity is concerned. What is needed to correct each of these cases of mistaken identity is, however, not simply a distinction between the mask and the face, but a distinction between what is and what is not a feature of the face. Moreover, this masking is at least in part under the control of the individual concerned (clearly not in the first case, but Humphrey Cobbler's eccentricity seems to be exaggerated to shock, and Higgin's behaviour is clearly designed to mislead). Hence that part of personal identity which we consciously control can be considered a form of illusion, because it creates a delusion among the group that what they see of the individual is who he is.

The element of conscious control in the development of personal identity is important for two other characters in *Leaven of Malice*: Pearl Vambrace and Solly Bridgetower. Significantly, we are introduced to each of them in the engagement announcement at the beginning of the book as the dependent child of a family unit and faced with the problem of developing an independent personal identity. The state from which they wish to escape – the state of not having an identity – has been illustrated by Freddy Webster (another, though much younger, dependent child) at the beginning of *Tempest-Tost*: 'At fourteen she had no defence against ... sudden shifts. People treated her as a child or an equal, whichever suited them at the moment' (TT 3). The defence she lacks is her independent personal identity which people will have to recognize and reckon with on its own terms. At fourteen Freddy has plenty of time, but Solly and Pearl have delayed the process somewhat because each is the only child of an abnormally possessive parent (Solly's father is dead, and Pearl's mother, although still living, is ineffective), and consequently the process is more difficult: it becomes both more urgent and more a matter of conscious effort.

This struggle for independent personal identity in Pearl and Solly links the illusion pattern with the underlying Jungian psychologem of individuation in *Leaven of Malice*. In their stories, there is a marked increase in complexity in the psychologem: both the anima and its counterpart the animus – the masculine soul-image characteristic of women – are present. A further complexity of the archetypes also introduced here is the ambivalence of both the anima and the animus. This ambivalence, characteristic of everything psychic, is described by Martin:

The nature of these beings is one of manifold ambivalence. They are infantile, undeveloped, semi-animal, semi-reptile even, and at the same time, semi-divine. They are completely indispensable and an insufferable nuisance. They have immense energy, extraordinary insight; and (so long as no adequate relationship is made with them) they will endeavour to use this energy and insight to run the man their own way – which will not be his way. They are immensely wise and can give the worst possible advice. They can be the truest guides and the most arrant deceivers. They are the light and the darkness, inspiration and madness, the new life and a perpetual distraction.[13]

The psychologem is, therefore, double-stranded, not only in that it concerns both Solly's attempt to free himself from his mother and Pearl's attempt to free herself from her father (these two strands being twisted together by the forced engagement), but also in that the archetypes themselves are shown to be double-faced.

The foundations for the individuation of Solly Bridgetower are laid in *Tempest-Tost* where he is shown from the beginning to be under heavy pressure from his mother. According to Jung, for a man 'the first bearer of the soul-image is always the mother' (cw 7:314:197), but this relationship must necessarily change.[14] The anima will be borne by other women, at least until the individual comes to terms with and repossesses his soul. Such a sequence is normal; what is not normal is that the mother should continue as anima-bearer. In such a case it is the demonic anima who is manifest. In Mrs Bridgetower's coaxing of Solly to acknowledge her as the girl 'at home ... waiting' (TT 92) the demonic anima is unmistakably manifest, for clearly she does not intend to relinquish her position as bearer of her son's soul-image. But Solly is at the stage where he must, according to Jung, break her hold on him: 'The important thing at this stage is for a man to be a man. The growing youth must be able to free himself from the anima fascination of his mother' (cw 9(i):146:71). The 'fascination' in the relationship between Solly and his mother is the fascination of the rabbit (Solly) by the weasel (Mrs Bridgetower) – the exercise of 'mana' or psychic power – disguised by her as a demand for reciprocal affection. Solly's needs are at this stage far removed from anything his mother can give him; he needs 'freedom ... a profession ... the love and reassurance of someone other than his mother' (TT 167).

In *Leaven of Malice* Scolly's forced engagement to Pearl Vambrace brings into his life, in the person of Pearl herself, a counter-image of the celestial anima which eventually prevails over his mother's influence. After he has seen Pearl struck by her father, Solly tries to forget about it. But the memory of 'the sound of Pearl Vambrace, weeping ... the ugliest sound he had ever heard, but none the less disturbing' (LM 167) persists, and is sufficient finally to enable him to resist his mother's interrogation about the true state of his relationship with Pearl: '"I don't think you can expect me to answer that question," said Solly, and was quite as surprised as his mother to hear himself say so' (LM 189). This resistance, slight as it is, is enough to begin the process of freeing himself from his mother for it leaves a barrier between them. Mrs Bridgetower's subsequent attempts to strengthen her grip on him come too late in a silent battle of wills. By winning this, Solly wins a victory in the battle for his freedom, but it is not decisive. As the aftermath of Mrs Bridgetower's death in *A Mixture of Frailties* reveals, it is barely more than a holding action.

The blow which encourages Solly in his first resistance to the negative anima figure of his mother is also the blow which encourages Pearl's own first step towards independence from the animus figure of her father. Initially her family situation is no better than Solly's own. Her difficult relationship with her father (for a woman, the first bearer of the animus is her father) is made clear: 'She saw him only as one who made constant demands on her, and was harshly displeased if those demands were not met' (TT 160). Like Mrs Bridgetower, Professor Vambrace exercises over his daughter the possessive tyranny of the demonic or negative archetype. In *Tempest-Tost* Pearl responds more passively to her situation than Solly to his, but she is conscious of the same need for freedom: 'Submissive to her father, loving and helpful to her mother, she was nevertheless conscious that she had a destiny apart from these unhappy creatures, and she waited patiently for the day of her deliverance' (TT 162). This submissiveness still envelops her at the beginning of *Leaven of Malice*.

In spite of her apparent passivity, Pearl is the stronger of the two, and becomes the first to win independence. Her quiet insistence on going to Norm and Dutchy's party precipitates the crisis in her relationship with her father: 'he pushed Pearl toward the gate, and as she fumbled with the latch he cuffed her shrewdly on the ear' (LM 166). The blow decisively releases Pearl from her father's demands and authority: 'She felt herself to be utterly alone and forsaken, for she knew that she had lost her father, more certainly than if he had died that night' (LM 167). From this point, Pearl continues towards complete independence:

in addition to spending a substantial sum on clothes, as an 'act of defiance' she has her hair 'cut to within three inches of her head, and curled' (LM 232–3). Her act of defiance is a symbolic act by which Pearl asserts her control over her own person; it is followed by a symbolic recognition of the emergence of the new identity when Solly rechristens her by her saint's name, Veronica. This rechristening, which makes her the first of Davies' 'twice-born,' confirms her new status as an autonomous adult woman. Pearl/Veronica has retrieved her soul-image from her father by removing from him all the power which she attributed to him as its first bearer. From this act springs her new ability to accept and love her father without submitting to his tyranny, to be able to talk to him, and with Solly to intervene with 'earnest affection' to stop the confrontation between Vambrace and Ridley.

The 'deep wisdom' which moves her in the same scene to kiss her father is the wisdom of a psyche increased by possession of a previously missing element of itself. It is the same wisdom with which Valentine Rich comforts and heals the shattered spirit of Hector Mackilwraith after his suicide attempt and with which Mrs Fielding has earlier comforted Gloster Ridley's misery over his wife's condition and his own responsibility for it. Possession and control of her own animus, her soul-image, brings Pearl/Veronica a stage nearer to individuation.

It is, moreover, this same wisdom, carried forward into her life as Solly's wife, which enables Veronica to help her husband finally free himself from Mrs Bridgetower's spirit. In the fate of Solly and Veronica's first child, stillborn, 'strangling as he moved towards the light' (AMF 272), Davies provides a parallel with Solly's psychic struggle: his very thrust towards freedom from his mother, by fathering a live son and completing the conditions of her will, tightens the hold she has on his soul. By the very energy of his efforts he is temporarily reduced to impotence, unmanned by his mother. With Veronica's help he recovers, but still Mrs Bridgetower asserts her power over him, turning him away from Veronica at the most crucial moments of their relationship: 'in the very climax of love he might have been struggling with the spirit of his Mother, so oblivious did he seem of Veronica' (AMF 273). Veronica, therefore, is confronted with the unleashed power of an opponent far stronger and more malignant than Professor Vambrace ever was. For Mrs Bridgetower is no longer constrained by physical limitations: 'Freed from the cumbrous, ailing body, freed from any obligation to counterfeit the ordinary goodwill of mortal life, her spirit walked abroad, working out its ends and asserting its mastery through a love which was hate, a hatred which was love' (AMF 273). Whereas

Professor Vambrace, first seen in *Tempest-Tost* as the demonic magus in contrast to his role as Prospero,[15] subsequently moves to the personal psychic level as Veronica's animus-figure in *Leaven of Malice*, Mrs Bridgetower, the demonic anima/mother during her life is removed by her death one step away from the personal psychic level to become the demonic sybil (or old wise woman).

Solly is by no means abnormally weak in his inability to cope with this archetype unaided, for the sybil is not usually projected onto the mother. In normal development, Solly would encounter the anima as Veronica encounters her animus, and his ego would be enlarged and strengthened by his conscious control of his soul-image, as hers is; only then would he move on to an encounter with the sybil. Deprived of this reinforcement and by his father's early death of the reinforcement to the ego often provided by the parent of the same sex (a forerunner of the magus figure in the case of a man, and of the sybil in the case of a woman), Solly is simply the victim of a psychic tyranny.

But he has married Veronica, who, being one step nearer individuation, is therefore stronger by one order of magnitude. For Solly, the demonic and the celestial anima are now split, and Veronica becomes his celestial anima. Accepting the burden of this partial projection out of love and compassion, and drawing on her more developed psychic power, Veronica battles on St Nicholas' Eve for the soul of her husband and the life of her son. Although Molly Cobbler believes that Veronica, 'confused by sleep,' wanders into Mrs Bridgetower's room accidentally and collapses, Solly himself knows that it has been a real battle against something, or someone, trying to prevent the live birth of his son and that it is at last defeated. The power of the hostile demonic archetype submits in the end to that of the celestial.

Solly is content to accept Veronica's victory on his behalf, and Davies is content to leave the narrative of their lives here. With the defeat of Mrs Bridgetower's spirit the psychologem of the encounters of the ego with the demonic contrasexual elements, embodied in Solly and Veronica's story and spanning the three novels, is complete. But their story is the subordinate narrative in *A Mixture of Frailties* (1958), in which Davies embarks on a yet further development of the themes of illusion and of identity in the narrative of Monica Gall's training as a concert soprano. This narrative traces her experiences in England and the effect they have on her personality. Consequently, the elements of the theme of illusion (fantasy, delusion, and insanity), although still present, arise only in so far as they contribute to the development of Monica's character. Again, however, the duality involved in illusion and the resolution of it in terms of the Jungian psychologem of the archetypes are as unmistakable as they were in *Leaven of Malice* and *Tempest-Tost*, although *A Mixture of Frailties* is less closely linked to the other two Salterton novels than they are to each other.

Of the three types of illusion in the novel, the element of fantasy is perhaps the slightest. It includes the theme of the three works (*The Discoverie of Witchcraft, Kubla Khan*, and *The Golden Asse*) which Giles writes in the period covered by the novel, all of which are concerned with magic or sorcery in one form or another. Important, too, as a piece of fantasy, is the production of *The Golden Asse* in which Monica takes the part of Fotis, the serving-maid turned enchantress. In addition, two rather more subtle forms of fantasy are introduced by John Scott Ripon. The first is his theory that books 'give shape and focus' to life (AMF 173), which assigns an interpretative function to fantasy, thus developing the nature of fantasy beyond its function as vision but not changing it significantly. His second theory, about off-stage role-playing as a defence of identity, introduces (in his recommendation that Monica should adopt a British mask) the concept of a deliberate use of illusion. Although in his theories the nature of fantasy remains essentially harmless, it is his discussion of the theory of role-playing which introduces the element of insanity in the thematic patterning of the novel.

The element of insanity is much more to the fore in *A Mixture of Frailties* and much more forcefully presented than in *Leaven of Malice*. Giles Revelstoke, whose descent into insanity we follow in *A Mixture of Frailties*, is a central character in the novel and vividly and engagingly portrayed. Ripon thinks that Giles is playing the role of genius 'a bit more obviously and consistently than most' (AMF 238). His analysis of the borderline nature of Giles' fantasy about himself as a genius is one of the first pointers towards Giles' slide from fantasy into delusion and from delusion into insanity: 'But that's what's so silly about Giles; he's obviously a real genius ... But he has to act the genius, as well ... And maybe he isn't play-acting. Ceinwen says that all that bad temper and sardonic laughter and nonsense is quite natural to him' (AMF 238). When Giles' role becomes reality because he has come to believe in it himself, it changes from fantasy to delusion, and from this point Giles' state of mind is shown (in his relationship with Aspinwall, Domdaniel, and, towards the end, Monica) as one of progressively deepening delusion. Finally, he cannot believe the truth when he hears it because it threatens to destroy his delusion; at that point delusion becomes insanity, and Giles commits suicide.

It is, however, delusion which is the focus of the thematic pattern of the novel, and it consists of Monica's deluded acceptance of the mundane reality which masks the transcendent reality. It is complex delusion and the narrative of her training as a concert soprano, supervised by Sir Benedict Domdaniel, details the extended process of its correction. Her delusion is, in effect, the sum of all the 'false' knowledge and attitudes which she has acquired from her upbringing and environment, and its correction involves not only the displacement of this false knowledge from her mind, but also the substitution of true knowledge. Davies presents the distinction between the false mundane and the true transcendent in terms of a polarity of eros and thanatos, worked out in a series of episodes in which Monica is forced to abandon more and more of the fabric of her delusion (such as her romantic notions about music and musicians, her sexual ignorance and inhibition, her 'unsuitable' manners, her mistaken loyalties, and her wrong priorities), and simultaneously to encounter the manifestations of the transcendent reality.

The distinction between eros and thanatos is a distinction between life (eros) and anti-life (thanatos).[16] Domdaniel's blunt opinion is that Monica's environment has been markedly anti-life, but not irreversibly so: 'there's a chance that you may be on the Eros side; there's something about you now and then which suggests it' (AMF 108). On the credit or eros side, Monica has a voice quite good enough to be worth training, 'sincerity, and absolute simplicity' (AMF 54), and aptitude. On the debit or thanatos side is her ignorance, the 'pseudo-religious twaddle' of her background, and her 'fat-headed nineteenth century notions ... about musicians' (AMF 135). Her training is intended to 'nurture the spirit,' a phrase which Giles defines in eros terms as the aim of her lessons with him, and it bears little resemblance to the genteel studies of May Wedderburn in *The First Violin*, from which most of Monica's ideas about musical studies and musicians derive.[17] What Monica undergoes at the hands of her three instructors closely resembles the passionate 'ridding-out' which she gives Giles' flat after she becomes his mistress: they turn upside down all her ideas about the nature and purpose of art.

At the beginning of her training she is presented with a notion of the transcendent reality which is to replace her old reality, and she is immediately responsive to 'the most elevating and releasing experience of her life' (AMF 63) and anxious 'to make [it] her own' (AMF 129). But, as Davies points out in his introduction to *Feast of Stephen*, 'In truth, only technique can be mastered; art masters those who serve it, in

whatever form,'[18] and the first thing Monica has to learn in acquiring
the technique of her art is humility. She cannot make the transcendent
world her own, but must instead allow herself to be mastered by it: 'I
want to go on in the life that has somehow or other found me and
claimed me' (AMF 379). 'Going on' involves first of all the development
of personal identity as an artist, which means establishing personal
autonomy in four areas of her life: family bonds, social relationships,
religious belief, and sexuality.

Autonomy in the face of family bonds is the most difficult to achieve.
Family directives are the most immediately emotional and hence the
most difficult to ignore. Monica is aware from the beginning that the
members of her family are 'thanatossers,' 'everything about them contrary to her great dream of life' (AMF 63), and her refusal to admit to
herself her criticism of her family is, she thinks, a form of loyalty. Her
new life not only enlarges her notion of loyalty but also plunges her into
a conflict of loyalties: 'she had not realized how costly such loyalty
might be. She had not foreseen that it could mean keeping two sets of
mental and moral books ... To close either set of books forever would
be a kind of suicide, and yet to keep them both was hypocrisy' (AMF
265–6). It is a conflict which, in keeping with Jung's statement that 'all
the greatest and most important problems of life are fundamentally
insoluble,'[19] she does not solve, but which in a sense is solved for her
by her mother's death. In wrestling with it, however, she discovers that
the only loyalty she can permit herself is loyalty to her art. Molloy
explains the implications to her on the occasion of the commemorative
concert for Giles: 'a public performer's first duty is to himself, and
unless he remembers that he can't do his duty to the public. You must
understand it rightly: cherish the art in yourself, not yourself in art'
(AMF 357). Cherishing the art in herself is, therefore, both freedom and
discipline.

Autonomy in social relationships not only releases her from the conventions of group behaviour but also supplies her with a new concept
of truth. Because 'pretence is wonderfully stimulating to the artistic
mind' (AMF 188), her social autonomy includes not only the 'freedom to
say one thing and think another' which she discovers during her visit
to the McCorkills but also the freedom to practise deception. Deception
is so far permissible for an artist that Domdaniel not only accepts
Monica's attempt to conceal her part in Giles' death but also makes himself an accessory after the fact. Moreover, with Aunt Ellen, whom it
would have been 'inexcusable cruelty' to disillusion about the real nature
of the musical world, deception is not merely permissible but obligatory.

Self-deception, however, as Domdaniel warns her, is the artist's greatest danger: 'Whatever deception you may have to practise on other people, you must not, under any circumstances, deceive yourself' (AMF 363). Self-deception precludes the development of the 'dual consciousness of the actress' which Monica will need as a singer in order 'to give herself to her part, and at the same time to stand a little aside, criticising, prompting and controlling' (AMF 321). If the artist believes in the part he is playing his total consciousness is involved, and there is no control and direction from a second consciousness. Self-deception, therefore, is not only delusion, but also bad art.

In order to develop autonomy in family and social relationships, Monica has to be instructed about the eros concepts of loyalty and honesty, respectively, so that in each of them, therefore, autonomy is achieved by the correction of her ignorance. Monica's 'cultural malnu-trition,' however, consists of inhibition as well as ignorance, and in those relationships where she is inhibited she achieves autonomy by the release of her inhibitions, allowing her to express previously repressed elements of herself. Davies' strategy here is to show Monica's develop-ment of autonomy of religious belief and of sexual morality in terms of the development of her function-type.

In Jungian theory music is closely associated with feeling, the mode of psychological functioning which 'imparts a definite *value* in the sense of acceptance or rejection' to whatever it is faced with (CW 6:724:434). Appropriately, Monica's function-type is shown to be feeling and is clearly illustrated in her reaction to death, which she understands en-tirely in terms of feeling, as Davies indicates on her visit to Giles' grave; 'She was glad that Giles lay there ... with open countryside beyond the churchyard walls; it stilled a deep feeling which had troubled her that he was somewhere, agonized, confined and alone' (AMF 355). Never-theless, a person whose dominant functions or function-type, is feel-ing does not necessarily have more capacity for emotion than anyone else. Consequently, although Monica is a feeling type, she is not in the usual sense of the words a particularly emotional person. In the course of her musical training she learns several things which are relevant to the development of her function-type. From Molloy she learns to 'com-mand emotion' (AMF 114), from Giles to 'feel a little, and understand, respect and cherish her own feeling' (AMF 158), and from Domdaniel to 'make out of the feelings life brings us ... something a little different, something not quite so shattering but very much more polished and perhaps also more poignant, than the feelings themselves' (AMF 214). But it is because she is forced to pay conscious attention to the command of emotion, and to the distillation of experience into art, that her 'feeling' becomes more accessible and more comprehensible to her, to the point where, at the tomb of St Geneviève, she can assert its total validity for her: 'Here was feeling, and feeling was reality' (AMF 247).

The autonomy in religious belief necessary for her if she is to develop as an artist is also achieved, therefore, through her feeling. The question is raised in the interpretation of sacred music, from which, as Domdaniel explains to her, sectarian or credal rigidity must be excluded: 'One's personal beliefs are peripheral, really, if one is an interpreter of other men's work; Bach was devout, but it is far more important for me to understand the quality of his devotion than to share it' (AMF 241). Hence, Monica is able to achieve autonomy by shedding the superficialities of the doctrines of the Thirteener Church, while retaining her innate religious sense: 'Christian myth and Christian morality were part of the fabric of her life, dimly apprehended and taken for granted behind the externals of belief. And it is what is taken for granted in our homes ... which supplies the bones of our faith' (AMF 233). Having achieved this autonomy, she welcomes the transcendent reality in religion, a reality which speaks to her through her religious feeling: 'Then, in the darkness beneath the canopy, there was something of a saint? ... She had never considered saints before. But, with a sense of awe and wonder that she had never known, Monica went to the tomb and, when no one was near, knelt and stretched her hand through the grille. "Help me," she prayed, touching the smooth stone ... ' (AMF 248). The comparison between the 'dark splendour' of the church of St Étienne du Mont where Monica finds the tomb of St Geneviève, and the 'bleak, naked horror of enthroned Reason' in the Panthéon from which she has just come, serves to emphasize further how deeply Monica's religious feeling is involved in this vision of transcendental reality.

Monica's autonomy in sexual morality is also achieved by a release from inhibition involving her feeling function. Her mother has taught her a 'morality of sexual prohibition' which Domdaniel attempts to counteract by telling her that 'chastity is having the body in the soul's keeping' and that the only sin passion can commit is to be joyless (AMF 242). That this is nearer to her own understanding is clear from her reflection that 'everything in her own experience supported it' (AMF 282). But the clearest indication is her response to Giles' seduction: 'miraculously, at this moment when she should have stood in awe of her mother, and Pastor Beamis and the whole moral code of the Thirteeners, she felt, on the contrary, free of them' (AMF 182). Part of Monica's response to Giles is a result of instinctive knowledge: 'she knew something which they [her mother and the Thirteeners] could never have known, or they would not have talked as they did,' to the extent that she feels 'as though reunited with something they sought to deny her.' Clearly then, by shedding the inhibitions imposed on her by her upbringing she can be released into a state of full autonomy in sexual morality.

Through the achievement of this fourfold autonomy, Monica is brought to a point at which experience of the transcendent reality is possible, and her most enduring experience of the transcendent reality is brought about through music. From the beginning of her training music has the power to move her, but her fullest understanding of the transcendent reality comes through hearing and taking part in a performance of Bach's *St Matthew Passion*: 'she was conscious as never before of the power of music to impose order and form upon the vastest and most intractable elements in human experience' (AMF 236). By taking part in the music, Monica moves beyond it into a transcendent state of being in which she not only recognizes the ordering power of music but also is enabled to apply that ordering power to her own life. In this state, as she sings, her most important decisions are made: about Domdaniel's proposal, for example: 'Monica sang, giving her full attention to what she was doing; sang well and happily, all her perplexities banished as she balanced the delicate vocal meditation above the great chorale in *Three Kings from Persian Lands.* When she was finished, she found that her mind was cleared, and she knew what she should do' (AMF 379). Monica finds a symbol for this transcendent state in Thomas Arne's song, *Water Parted*, which she sings in public for the first time at her mother's funeral. In thinking about the effect of the song she concludes that in this transcendent state she is in a 'condition of being ... beyond' the Monica Gall of her outer everyday life (AMF 311) and has taken on a new identity. The question of identity now becomes more complex. The two selves she appears to recognize – herself in this transcendent state and her everyday self – are clearly different but not separate, and the personal identity she has so painfully achieved is not a simple but at least a dual identity.

It is at this point that Davies makes the crucial link between the theme of illusion (developed through the autonomous personal identity of the artist) and the theme of psychic identity (developed in terms of the Jungian psychologem of individuation): the duality of identity which Monica has discovered in herself is in Jungian terms the duality of the ego and the self. Hence it is in terms of Jungian theory that the implications of her discovery can properly be understood.

The concept of the self is one of the most fundamental principles of Jungian psychology, as well as one of the most difficult. In *Ego and Archetype*, his study of the development of the self in the individual, E.F. Edinger describes the discovery of the self as second in importance only to the discovery of the collective unconscious:

> Jung's most basic and far-reaching discovery is the collective unconscious or archetypal psyche. Through his researches, we now know that the individual psyche is not just a product of personal experience. It also has a pre-personal or trans-personal dimension which is manifested in universal patterns and images such as are found in all the world's religions and mythologies. It was Jung's further discovery that the archetypal psyche has a structuring or ordering principle which unifies the various archetypal contents. This is the central archetype or archetype of wholeness which Jung has termed the Self.
>
> The Self is the ordering and unifying center of the total psyche (conscious and unconscious) just as the ego is the center of the conscious personality. Or, put in other words, the ego is the seat of *subjective* identity while the Self is the seat of *objective* identity. The Self is thus the supreme psychic authority and subordinates the ego to it. The Self is most simply described as the inner empirical deity and is identical with the *imago Dei*.[20]

The development of the human personality can, according to Edinger, be described in terms of the relationship between the ego and the self. The normal human being moves from 'a total state of primary ego-Self identity' as an infant (inflation), through an emergent state in which ego and self begin to separate but still overlap (alienation), to a state in which only 'a residual ego-Self identity still remains' (individuation). In individuation the 'ego-Self axis,' which up to this point has been 'completely unconscious and therefore indistinguishable from ego-Self identity, has now become partly conscious,' and individuation is 'characterized by a conscious dialectic relationship between ego and Self.'[21] Evolution from alienation to individuation is accomplished through the resolution by the ego of the successive archetypal figures of the unconscious, thus establishing the ego in charge of the ego-Self axis: 'The ego-Self axis represents the vital connection between ego and Self that must be relatively intact if the ego is to survive stress and grow. This axis is the gateway or path of communication between the conscious personality and the archetypal psyche. Damage to the ego-Self axis impairs or destroys the connection between conscious and unconscious, leading to alienation of the ego from its origin and foundation.'[22] If the conscious personality does not control the path of communication then it will be subject to attack by the unconscious.

In *A Mixture of Frailties* the evolution from alienation to individuation is followed in considerable detail. It is figured by Monica's relationship with three of the other major characters. Monica, as the ego-figure, must encounter the animus (Giles), sybil (Ma Gall), and magus (Domdaniel) and, by the adjustment of her relationship with each of them, resolve the psychic element which each represents into harmony with her conscious personality. There is some support for considering Alice Gall (Monica's sister) and Persis Kinwellmarshe as shadow figures in relation to Monica at different stages in the narrative, but this is a minor point in the dramatic structure.

The first of the three to be introduced is, in compliance with narrative demands rather than clinical analytic pattern (which would suggest that the animus would be first), the sybil, manifested in the person of Mrs Gall, Monica's mother, who thinks of herself 'as a Character, with a capital letter' (AMF 62). At Monica's farewell party the 'Character' which Mrs Gall likes to play, the psychic element which she represents in Monica's life, and her actual physical relationship to Monica merge in the figure of 'the Earth-Goddess, the Many-Breasted Mother, dispensing food and drink' (AMF 81). The earth-goddess role is one of the many manifestations of the sybil which she represents in Monica's psychic make-up. Like all the archetypes, the sybil is ambivalent, appearing in both demonic and celestial manifestations. In Mrs Gall we see one of the demonic manifestations but, in spite of this, she is not only potentially but actually Monica's ego-source.

Certainly Monica has to reject a great deal which she inherits from her mother. Nevertheless, rejection of what is demonic in her ego-source must not lead to rejection of the ego-source as a whole, for that would damage the ego-self axis. Some bond with the ego-source is required, as Monica instinctively recognizes: 'If these ideas [of good and bad] were invalid for her, what else that was valid had her mother to give her? Nothing, thought Monica; not with any sense of freedom, of breaking a lifelong bondage, but sadly and with pity for her mother and herself' (AMF 282). Mourning the absence of a positive bond between herself and her mother, she acknowledges implicitly the existence and propriety of a bond of some sort. Immediately after this acknowledgement comes the first understanding between Monica and her mother, and this provides the positive element necessary in the bond. In a brief lucid period before her death Mrs Gall tells her daughter: 'I've got quite an imagination. That's where you're like me, Monny. Always remember that. You get that from me' (AMF 282). Made aware of the positive bond, Monica can then accept some of the negative element which she cannot lose or change. By accepting it, she can control it, even when it attacks her in the form of depression about her singing: 'By now she had some experience of this state, and recent reflection had convinced her that it was part of her heritage from Ma; her imagination, and her ups and downs of feeling, were Ma's ... she must not let them dominate her life' (AMF 298). After she has accepted this element, she can begin to understand herself and her mother and the way in which they are alike: 'For in Ma ... was an artist – a spoiled artist ... who nevertheless possessed the artist's temperament' (AMF 303). The result is an ironic reversal of the apparent importance to Monica of Ma Gall and Aunt Ellen. Aunt Ellen, a 'specialist in romance,' has seemed to provide Monica with her music; what she has actually given is merely technical instruction. All her non-technical instruction, drawn from *The Victor Book of the Opera* and *The First Violin*, has to be jettisoned. But Mrs Gall, who has in Monica's first estimate 'given her everything, except music' (AMF 67), has in fact given her music and nothing else; it is from Mrs Gall, the spoiled artist, that Monica derives her artistic gift without which Aunt Ellen's instruction is useless.

In terms of the psychologem of individuation, Monica's adjustment of her relationship to her mother (from uncomprehending antagonism to understanding and control of what she has inherited from her) shows the resolution of the archetype of the sybil. Monica confronts the archetype, learns to control its inimical element, and takes up the unconscious libido attached to it into her conscious personality. In this way she enlarges and strengthens her conscious personality and establishes one healthy strand in the ego-self axis.

In a similar way she finally wins control over her animus, as figured by Giles Revelstoke. Giles, who is 'smiling like a demon' in Monica's first encounter with him (AMF 149), proceeds to show himself to be truly demonic. To begin with, he is, as animus figures usually are, domineering: 'Revelstoke had made her sing against her will, and she knew that he could make her speak' (AMF 150). Moreover, in spite of his gentleness with her when he seduces her and later when she becomes his mistress, he has no love for her: 'I don't love you ... But if ever I do love you, I'll tell you' (AMF 221). Recognizing his power over her, he exploits it to the full, always to his own advantage: 'Giles liked comfort ... and once the flat was running in a reasonably orderly manner, he wanted it to continue that way ... And he began to work her mercilessly at her singing lessons ... He hunted out and revised his songs ... and it was her task to copy the new versions neatly' (AMF 229). These are signs not only of human domineering but also of the working of the demonic animus, inimical and threatening to the ego.

Instinctively Monica recognizes the threat, and her recognition prompts her self-preservative actions on the night of his death. The dreams she has of Giles later confirm the threat: 'Three times she dreamed that Giles came to her, his eyes ablaze, his mouth distorted with rage, and menaced her with a bloody knife. But although this dream paralyzed her with terror, its after-effect was life-enhancing, and she woke moist, panting and stirred to the depths of her being' (AMF 352). The dream is significant on more than one level. First, it presents to Monica's conscious mind the unconscious reason for what she did, making her aware of the totality of the threat to her life which Giles represented. By recognizing that she acted defensively, she can begin to cope with her feelings of guilt, which are anti-life, and hence the dream is life-enhancing. Second, the dream signifies that the animus has been contained within the conscious personality (Giles is no longer a person outside her but a figure in her dream). The conscious personality therefore has the animus-libido integrated within it to draw upon, and this again is life-enhancing in that it enhances the ego.

Furthermore, once the threat is recognized and dealt with, Monica can begin to see things in a truer perspective. Her ability to detach herself from Giles' death may appear somewhat callous: 'to her surprise and shame, Giles seemed to be behind her, too. She grieved for him, but her guilt was retreating from her' (AMF 365). But in terms of the psychic struggle of the ego against the archetype of the unconscious such an ability is absolutely essential. The ego must preserve its integrity and command the ego-self axis or it will be destroyed in psychosis. The animus, moreover, does not disappear as a result of being taken up into the conscious personality any more than Giles' memory disappears from Monica's consciousness: 'she would never be free of him. By his suicide he had put his mark on her forever' (AMF 378). What remains is the positive aspect of the animus. Giles, in the course of their relationship, does benefit Monica; however exhausting and tyrannical his instruction in the literature of song may be, he has not only nurtured her spirit but also provided her with music especially designed to show the qualities of her voice: 'he had prepared an accompaniment for it [*Water Parted*], for her special use, and had set it in a key which made the best use of what he called her "chalumeau register," as well as the brilliance of her upper voice' (AMF 305). In addition, under his guidance, she was developing 'a faculty of finding worth where others had missed it' (AMF 306). It is only when the animus is integrated into the conscious personality that the ego can discriminate between the demonic and the celestial, the negative and the positive aspects, and that Monica can fully appreciate Giles. Moreover, resolution of the animus further strengthens the ego-self link as the Ego then incorporates the attached libido.

The magus figure in Monica's life, Sir Benedict Domdaniel, differs in two important respects from the sybil and the animus figures. First, his name, unlike theirs, is directly symbolic of his archetypal function: Domdaniel is the 'fabled abode of evil spirits, gnomes, and enchanters under the roots of the ocean,'[23] and his name therefore hints not only at his archetypal mana as similar to the power of an enchanter (or magus), but also at his function as one of the deep-lying powers of the unconscious (the unconscious is typically symbolized by the ocean, but Domdaniel is 'under the roots' of it). His given name, Benedict (blessed), moreover, hints at the second difference between this archetype and the other two: this archetype is manifest in its celestial, rather than its demonic, aspect. Consequently, the nature of the encounter with this archetype follows a different pattern from the two previous encounters. In dealing with the sybil and the animus, Monica is dealing with demonic manifestations, directly inimical to the ego, and the effort needed to resolve them and to integrate them into the conscious personality is considerable; this effort is reflected in the conflicts in the relationships in the narrative which terminate in the deaths of the characters concerned. The celestial manifestation of the magus, however, can be resolved without so much of a struggle.

Monica's relationship with her magus goes well from the start. She correctly identifies his role in her life on first meeting him when she casts him as the counterpart of von Francius in *The First Violin*, recognizing even as she does so, however, that he is not a demonic figure like von Francius (AMF 66). Domdaniel is, furthermore, the first person she meets who can reveal the transcendent reality to her, and his attitude to her throughout the novel is kindly. Nevertheless, her relationship with him, although it involves less conflict than her other relationships, does demand that he be confronted at least once. This confrontation develops out of Monica's refusal to fall in love at his bidding in order to 'extend [her] range;' her refusal is couched in such forthright and uncompromising terms that Domdaniel is forced to apologize (AMF 213). This confrontation demonstrates the need for the ego's assertion of control over the libido even of the celestial magus in order to command

the ego-self axis and to maintain full unhindered communication between the conscious personality and the unconscious. Because the conflict here is so much less strenuous, the resolution of the magus is
accomplished without violence by Monica's marriage to Domdaniel,
rather than by his death and transformation into a voice within her
mind.

Davies chooses as the appropriate narrative device of the operation of
the archetypes within the conscious personality that of the 'inner voice.'
Monica begins to hear the voices of her sybil and her animus inside
her head. Mrs Gall's, as the sybil's, is the first to manifest itself in this
way: 'Miss Kinwellmarshe ... went to the kitchen. *She's got a butt-end on
her like a bumble-bee,* said the voice of Ma Gall, very clearly, inside Monica's head – so clearly that Monica started' (AMF 148). At first Monica
finds the intrusion of her mother's voice not only confusing but frighten-
ing: 'sometimes it seemed like a form of possession' (AMF 163). The
next voice is that of Giles as her animus: 'the inner voice ... said: *Don't be a
hypocrite; you're ashamed of them* ... in this case it used the voice of Giles
Revelstoke' (AMF 285–6). At first she identifies the voices as a single
'intruder' using different voices and having different functions: 'a
new conscience' (AMF 285) or an 'inner critic,' or something which 'complicated her life, and at the same time kept her romanticism from
running away with her' (AMF 371). Later, as she listens to Dean Knapp
read the lesson at the Bridgetower memorial sermon, she recognizes
the voices as separate entities and examines their function in her life:
'Monica paid little attention after the words ... *thy voice shall be, as one
that hath a familiar spirit* ... reached her ears. Like me, she thought; only I
have two ... Is it perhaps my substitute for thinking – orders and hints
and even jokes from deep down, through the voice and personality of
someone I've loved – yes, and feared.' (AMF 372). She is perhaps
correct in thinking of them as familiar spirits, but otherwise incorrect.
Since feeling is Monica's superior or differentiated conscious function,
the inferior opposite function, lying in the unconscious, is thinking.
The inner voices are, therefore, not a substitute for thinking, but a way
in which her unconscious function can supplement her conscious function, and an image of how the ego-self axis works within the individual.
It can operate before the archetypes are fully integrated into the
conscious mind, so that it is long before Mrs Gall's death that her voice
begins to speak in Monica's mind, but it only becomes fully operational
when Monica understands what is happening and why.[24]

With the integration of the last of the archetypes and the resolution of
the ego-self axis, the examination of the movement from alienation to

individuation ends, and the reconciliation of the dualities involved in the novel's examination of illusion is complete. Davies closes the parallel narratives of the novel simultaneously, ending both the narrative of Monica's training as a singer and the narrative of Solly and Veronica's marriage with the breaking of the Bridgetower Trust. In the final pages Solly, Veronica, and Monica all celebrate the safe arrival of the baby boy who breaks the Trust, and both *A Mixture of Frailties* and the trilogy as a whole are, with not too many loose ends, concluded on this triumphant note.

Certain general conclusions can be drawn about the nature of the duality examined in each novel and about the mode of its resolution. In *Tempest-Tost*, the duality involved is that of the transcendent and the mundane, presented not as a duality of fact and appearance but as two worlds. Individuals who are shown to have moved nearest to true identity (Valentine Rich and Humphrey Cobbler) are those who have accepted both worlds as equally real, or as two modes of reality. It is only within the human psyche that the transcendent and the mundane coexist; the human psyche is the interface between the modes. The individual who comprehends only one mode (the mundane) is incomplete; to move to his true identity he must comprehend the reality of the transcendent. The modes are separated within the psyche by a very thin membrane. Unless the ego learns to pass through the membrane and recognize both modes, the higher-energy transcendent will invade and possess the mundane. This process is shown in Hector Mackilwraith's struggle to cope with the influx of the transcendent reality into his life, figured by the Jungian psychologem of the incursion of the anima. Because the anima lies in the unconscious it is a part of the transcendent reality, and the resolution of the anima is synthesis of the dual modes of reality, transcendent and mundane, as well as synthesis of the ego and its contrasexual element. Analysis in *Tempest-Tost* separates and distinguishes the dual modes of reality; synthesis is achieved by the individual's simultaneous comprehension of both modes.

Within the dual modes of reality, however, each mode involves a further duality. In *Leaven of Malice* the duality is the mundane duality of true and false identity. In the mundane reality of each individual the elements involved in the creation of personal identity are either extrinsic or intrinsic to that identity. The problem of personal identity in the mundane reality parallels the problem of psychic identity in the transcendent reality: this is worked out in the story of Pearl Vambrace whose achievement of a personal identity, independent of her identity as her father's daughter, is also the achievement of the resolution of the animus in her psyche, which again is a stage in the achievement of true psychic identity (the self). Pearl retains her affection for her father after she has achieved her independence, but she does so by loving him without identifying with him. Analysis is here achieved by the separation of the intrinsic elements of personality from the extrinsic, so that the intrinsic personality is left whole but uncontaminated; synthesis is achieved by that personality's command of both itself and the rejected extrinsic elements.

The duality of the transcendent mode of reality explored in *A Mixture of Frailties* lies between the dark and the light, the demonic and the celestial. But the resolution of this duality involves each of the other two. Monica Gall is, like Valentine Rich and Humphrey Cobbler, an interpretative artist and the narrative follows her training as a singer as a method of resolving all three dualities. To begin with Monica must resolve the duality of mundane and transcendent: she must learn to analyze the duality by recognizing the separate modes and to synthesize it by inhabiting both modes simultaneously. In addition, she must in the mundane mode resolve the duality of the true and false, life and anti-life, elements of her personality by commanding both from the standpoint of her true, autonomous eros (life) personality. In the transcendent mode she must analyze the demonic and celestial aspects of the archetypes, and synthesize her self by the resolution of the celestial side of the archetypes into her conscious personality by the creation of the ego-self axis, while still commanding the demonic side of the archetypes.

The completion of the Salterton trilogy brought to an end for some time Davies' discussions of illusion and identity, of the modes of reality, and of individuation. But it did not exhaust his preoccupation with them. Twelve years later, in *Fifth Business*, he returned to the same themes with renewed vigour and increased intellectual and artistic involvement.

4 / Interface

In *Fifth Business* (1970), Davies continues to pursue his attempt to
define human identity, and comes up with a novel which is very different
from any of his preceding ones. He uses the paradigm of illusion and
the Jungian psychologem of individuation, but between *A Mixture of
Frailties* and *Fifth Business* the focus of his interest shifts, and his artistic
skill develops, so that in *Fifth Business* his treatment of illusion and of
individuation is not only more complex but also more closely integrated.
In his discussion of illusion he is concerned at this stage not with the
synthesizing of dualities which preoccupied him in the Salterton trilogy,
but with the nature of what we know as reality, whether it is the
transcendent psychic reality or the mundane physical reality, and he
explores this theme in four psychosymbolic patterns of opposition.
The increased integration of the illusion theme with the theme of individuation results from his carrying over the examination of reality
from one theme to another. He achieves this carry-over by making the
examination of reality the explicit concern of his narrator and a central character, Dunstan Ramsay, in whose autobiographical narrative the
psychosymbolic patterns are manifest as he progresses towards individuation and the development of the autonomous Jungian self. The carry-
over is further supported by the considerable increase in narrative skill
which enables Davies to free his presentation of individuation from
the rather simplistic pattern of a series of encounters with archetypal
manifestations. Through Dunstan Ramsay's exploration of the nature
of reality in his life, Davies therefore explores not only the paradigm of
illusion, but also the gradual development towards individuation of a
fully realized character. Moreover, by focussing that exploration on religious belief, Davies both extends the paradigm of illusion and also
brings into his discussion of the concept of reality an ambivalence which
appears to erode the distinction between actuality and appearance.

The initial factor which must be taken into account in considering Davies' treatment of the theme of illusion is that his concept of illusion changes radically between the conclusion of *A Mixture of Frailties* and the beginning of *Fifth Business*. In the Salterton trilogy, as I have pointed out, illusion is shown to deceive the observer about the nature of reality by functioning as a mask. In *Fifth Business*, however, illusion is shown to illuminate reality for the observer by functioning as a metaphor. Some such bridge as illusion, it is implied, is necessary between reality and the observer because unmediated reality is not apprehensible by the observer's limited human nature. This changed concept of illusion is expressed in the treatment of the illusion paradigm in which, from the beginning of the novel, all the elements of illusion explored in the Salterton trilogy are re-explored at greater depth: the nature of insanity is examined through the history of Mary Dempster's mental condition; the nature of fantasy is examined through Paul's career as a magician; and the nature of delusion is examined through Ramsay's fixed belief that Mary Dempster is a saint. It is through Ramsay's efforts to substantiate this belief that Davies introduces his examination of the nature of religious belief (faith) as a type of illusion not previously discussed (illusion which is voluntary and incorrigible); he moves from there to a consideration of the nature of good and evil and, finally, to a consideration of the nature of reality. The theme of illusion, therefore, occupies the foreground of the novel, and is presented much more explicitly as Davies allows his thoughtful and articulate narrator to brood upon the ideas suggested to him by the events of his life.

Ramsay's declared interest in insanity introduces that element of illusion to the reader early in the novel. It begins as a childish curiosity in 'poor demented' Miss Athelstan, but develops, in the history of Mary Dempster, into a deeply compassionate understanding as Ramsay's visits to her in the asylum teach him that 'though reason may be injured, feeling lives intensely in the insane' (FB 210). The onset of Mary Dempster's insanity is first described by Mrs Ramsay, who observes a change in her after Paul's premature birth: 'She's as quiet and friendly and sweet-natured as she ever was, poor little soul, but she just isn't all there' (FB 20). After the episode with the tramp in the gravel pit, however, Ramsay's own attitude becomes more complex: 'there was an aspect of Mary Dempster which was outside my ken; and ... I decided that this unknown aspect must be called madness' (FB 56). This attitude of the sexually uninitiated adolescent is modified by his interest in 'madness': 'She was a little strange because she had been so lonely, but she made good sense' (FB 53–4). Later in his life Ramsay is able, in the light of his adult knowledge, to analyze Mrs Dempster's strangeness as a 'lack of fear.' But he makes it clear that it is not this fearlessness alone, but its coexistence with another quality (which he recognizes at the time), which enabled him to avoid the villagers' mistaken fear: 'she was wholly religious ... She lived by a light that arose from within; I could not comprehend it, except that it seemed to be somewhat akin to the splendours I found in books, though not in any way bookish. It was as though she were an exile from a world that saw things her way' (FB 55). This passage is important in the characterization of Ramsay because it demonstrates the early roots of his interest in the nature of religious belief, as well as confirming his interest in madness and the strange. But more importantly it suggests, by implying a fusion between insanity and religious belief, the ambivalence of the latter. There are, moreover, two points in the same paragraph which do a great deal to undercut the previous suggestion that insanity, like other forms of illusion, takes account of appearance only. First, there is Ramsay's speculation that there might be 'a world that saw things her way,' where someone like Mrs Dempster belonged. Second, there is the linking of this world and the inner light by which Mrs Dempster lives with 'the splendours ... found in books' – splendours certainly not evident in Deptford. Some of these splendours are found in the *Arabian Nights* and some in the books of stage-magic which inspire Ramsay to want to become an illusionist and, subsequently, after discovering his own clumsiness, to teach Paul. The early juxtaposition of madness, magic, and religious theory, in the context of Ramsay's incomprehension of what he saw in Mrs Dempster and his speculation about a possible 'other' reality, begins to prepare the reader for a reconsideration of the nature of reality.

The narrative of Paul Dempster's career as an illusionist, which has a great deal of structural importance in the plot of the book (because it enables Paul, as Magnus Eisengrim, to return unrecognized by Boy Staunton) also provides the major element of fantasy in the book. Paul's career owes more to Ramsay than the mechanics of card-tricks and sleight-of-hand with eggs. Ramsay also inadvertently teaches Paul two attitudes to illusion which will be carried into Paul's life as Magnus Eisengrim. The first is the equation of magic with power, which Ramsay makes on seeing the books of magic: 'as soon as I saw them I knew that fate meant them for me. By studying them I should become ... a great power' (FB 31). At this point the equation is made in a very general way, but at its second appearance it refers specifically to power for Ramsay needs power to escape from his mother: 'It was necessary for me to gain power in some realm into which my parents – my mother particularly – could not follow me' (FB 35). In Paul's life this equation of magic and power has a double effect. It enables him (as in fact it does not enable Ramsay, whose only avenue of escape is to enlist) to escape from his mother by running away as an apprentice conjuror, for Paul's own narrative of his escape implies that his showing-off of his ability as an illusionist to Willard, as well as the latter's morphia-induced carelessness and sexual impulse, contributed to Willard's abduction of him (FB 305). Furthermore the equation of magic and power also causes Paul to take his illusions seriously: 'Eisengrim now introduced himself to us ... He received us as honoured guests and promised us an evening of such visions and illusions as had nourished the imagination of mankind for two thousand years – and a few trifles for amusement as well. This was a novelty – a poetic magician who took himself seriously' (FB 236). As Paul is aware, the dignity of his show is an important part of his success, but so is his insistence on the innocence of his make-believe, which is the second attitude to illusion that he has learned from Ramsay. Ramsay cannot accept the Reverend Amasa Dempster's view of magic as 'mere cheating and gambling; it had seemed to me to be a splendid extension of life, a creation of a world of wonder, that hurt nobody' (FB 43). Paul adopts Ramsay's view and uses it as one of his arguments to persuade Ramsay to write Magnus Eisengrim's autobiography: 'What we offer is innocent – just an entertainment in which a hungry part of the spirit is fed' (FB 244). The autobiography is itself another example of innocent illusion, allowing Ramsay to enjoy the pleasures of creating one 'full of romance and marvels' (FB 269). As such it plays an important part in the development of his self-knowledge. It is, moreover, the innocence of magic which betrays the ambivalence of this form of illusion. The undercutting phrase is that which refers to magic as 'a splendid extension of life, a creation of a world of wonder.' The link with splendour is again made, as it is in the phrase which reveals the ambivalence of insanity. It is important, too, that Ramsay suggests that magic creates not an appearance which obscures life but an extension of life. The phrase 'a world of wonder' echoes the idea that Mary Dempster is an exile from another world and suggests that in their ambivalence there is a link between fantasy and insanity. The same question is implied about both: how far are they, after all, only appearances?

The main element of delusion in the book, Ramsay's fixed belief that Mary Dempster is a saint, is shown to be equally ambivalent. Ramsay develops a liking for saints early in his life from *A Child's Book of Saints*. This liking runs contrary to the general attitude in puritan Protestant Deptford, which is represented at its extreme by Amasa Dempster's opinion that 'the veneration of saints was one of the vilest superstitions of the Scarlet Woman of Rome' (FB 42). Either from his *Child's Book of Saints*, or more probably from his encyclopedia, Ramsay learns that three authenticated miracles are demanded before an individual can be canonized. Disconcertingly, the first mention of miracles in connection with Mary Dempster is not her first, which for the time being is passed over without comment, but the second: 'For me, Willie's recall from death is, and will always be, Mrs. Dempster's second miracle' (FB 67). The third miracle is recognizable without being described as such: Ramsay, wounded in the taking of an enemy machine-gun placement, drags himself to shelter in the ruins of a church: 'As the hissing flame dropped I saw there about ten or twelve feet above me on an opposite wall, in a niche, a statue of the Virgin and Child. I did not know it then but I know now that it was the assembly of elements which represent the Immaculate Conception ... But what hit me worse than the blow of the shrapnel was that the face was Mrs. Dempster's face' (FB 84–5). Only a considerable time later, after Ramsay's encounter with Joel Surgeoner, whom he recognizes as the tramp in the gravel-pit, are we told that Mary Dempster's giving of herself to the tramp as an act of charity constituted her first miracle because it led to his conversion.

Ramsay's delusion about Mrs Dempster's sainthood gives the impetus to his search for the 'little Madonna' of his experience at Passchendaele: 'The little Madonna was a bee in my bonnet; I wanted to see her again, and quite unreasonably ... I kept hoping to find her' (FB 140). This search expands into a lifelong preoccupation with the nature of saints in general which leads to his various books and to his extensive travelling. During the course of this delusion various people make an effort to 'correct' it: the new minister, the Reverend Donald Phelps, Diana, Boy Staunton, and Father Regan. He remains obstinately deluded, however, until he finds the little Madonna herself in an exhibition of *Schöne Madonnen*: 'There she was, quite unmistakable, from the charming crown that she wore with such an air to her foot set on the crescent moon ... But the face of the Madonna – was it truly the face of Mary Dempster? No, it was not, though the hair was very like; Mary Dempster, whose face my mother had described as being like a pan of milk, had never been so beautiful in feature, but the expression was undeniably hers – an expression of mercy and love, tempered with perception and penetration' (FB 295). In these comments we see Ramsay attempt to match his remembered vision with the reality which has eluded him for so long, and to assess objectively the relative weight of fact and illusion. For an objective assessment, however, the description is oddly ambivalent. His conclusion is that the features are not those of Mary Dempster, but that the expression is hers. The emphasis on the difference between Mary Dempster's plainness and the statue's beauty suggests that Ramsay thinks that the resemblance which he saw in the light of the flare has been a mistake, not a miracle, and that therefore Mary Dempster cannot be a saint. But the comment that the expression was hers suggests that what he recognized was the inner resemblance and, consequently, that he was *not* mistaken, but witness to a genuine miracle, in which case Mary Dempster *is* a saint. Reinforcing this ambivalence is his final comment when he leaves Salzburg: 'when my week was up I never saw it [the Madonna] again. Photography in the exhibition was forbidden. But I needed no picture. She was mine forever' (FB 295). This ambiguity of phrasing leaves uncertain whether it is the corrected image or the original image which he retains.

The search for the Madonna is the origin of his interest in hagiography generally and in the nature of faith, and a similar ambivalence characterizes this interest. At Ramsay's farewell dinner at Colbourne College, hagiography is referred to as Ramsay's 'explorations of the borderland between history and myth' (FB 7). But in Ramsay's own mind it is simply the outcome of an interest in the nature of religious ideas which had begun early in his childhood: 'when the Reverend Andrew Bowyer bade all us Presbyterians to prepare ourselves for the Marriage Feast of the Lamb, it seemed to me that *Arabian Nights* and the *Bible* were getting pretty close – and I did not mean this in any scoffing sense' (FB 43). In later years his reading of the New Testament confirms and sustains his interest: 'I read it not from zeal but curiosity and ... long passages of it confirmed my early impression that religion and *Arabian Nights* were true in the same way' (FB 77). In the course of his travels in search of the Madonna, accumulating a great deal of information about saints, he at first merely confirms what he has already grasped about the nature of faith, 'that religion was much nearer in spirit to the *Arabian Nights* than it was to anything encouraged by St James' Presbyterian Church' (FB 142). But the close acquaintance he makes with religious legend, through its manifestations in art, leads to a deeper preoccupation with the meaning of what he is studying, the *numinosum* which is the object of belief:[1] 'I knew that I was rediscovering religion ... I was not such a fool or an aesthete as to suppose that all this art was for art's sake alone. It was about something, and I wanted to know what that something was' (FB 140–1). Subsequently Ramsay is shown moving towards a direct examination of the nature of faith. From his investigation of the factual element in religious legends he advances to an investigation of its source in the human psyche involving, he explains, 'a much bigger piece of work, to be called *The Saints: A Study in History and Popular Mythology*, in which I wanted to explore first of all why people needed saints, and then how much their need had to do with the saintly attainments of a wide range of extra-ordinary and gifted people' (FB 211–12). But what he finds himself ex-amining is more than belief in saints – it is the nature of faith itself: 'what I was writing, slowly, painstakingly, and with so many revisions that the final version was not even in sight, was a sort of prologue to a discus-sion of the nature of faith' (FB 234). And it becomes clear in the course of the novel that faith is a highly ambivalent concept.

The ambivalence of faith is presented in such a way that Davies' concept of the metaphoric function of illusion is unmistakable. Ambi-valence is first suggested by Ramsay's early recognition that 'religion and *Arabian Nights* were true in the same way ... they were both psycho-logically rather than literally true' (FB 77–8). Because he recognizes that truth may be manifest in more than one way, Ramsay is also able to recognize the flaw in the rationalistic arguments of Sam West, the Dept-ford atheist, who is unable to recognize the metaphoric nature of religious language: 'If he hoped to make an atheist of me, this was where he went wrong; I knew a metaphor when I heard one, and I liked metaphor better than reason. I have known many atheists since Sam, and they all fall down on metaphor' (FB 57). Metaphor, then, is a key factor in religious belief. But there is more to the problem than simply recognizing the metaphoric nature of religious language. Ramsay re-fuses to tell Boy about the subject of his article in *Analecta* on the grounds that Boy is unable to make the distinction between what is literally and what is psychologically true, and would, therefore, be un-able to make any sense of it: 'he was no audience for such psychological-mythological gossip, which appealed only to the simple or the truly sophisticated' (FB 193). The implication of his refusal is that religious beliefs (as expressed in religious art, saints' legends, and so on, as well as in religious language) are metaphoric expressions of religious reality (the numinosum). A metaphor may be taken either literally (without understanding that it is a sign for something else), which leads to delusion, or symbolically (understanding that it is a sign for something else), which makes it a form of fantasy; the former is the way of the 'simple,' the latter the way of the 'truly sophisticated.' Both fantasy and delusion, however, are in Davies' terms forms of illusion. Consequently an apprehension of the numinosum is possible only through the medium of illusion.

This apprehension of the numinosum, which we call faith or belief, is the fourth category of illusion, being both voluntary and incorrigible. It is voluntary because it is neither the result of a mistake by the observer nor the result of a deception of the observer by another person. It is incorrigible because there can be no substitution of reality for the illusory form which is perceived for, when simple 'literal' faith is corrected, it may be corrected only to sophisticated 'symbolic' faith (which seems to be Ramsay's position from the beginning). But 'symbolic' faith is another form of illusion and should also, therefore, be corrigible, at least in theory; in practice, it is not. Those who will not accept the metaphor either literally or symbolically end up with nothing: they lose their faith and must find some such substitute as Boy's muddle-headed secularism or Sam West's thoughtful atheism. The only way to correct 'symbolic' faith would be to substitute a direct apprehension of the numinosum which, on the evidence of *Fifth Business*, is not possible.

But the emergence of faith as an ambivalent form of illusion does more than complete the paradigm of illusion. By twisting the concept of illusion back on itself, by changing its function from that of mask to that of metaphor, Davies throws into doubt the nature of reality. For if belief apprehends something which is only a metaphor for reality, then there is no way to validate the reality for which the metaphor stands. Hence reality becomes a variable rather than a constant. This point is made clear in Father Blazon's comment on Ramsay's attempts to decide whether Mary Dempster is a saint: 'If you think her a saint, she is a saint to you ... That is what we call the reality of the soul; you are foolish to demand the agreement of the world as well' (FB 203). The obvious implication is that the individual's view of reality becomes reality, but this is true in a qualified sense only, for Father Blazon limits this reality to 'the reality of the soul.' Two realities, then, are implied: the physical or mundane, and the psychic or transcendent. In the physical reality the individual has to obtain 'the agreement of the world' to validate his or her individual experience because in the physical realm we exist as social animals for whom general agreement about physical experience is necessary for communication. In the psychic or transcendent reality, however, each of us is truly an individual, independent of any group; the psychic life is lived alone, and each individual is his or her own interpreter of events. The two realities are distinct and separate. Ramsay's mistake, in Father Blazon's view, is that he is trying to obtain external validation (from Father Blazon himself, as a representative of the Roman hierarchy) for an internal psychic event (the knowledge of Mary Dempster's sainthood).[2] As a result of the separation of the two realities, external validation is not only irrelevant in validating psychic events, but impossible; only Ramsay can validate Ramsay's psychic experience.

Davies uses the theme of illusion in *Fifth Business* to present not only an ambivalent concept of reality but also a most emphatic distinction between two modes of reality (the transcendent psychic reality and the mundane physical reality) in order to throw as much light as possible on their interface within the individual human being. The interface of the modes is governed by two of Jung's principles of psychic action, and it produces the major psychosymbolic patterns of the novel. Both governing principles are principles which determine the operation of psychic systems, and specifically the operation of pairs of opposites as parts of the *pleroma* (the sphere of totality consisting of all possible pairs of opposites).[3] The first principle is that of the relativity of values in pairs of opposites. The nature of this relativity, and of the consequent necessity for conserving both of any given pair of opposites, is discussed by Jung as part of the process of psychic maturation:

The transition from morning to afternoon means a revaluation of earlier values. There comes the urgent need to appreciate the value of the opposite of our former ideals, to perceive the error in our former convictions ... It is of course a fundamental mistake to imagine that when we see the non-value in a value or the untruth in a truth, the value or the truth ceases to exist. It has only become *relative.* Everything human is relative, because everything rests on an inner polarity; for everything is a phenomenon of energy. Energy necessarily depends on a pre-existing polarity, without which there could be no energy. There must always be high and low, hot and cold, etc., so that the equilibrating process – which is energy – can take place ... The point is not conversion into the opposite but conservation of previous values together with recognition of their opposites. (cw 7:115:74–5)

In this context Jung is speaking of the psyche as a whole system in relation to the partial systems which constitute it. As Jacobi points out, however, 'the law also holds good in ... partial systems.'[4] Within the pleroma the psychic reality forms, with the physical reality, another pair of opposites (a partial system). Consequently, in taking the psychic and the physical modes of reality as the opposites or poles of his symbolic organization Davies selects a partial system which comes under this law of 'relativity.' (Good and evil and truth and falsehood, like psychic and physical, form similar partial systems obeying the same law of relativity.) The paradoxical nature of faith is, therefore, not merely an exhibition of sheer ingenuity but a statement of a fundamental principle of the symbolic organization of the novel. Jung's second principle, moreover, which governs all pairs of opposites, asserts that 'pairs are opposites not only in content but also in respect to their energetic intensity.'[5] Equal potential for symbolic significance of the narrative structures which embody the psychic and the physical modes of reality is therefore present. Both principles, it should be noted, demand the separate recognition of each member of any pair before the adjustment of any value can take place. The totality is, therefore, not an unanalyzed muddle, but a synthesis based on analysis, and hence the thrust of both principles is always towards the construction of this spagiric whole.[6]

In *Fifth Business* Dunstan Ramsay is the individual in whose life the interface of the modes is observed in the process of producing a spagiric whole. From this process of analysis-synthesis arise the four major psychosymbolic patterns of the novel. The first is the simple opposition of the psychic and the physical as manifest in Ramsay's experience. Two others – the opposition of truth and falsehood, and the opposition of good and evil – emerge from Ramsay's struggle towards self-knowledge and individuation. The fourth pattern is the reciprocal relationship between Boy Staunton's life and Ramsay's.

The first pattern, the opposition of the psychic and the physical realities, is introduced into the narrative as an emphatic and balanced disjunction between the solid naturalism of Ramsay's family and background in Deptford and the preternatural or fantastic elements which impinge upon his life there. The rural setting is presented naturalistically and with vivid detail:

It was called Deptford and lay on the Thames River about fifteen miles east of Pittstown, our county town and nearest big place. We had an official population of about five hundred, and the surrounding farms probably brought the district up to eight hundred souls ... We had two doctors ... We had a dentist, a wretch without manual skill, whose wife underfed him, and who had positively the dirtiest professional premises I have ever seen; and a veterinarian who drank but could rise to an occasion. We had a canning factory, which operated noisily and feverishly when there was anything to can; also a sawmill and few shops. (FB 10–11)

Within this village setting the Ramsay family is presented as 'representative of the better sort of life' (FB 12). Nevertheless, Mrs Ramsay, although she is a leader within the village community, is a leader of the same persuasion as her followers, scornful of personal appearances and very practical in her speciality of 'matters relating to pregnancy and childbirth.' After the incident in the gravel pit her 'furious rectitude' exemplifies the moral attitude of the community.

In Ramsay's own view he resembles his mother rather than his father. He is, for example, 'all thumbs' at his father's trade of printing. What we see of him through the narrative of his life demonstrates this heredity: Liesl's picture of Ramsay as a 'moral monster' echoes strangely his own portrait of his mother. Even his mother's 'strong features' are perhaps reflected in his own: 'a cadaverous and scowling cast of countenance and a rather pedantic Scots voice' (FB 123). And in spite of his disclaimer that his parents' 'Scottish practicality' is 'not really in grain' with him, he demonstrates that in some ways it is engrained in him and needs only the right circumstances to bring it out: 'I had not waded through the mud-and-blood soup of Passchendaele to worry about foolish things; blasphemy in a good cause (which usually means one's own cause) is not hard to stomach' (FB 104). He describes himself as a boy in harmony with his setting not only physically (in contrast to Boy Staunton), but also temperamentally. For although his attitude to Mary Dempster after the incident with the tramp is not exactly that of the villagers, it does resemble it: 'I was trying to forget ... my first encounter with a particular kind of reality, which my religion, my upbringing, and the callowly romantic cast of my mind had declared obscene' (FB 56). This closing of the mind comes, it is implied, as a consequence of Deptford's lack of any imaginative quality: 'one of the things it conspicuously lacked was an aesthetic sense; we were all too much the descendants of hard-bitten pioneers to wish for or encourage any such thing, and we gave hard names to qualities that, in a more sophisticated society, might have had value' (FB 21). The aesthetic sense, the imagination, is one of the openings into the transcendent reality, and it is this transcendent reality to which the villagers as a whole have closed their minds. Whereas a mind open to the transcendent mode receives it fully – so that Ramsay enjoys the wonder of magic as well as the terrors of threatened damnation – a mind which is closed to the mode will nevertheless feel the pressure of its manifestations, without understanding what is happening. This is the reason why the villagers fear that Mary Dempster will 'bewitch ... by the unreason of her lust.' She represents something outside their experience, and they fear the unknown. For them, stolid and unimaginative, the unknown includes all the different manifestations of the transcendent – both magic and madness.

It is against the solid realism of his village and family life that Dunstan Ramsay's experience with the preternatural and the fantastic begins. His incursions into the 'strange and unchancy world of the Dempsters' are set in emphatic contrast to the solid reality of his everyday existence. A similar contrast is visible between the blood, mud, and stench of trench warfare and the 'miracle' of Mary Dempster's appearance as the little Madonna. The visionary state which he experiences after he is wounded is his next encounter with the transcendent mode. Others follow, notably his renewed relationships with Mary Dempster, Joel Surgeoner, and Paul Dempster as Magnus Eisengrim, and, above all, his meeting with Liesl. The contrast between the elements of the mundane physical reality and the transcendent psychic reality in Ramsay's experience serves to emphasize the autonomy of the two modes of reality within the narrator's psyche. The full weight of the physical reality must be brought out in order to balance the strength of the transcendent vision.

Primarily this balancing of modes is necessary to conform with the Jungian idea that 'pairs are opposites not only in content but also in respect to their energetic intensity.'[7] In terms of narrative structure this means that they must appeal equally to the reader so that he or she gives equal attention to all parts of the narrative. Additionally, the strength of the mundane element in the narrative serves to anchor the transcendent in the mundane by making it more comprehensible to a reader more familiar with the mundane than with the transcendent.[8] Ramsay's own view, that 'the marvellous is indeed an aspect of the real,' is partial and misleading. For the point which Davies is making in the novel as a whole is not that the marvellous is an aspect of the real, but that what we call the 'marvellous' and what we call the 'real' (the transcendent and the mundane, the psychic and the physical) are in fact two equal, opposite, and autonomous realities or modes of reality.

The autonomy of the two modes is also a Jungian concept. In Jung's view the psychic mode is both as real as the physical and quite different from it: 'For Jung the psyche is no less real than the body. Though it cannot be touched, it can be directly and fully experienced and observed. It is a world of its own, governed by laws, structured, and endowed with its own means of expression.'[9] Because of this autonomy the psychic mode cannot be interpreted in terms of the physical: we cannot understand the transcendent in terms of the mundane, the marvellous in terms of the real.[10] If the modes are opposites, the terms in which each may be understood may be not merely different but opposite. For example, events in the psychic mode must appear 'arbitrary and unconvincing' in terms of experience as real,[11] because our require-

ment that experience be non-arbitrary and convincing, being formulated by the conscious mind which operates only in the mundane reality
on the principles of cause and effect and demonstration and proof,
can, if the two modes are equal, opposite, and autonomous, apply only
to physical and mundane events. At least a part of what Davies is saying
in *Fifth Business* is that not enough attention is paid to the autonomy of
the psychic mode, a point emphasized by Jung himself.[12] The experience
of Dunstan Ramsay is not, therefore, experience in terms of either one
or the other mode of reality, but experience of each on its own terms.

The emphatic disjunction between the two modes – the discrepancy
between the two aspects of Ramsay's life – has to be balanced by an
equally emphatic synthesis which in purely structural terms is achieved
by the first-person narrative. The human psyche is the interface between the two modes of reality because it is only there that they coexist.
Fifth Business takes place entirely within Dunstan Ramsay's psyche,
and from what he remembers, reflects on, and narrates, we construct a
map of the interface. His single consciousness constructs from the
dual reality a single vision.

From a Jungian viewpoint the only respect in which Ramsay's narrative is unusual is that his experience of the psychic mode of reality in
his life is on a conscious level. Normally, although our psychography
has analogues in our biography,[13] our experience of the psychic mode of
reality is accessible only in a limited way (dreams, active imagination,[14]
and fantasy) to the conscious ego. We experience the psychic reality
unconsciously unless we undergo the psychotherapy of raising unconscious content (psychic experience) to consciousness as part of individuation. Even so, Ramsay's narrative is more than a justifiable artistic
liberty. Because Ramsay's physical life is nearly completed, so is his psychic life, and it is the light of the latter which he turns back on his
physical life, bringing out the psychic reality unconsciously experienced
in and through physical events. Thus, between the visible lines of his
biography the invisible lines of his psychography are made visible, just as
ultraviolet light makes some invisible inks visible. The narrative is
reflective also in the sense that Ramsay uses past events as a mirror in
which to discover himself. This self-discovery is a cumulative process
in the form of a conscious quest throughout Ramsay's whole life, but
taking shape only towards the end of it. Two patterns of opposites are
involved in this self-discovery: Ramsay must discriminate between the
fact and the illusion of his life, and between the light and the dark
elements in it. As Ramsay looks back at his life from the point of view of
his old age he reflects on it in a double sense.

He is able to articulate the nature and purpose of his quest for self-knowledge, which is the context of the second of the major psychosymbolic patterns in the novel (the pattern of the opposition of truth and falsehood), only towards the end of the novel. The occasion comes when he is forced to consider the question of self-knowledge in relation to that part of his past embodied in his 'lifelong friend and enemy Percy Boyd Staunton.' For Ramsay an essential element of self-discovery is the ability to remember the past but, as Paul Dempster remarks, 'We all forget many of the things we do, especially when they do not fit into the character we have chosen for ourselves' (FB 308). Boy has forgotten much of his past, including the snowball that he threw at Mary Dempster, in precisely this way. Ramsay has to accept that it is genuinely forgotten: 'I could hardly believe he spoke the truth, but as we talked on I had to accept it as a fact that he had so far edited his memory of his early days that the incident of the snowball had quite vanished from his mind' (FB 307). Yet, as Ramsay's use of the word 'editing' implies, the forgetting is a deliberate act, not an accident. Nor is it merely a single act but, as Boy himself makes clear, part of his general policy: 'I don't remember what is of no use to me' (FB 307). He justifies himself by claiming that the act he does not remember committing did not change events: 'It precipitated something which was probably going to happen anyhow. The difference between us is that you've brooded over it and I've forgotten it' (FB 310). From this conviction he will not be shifted, even by Ramsay's insistence that the incident reveals something so essential to Boy that he cannot afford to discard all memory of it.

Ramsay's reason for his insistence reveals what he sees as the purpose of his quest for self-discovery. He asserts that he is trying to recover for Boy 'the totality' of his life, so that he can 'possess it as a whole – the bad with the good' (FB 311). Self-discovery or self-knowledge, available through memory, is apparently the key to self-possession without which the individual possesses nothing. Self-possession is perhaps also the 'meaning' of age, discussed earlier in a conversation between Ramsay and Staunton: 'You must grow old, Boy; you'll have to find out what age means, and how to be old. A dear friend of mine once told me he wanted a God who would teach him how to grow old. I expect he found what he wanted. You must do the same, or be wretched. Whom the gods hate they keep forever young' (FB 284). But Boy Staunton refuses self-knowledge by refusing to accept what Ramsay has remembered for him (and in so doing has deliberately acted as 'fifth business' and the keeper of Staunton's conscience). By this refusal he not only makes self-possession impossible, but also delivers himself over to an ironic fulfilment of Ramsay's observation that those 'whom the gods hate they keep forever young.' Boy is kept forever young by his death, which happens before he has time to grow old (in the sense of being psychologically mature). Paul Dempster, moreover, unwittingly prac- tises the same kind of memory-editing as Boy even though he knows that it is a general human trait. He forgets Mrs Ramsay's kindness to his mother, and recollects Ramsay's parents as 'hard people—especially your mother,' so confirming Ramsay's comment that he had 'edited his memories so that only pain and cruelty remained' (FB 307). Consequent- ly, even Paul is as far from self-knowledge and therefore from self- possession as Boy.

Confrontation with so much memory-editing makes Ramsay recon- sider his own memory and self-knowledge: 'I began to wonder what I had erased from my own recollection' (FB 307). It is the effort to as- semble a 'true recollection' which brings to the fore the first of the two patterns involved in Ramsay's quest: the discrimination between the true and the false in his life. Ostensibly he is writing an account of his life because he is dissatisfied with the official account published in the Col- bourne College magazine on his retirement from the teaching staff. To set things straight he addresses his narrative to the headmaster: 'I am driven to explain myself to you, Headmaster, because you stand at the top of that queer school world in which I seem to have cut such a meagre figure' (FB 9). His first discrimination then is between the ap- pearance he has made in the world (illusion), particularly in his profes- sional world, and the life he has been living behind that appearance (truth), corresponding to a discrimination between his biography, of which the facts are available to everybody, and his psychography, to which he alone has access.

There is, however, a second discrimination involved, which he makes clear from the beginning. His own account is to be an essay in writing truthfully about himself after real self-examination without distortion by 'that disgusting self-love.' As the narrative proceeds, several hints (such as the mention of 'an odd thing that I almost fear to record') are introduced which are designed to remind the reader of the impulse towards 'truth' which governs it. Another of these hints is found in Ramsay's attitude to the 'official' biography of Boy Staunton which Boy's widow (Denyse) wishes him to write. Ramsay questions whether, after all his professional training, he could write anything of which Denyse would approve, because he has learned 'something about the variabil- ity of truth as quite rational people see it' (FB 299). The parallel between his attitude to the biography and to the autobiographical narrative in which it occurs is clearly implied, and elsewhere in the course of the

narrative Ramsay adduces other parallels between himself and Boy
Staunton. In the description of Boy's life after his second marriage,
Ramsay notes that childhood traits 'often ... make a vigorous appearance after the meridian of life has been passed' and he recognizes this
pattern in his own life as well as in Boy's: 'my boyhood trick of getting
off "good ones" that went far beyond any necessary self-defence and
were likely to wound, had come back to me in my fifties. I was going to
be a sharp-tongued old man as I had been a sharp-tongued boy' (FB 285).
For Ramsay the recognition of this pattern in his life and in Boy's
provides an opportunity for the objective recognition of something about
himself. The unpleasant characteristic which he might wish to ignore is
recognized as part of his essential or real self, and he is able also to
recognize its function in his future—or the remainder of his future. A
similar attempt at objectivity is seen in his analysis of his contribution
to the friendship between himself and Boy.

Two other childhood characteristics, however, also contribute to
Ramsay's receptiveness to the importance of self-examination and self-
knowledge: his desire for knowledge and his introspection. Neither
disappears, although both change somewhat in his later life. They form
a double strand running through his account until they come together
to create his capacity for self-knowledge.

His desire for knowledge is first presented as the result of a wish for
power, primarily to escape from his mother. When he fails in his attempt
to become a conjuror, one of the insults of his school life prompts
another attempt to escape: 'I set to work to become a polymath' (FB 56).
The desire for knowledge persists through his adult life, but begins to
be seen in adult terms; his enlistment effectively frees him from his
parents, and he can then pursue knowledge unhindered by external
pressures. His adult regard for knowledge is formulated in the face of
internal pressures—his own doubts about his career as a hagiographer:
'I clung to my notion, ill defined though it was, that a serious study of
any important body of human knowledge, or theory, or belief, if
undertaken with a critical but not a cruel mind, would in the end yield
some secret, some valuable permanent insight, into the nature of life
and the true end of man' (FB 196). The important difference between his
earlier and his later desire for knowledge lies in his changed concept
of the purpose of knowledge. As a child, he sees knowledge as the way to
power. As an adult, he sees it as insight into the nature of life and the
true end of man and, consequently, insight into his own nature and true
end.

His concept of knowledge as insight and his introspection (which is suggested principally by the structural use of the first-person narrative voice) combine to prepare him for the advent of true self-knowledge through the synthesis of his total experience. Ramsay's interest in hagiography, which he has taken as the subject of his 'serious study,' is used to bring him to the attention of Liesl and Paul as a suitable candidate to write Magnus Eisengrim's autobiography. *The Soirée of Illusions* provides the context in which Ramsay comes to terms with that side of life which Liesl represents and he finally receives from her the ordering pattern of the totality of his experience: the fifth business mandala.

Liesl Vitzlipützli is by function and by name a manifestation of the devil himself, and that portion of the narrative which concerns her presents the third major psychosymbolic pattern in the novel, the pattern of the opposition of good and evil. The significance of her surname, which Ramsay originally finds merely 'absurd,' is never made explicit in *Fifth Business*; all that is given is Liesl's own hint that it is a 'new name' which she has taken on becoming one of the 'twice-born' like Ramsay (becoming Dunstan rather than Dunstable) and Paul (who becomes Magnus Eisengrim). It is in fact a Swiss-German dialect corruption of the name of the Aztec war and sun god, Huitzilopochtli, and denotes, as well as the devil, any sort of bogey-man used to frighten children into being good.[15] There is some ambivalence here: although the name has the overtones of cruelty and human sacrifice connected with the Aztec original, its use as a nursery threat gives precisely that absurdity on which Ramsay comments, drawing it explicitly to our attention.

Ambivalence is present from the beginning in the descriptions of Liesl. Her first appearance introduces her as both physically ugly and sexually ambivalent: 'The person who was speaking to me ... was probably a woman but she wore man's dress, had short hair, and was certainly the ugliest human creature I had ever seen' (FB 240). Her sexual ambivalence is confirmed in that she acts as a sexual partner for both Faustina and Ramsay. Even her ugliness becomes ambivalent in Ramsay's further observation: 'Nothing could mitigate the extreme, the deformed ugliness of her face, but she was graceful, she had a charming voice, and gave evidence of a keen intelligence' (FB 243). The effect of her ambivalence is to create in Ramsay a response which at first is merely uncertain, but later, as it becomes more conscious, it can better be described as adapted. The change is shared by the reader. In the Marchbanks material a similar response was evoked and directed towards the shadow side of personality represented by Marchbanks himself. But in the early material Davies' concern is limited to the individual shadow and to only a suggestion of its relationship to the problem of good and evil. In *Fifth Business* his concern is extended to the general nature of the shadow and a deep consideration of its relationship to the problem of good and evil.

It is clear that the consideration of good and evil takes place in a Jungian context. It demands a 'revision' (in a very basic sense of the word) by the reader, similar to that suggested by Jung:

Although good and evil are unshakable as moral values, they still need to be subjected to a bit of psychological revision. Much, that is to say, that proves to be abysmally evil in its ultimate effects does not come from man's wickedness but from his stupidity and unconsciousness ... One of the toughest roots of all evil is unconsciousness, and I could wish that the saying of Jesus, 'Man, if thou knowest what thou doest, thou art blessed, but if thou knowest not, thou art accursed, and a transgressor of the law,' were still in the gospels, even though it has only one authentic source.[16]

Such a revision demands considerable ethical adaptability on the part of the individual who has to overcome the rigidity of the ethical concepts within Western Judaeo-Christian tradition. That such a revision is indeed part of the structure of *Fifth Business* is indicated by the apparently casual juxtaposition of psychology and religion early in the narrative, when Ramsay refers to his early impression that religion and *Arabian Nights* were 'both psychologically rather than literally true, and that psychological truth was really as important in its own way as historical verification' (FB 77–8). Concern with the psychological truth of religion is also underlined by Ramsay's justification of his hagiographical researches. The latter illustrate particularly aptly the effect of the revision involved, because his research demands that neither the Protestant denial of saints nor the Roman Catholic belief in them be accepted, both being responses to the outward form of sainthood without reference either to the psychology of sainthood or to the psychology of belief and denial. Ramsay's research is bound to affect both those who believe and those who deny and so create maximum disturbance.

On a larger scale, this is what Davies himself does in presenting a revision of good and evil. The increased concern in the novel (beyond that demonstrated in the Marchbanks material) demands a correspondingly greater ethical adaptability in the reader. Such adaptability is encouraged by presenting in the narrative a general shake-up of common attitudes to the manifestations of good and evil in human society. This begins comparatively gently, but becomes increasingly tougher up to the

point of Ramsay's comment to Father Blazon, that 'the Devil proved
to be a very good fellow,' which tests the full extent of the reader's
adaptability to the revised notion of good and evil being presented.

The shake-up begins with Deptford's ideas of good as presented at the
opening of the novel. They are psychologically unrevised: they manifest an old-fashioned puritanism whose cardinal virtues are prudery,
prudence, and hard work. How far this differs from the psychologically revised idea of good is apparent in Davies' own definition of a truly
good life: 'I think ... it's the fully realized human life, the fulfilling of
one's potential. The person who lives that way can't help but be enor-
mously valuable to an awful lot of people. And he's not going to do
harm, because he knows himself.'[17] Deptford 'good,' on the contrary, is
life-denying and exists without awareness of the numinosum; it is
essentially the world of thanatos, or anti-life, as Davies described it in *A
Mixture of Frailties*. This concept of good is represented by the Deptford
clergy in general and the Reverend Amasa Dempster in particular.
Stupid, timid, self-righteous, and over-emotional, he smothers his wife
with unnecessary attention, but denies her protection and understanding
when she most needs them. In morals and in moralizing, the inhabitants
of Deptford share with their so-called 'spiritual leaders' the anti-life of
thanatos.

Ironically, it is Mary Dempster, whom even the most unspiritual of
Deptford's 'good' citizens may presume to despise, who has the spiritual-
ity they so evidently lack. Ramsay can recognize, without at the time
understanding the quality of a life in constant contact with the numinosum: 'it was impossible to talk to her for long without being aware
that she was wholly religious ... she ... seemed to live in a world of trust
that had nothing of the stricken, lifeless, unreal quality of religion about
it ... She lived by a light that arose from within' (FB 55). This is the eros life
(to use Davies' earlier distinction) and as its representative she initiates Ramsay into the feeling side of that life: 'But, looking back on it
now, I know I was in love with Mrs Dempster ... I had made her what
she was and in such circumstances I must hate her or love her. In a mode
that was far too demanding for my age or experience, I loved her'
(FB 27–8). In contrast to her husband and the rest of Deptford she
demonstrates the nature of the eros concept of good when she puts
charity above morality in giving herself to the tramp in the gravel-pit.
Here Davies translates into terms of everyday human action not only
the difference between the eros and the thanatos concepts of good but
also that between the conventional moral decision and the autonomous ethical decision of a revised concept of good and evil described by

Jung: 'Nothing can spare us the torment of ethical decision. Nevertheless, harsh as it may sound, we must have the freedom in some circumstances to avoid the known moral good and do what is considered to be evil, if our ethical decision so requires' (MDR 330).

The character of Mary Dempster is only one of the ways in which the eros life is manifest. Davies assails traditional concepts of good again in his portrait of Father Blazon who is set in contrast to Father Regan, the Roman Catholic priest in Deptford. Like Mary Dempster, Father Blazon illustrates the life in contact with the numinosum. Whereas she initiates Ramsay into the feeling side of the eros life (spiritual love), Father Blazon initiates him into its intellectual side (spiritual wisdom): 'Forgive yourself for being a human creature, Ramezay. That is the beginning of wisdom' (FB 208). Love and wisdom are complementary in the eros life, and the numinosum must be known or experienced through both.

Although Davies indicates in these portraits the eros element which is lacking in traditional concepts of good, and which is clearly necessary to the revised concept he presents, there is something more in each. Mary Dempster's simple-mindedness and the grotesqueness of Father Blazon's appearance and his much-vaunted chastity are intended not only to break down the reader's resistance to the process of revision, but also to warn the unwary. In Mary Dempster's case, the warning is given in the description of her as a 'fool-saint.' According to Father Regan, the fool-saint is one without prudence (FB 159). In revised psychological terms, prudence can be said to be knowing what one is doing and taking responsibility for it, and in this sense Mary Dempster is not living a truly good life according to Davies' definition. The earlier life of Father Blazon is similarly unexamined; as he points out, the questions he should have been asking himself all along did not occur to him until he was forty (FB 205). Davies says that 'Just to go ahead living blindly, assured you're on the right path, is almost certain damnation.'[18] Living blindly leads Mary Dempster to the mental hospital (a certain damnation), but the questions which torment Father Blazon and which he attempts to answer are his way of taking responsibility for himself, and they lead him, in the end, to the God who will teach him to be old (FB 294).

Before he reaches this point, Father Blazon asks if he is at fault in wanting a God who will teach him to be old, and it is clear that what he says about the youth of Christ is designed to challenge the reader's preconceptions about the perfection of Christ. Equally clearly he is not at fault in asking; the ones at fault are those who do not know what they want of God—who do not examine their ideas of God or of good and evil, but act unthinkingly in the context of what they have been taught. Consequently, they fall into one of the dangers which Jung points out: 'Touching evil brings with it the grave peril of succumbing to it. We must, therefore, no longer succumb to anything at all not even to good. A so-called good to which we succumb loses its ethical character. Not that there is anything bad in it on that score, but to have succumbed to it may breed trouble. Every form of addiction is bad, no matter whether the narcotic be alcohol or morphine or idealism' (MDR 329). To succumb to good is to act without examining it, as though it were the only possibility, and good, if unexamined, turns to evil. Davies supports this by citing Jung: 'It is Dr. Carl Jung who is always quoting a saying of Jesus from the Gospel of Thomas to the effect that if you know fully what you're doing, you are blessed; if you don't know, you are damned. This is a very great saying and I wish we had it in the orthodox Gospels.'[19] In one reference to this saying, Jung himself notes: "It might well be the motto for a new morality" (CW 11:291:197). Elsewhere, he comments:

In Christ's sayings there are already indications of ideas which go beyond the traditionally 'Christian' morality—for instance the parable of the unjust steward, the moral of which agrees with the Logion of the Codex Bezae, and betrays an ethical standard very different from what is expected. Here the moral criterion is *consciousness*, and not law or convention. One might also mention the strange fact that it is precisely Peter, who lacks self-control and is fickle in character, whom Christ wishes to make the rock and foundation of his Church. These seem to me to be ideas which point to the inclusion of evil in what I would call a *differential moral valuation*. For instance, it is good if evil is sensibly covered up, but to act unconsciously is evil. One might almost suppose that such views were intended for a time when consideration is given to evil as well as to good, or rather, when it is not suppressed below the threshold on the dubious assumption that we always know exactly what evil is.[20]

The change of the 'moral criterion' (the criterion of distinction between good and evil) from law or convention to consciousness necessarily revises our idea of evil as well as of good. By this criterion the 'good' citizens of Deptford are damned, for the life they lead, the thanatos life, is an unexamined life governed by law and convention. Mary Dempster's eros life is equally damned, however, because equally unexamined.

Because the revision of our concept of good and evil necessarily introduces a revision of the concept of the devil, Mary Dempster could equally well be considered a devil, in terms of Davies' definition: 'The devil seems to me to be not the commonplace symbol of evil but the symbol of unconsciousness, of unknowing, of acting without knowledge of what you're intending to do. It's from that that I think the great evils spring. The devil is the unexamined side of life; it's unexamined but it's certainly not powerless.'[21] *Fifth Business*, in which the devil is manifest in the person of Liesl Vitzlipützli, certainly revises our idea of the devil, and the ambivalence with which she is presented is the key to the theme of differential moral valuation in the novel.

On the level of the personal unconscious, the unexamined side of psychic life is represented by the archetype of the shadow. Liesl, however, becomes more than merely an embodiment of Ramsay's unlived psychic elements: she is the agent who brings these unconscious elements to his conscious notice and who, by the psychological pressure she exerts on him, forces him to acknowledge them and to integrate them into his conscious life. Her function is to introduce him to his internal, non-mythological shadow, confusingly also personified as a personal devil: 'But every man has a devil, and a man of unusual quality, like yourself, Ramsay, has an unusual devil. You must get to know your personal devil. You must even get to know his father, the Old Devil' (FB 266). This echoes Jung's statement that, 'Everyone carries a shadow, and the less it is embodied in the individual's conscious life, the blacker and denser it is' (CW 11:131:76).

The shadow is hostile to the ego and, if it is not examined or made conscious, it forms a definite threat to the ego. As Jung points out: 'The shadow is a moral problem which challenges the whole ego-personality' (CW 9(ii):14:8). The practical resolution of this is seen when, as a result of Liesl's manipulation, Ramsay is persuaded to write Eisengrim's autobiography. The structure of his conscious life becomes a little shaky: 'Working on these illusions was delightful but destructive of my character ... I was regaining the untruthfulness, the lack of scruple, and the absorbing egotism of a child. I heard myself talking boastfully, lying shamelessly. I blushed but could not control myself' (FB 252). He is further shaken by Faustina, who represents that unthinking animal side of him which he has rigidly suppressed in the furtherance of his career: 'for the first time in my life, I began to wonder if education could be quite the splendid vocation I had, as a professional, come to think it' (FB 257). As the ego falters, the shadow gains strength.

Ramsay's shadow, moreover, is unusual in that the qualities which begin to emerge are not unattractive. The distinction Liesl makes,

however, between the personal devil and his father, the old devil
accounts for the curiously bloodless 'evil' of Ramsay's life, since his evil,
his shadow, is the unlived side of a life whose conscious side is, for a
schoolmaster, somewhat ruthless, cruel, cold, and acquisitive. As Liesl
points out he is, thanks to his environment, ' a moral monster' for
whom 'life is a spectator sport' in which he manages to avoid becoming
involved. He is, for Liesl, 'a man full of secrets' – 'grim-mouthed and
buttoned-up and hard-eyed and cruel' (FB 255); such secrecy, as she
points out, demands a high price for, in Jung's words: 'It is not we
who have secrets, it is the real secrets that have us' (CW 10:886:468). Liesl
also brings home to him his contempt for other people, even for her,
and the obsession which has given to Mary Dempster 'the affection you
should have spread among fifty people' (FB 255). His is a severely
logical and rational life. That his ruthlessness and cruelty and coldness
are turned against himself as much as others is not the point at issue,
which is that they are lived as part of his conscious ego-structure, while
their opposites (gentleness, warmth) remain unlived shadow qualities.

Ramsay's shadow has to be raised to consciousness so that his warmth,
kindness, illogic, and irrationality can be part of a whole life. This is
the life possessed 'as a whole – the bad with the good' of which Ramsay
speaks to Boy Staunton, in terms which reflect Jung's dicta that 'without the integration of evil there is no totality' (CW 11:232:156), and that
such integration 'cannot take place and be put to a useful purpose
unless one can admit the tendencies bound up with the shadow and
allow them some measure of realization – tempered, of course, with
the necessary criticism' (CW 11:292:198). The integration of his shadow
is needed to make Ramsay fully human, as Liesl points out in explaining her reason for coming to his room: 'I wanted to tell you that you are
human, like other people' (FB 264).

The integration of Ramsay's shadow is also the aim of her invitation to
Ramsay to acknowledge his devil: 'Why don't you shake hands with
your devil, Ramsay, and change this foolish life of yours? Why don't you,
just for once, do something inexplicable, irrational, at the devil's bidding, and just for the hell of it? You would be a different man' (FB 266).
For the same purpose, she has issued her earlier invitation: 'Shall we
go to bed together?' (FB 261). The parallel with the legend of St Dunstan
makes it clear that Liesl's invitation to integration involves a temptation to evil. Like St Dunstan, however, Ramsay successfully resists the
temptation.[22] The evil involved, however, is not to live the unlived side
of his life but to live it 'at the devil's bidding' (FB 266), that is, as a
response to an autonomous impulse of the shadow itself. Since the

shadow is part of the unconscious this would necessarily involve acting unconsciously and, as Jung says, 'to act unconsciously is evil' (CW 11:696:434). Ramsay, if he surrenders immediately to Liesl, acts unconsciously; the unlived side of his life has to be examined before he can live it out in the full knowledge of what he is doing. Thus he must force Liesl, through physical domination, to explain what she means by the unexamined side of his life before he consciously decides to live it out.

Within the context of the psychologically revised concept of good and evil Dustan Ramsay's temptation is as real as his namesake's, as is the evil to which he is tempted. Within this context, however, the evil is relative – it is what is unconscious and uncontrolled within the individual. Liesl's distinction between the 'personal devil' and his father, the old devil, points to the fact that, within the psychologically revised Jungian concept of evil, it is no longer possible to say 'the evil in man,' but only 'the evil in *a* man.' Jung points out: 'everything begins with the individual' (CW 10:45:27), and a man who takes on the evil in himself takes on as much as he can or needs to of the evil of the world: 'Such a man knows that whatever is wrong in the world is in himself, and if he only learns to deal with his own shadow he has done something real for the world. He has succeeded in shouldering at least an infinitesimal part of the gigantic, unsolved social problems of our day' (CW 11:140:83). Moreover, once recognized and controlled such evil becomes something else, as Davies points out: 'I think it is absolutely necessary for a man to recognize and accept the evil in himself. If he does that he is in a position to make the evil work in a different way; the charges of psychological energy involved can be re-directed in not necessarily good paths, but at least in understood paths.'[23] It is this state of redirected psychic energy which is reflected in Father Blazon's final comment on Ramsay's spiritual state: 'Well done, well done! You met the Devil as an equal, not cringing or frightened or begging for a trashy favour. That is the heroic life, Ramezay. You are fit to be the Devil's friend, without any fear of losing yourself to Him' (FB 294). It is from the standpoint of the 'heroic life' that Ramsay has the power to say, 'The Devil proved to be a very good fellow' (FB 293), and it is only from the standpoint of the psychologically revised concept of good and evil, within which the statement is made, that this aspect of *Fifth Business* can properly be understood.

At the moment when Ramsay achieves the heroic life Liesl gives him the fifth business mandala: the ordering pattern for the totality of his experience, which is also the fourth and final psychosymbolic pattern in the novel. The term 'fifth business' which gives the novel its title is introduced in the epigraph, as a quotation attributed to Thomas Overskou: 'Those roles which, being neither those of Hero nor Heroine, Confidante nor Villain, but which were none the less essential to bring about the Recognition or the denouement were called the Fifth Business in drama and opera companies organized according to the old style; the player who acted these parts was often referred to as Fifth Business' (FB vi).[24] Some hint of the function of this idea in the narrative is given by Ramsay's remarks about this 'vital though never glorious role' in the first chapter. The idea is elaborated by Liesl when she suggests to Ramsay that it may be the interpretative pattern for his life: 'I think you are Fifth Business ... the odd man out ... who knows the secret of the hero's birth, or comes to the assistance of the heroine ... or keeps the hermitess in her cell, or may even be the cause of somebody's death' (FB 266–7). But this exposition takes place only when demanded by Ramsay's psychic development, as soon as he reaches a position from which he can recognize the patterns of opposition in his life – the opposition of psychic and physical, of truth and illusion, of good and evil – and can attempt to synthesize them into some sort of totality. Such a totality must, because of its complexity, be expressed in symbolic form, and the symbolic form of totality is the mandala:

The archetypal image of this *coincidentia oppositorum*, this transformation of the opposites into a third term, a higher synthesis, is expressed by the so-called *uniting symbol* which represents the partial systems of the psyche as united on a *superordinate*, higher plane ... Symbols of this kind, representing a primordial image of psychic totality, always exhibit a more or less abstract form, because their basic law and essence demand a symmetrical arrangement of the parts round a midpoint. Such symbolic figures have been fashioned from time immemorial in the orient; the most significant examples being the so-called *Mandalas*, or 'magic circles.'[25]

Jung borrowed this term, discovered in the course of his research into the psychology of eastern meditation, to signify the 'concentric or radial order which constitutes the true centre or essence of the collective unconscious.'[26] Elsewhere he defines its various manifestations:

The Sanskrit word *mandala* means 'circle' in the ordinary sense of the word. In the sphere of religious practices and in psychology it denotes circular images, which are drawn, painted, modelled, or danced ... As psychological phenomena they appear spontaneously in dreams, in certain states of conflict, and in cases of schizophrenia. Very frequently they contain a quaternity or a multiple of four, in the form of a cross, a star, a square, an octagon, etc. In alchemy we encounter this motif in the form of *quadratura circuli*.[27]

The mandala is not the completed totality itself: it is the mode of realization of such a totality. Discussing the functional significance of mandalas, Jung says: 'They are *yantras* in the Indian sense, instruments of meditation, concentration, and self-immersion, for the purpose of realizing inner experience ... At the same time they serve to produce an inner order – which is why, when they appear in a series, they often follow chaotic, disordered states marked by conflict and anxiety. They express the idea of a safe refuge, of inner reconciliation and wholeness' (CW 9(i):710:383).[28] The mandala, then, is characteristically a tetradic figure whose components are arranged symmetrically around a central point, more or less abstract in design, and presenting a forward-looking vision of wholeness.[29]

Although Jung's exposition of the mandala's manifestations makes no mention of its occurrence in the literary arts, mandalas can nevertheless be found in all of them. In literature the mandala is more often expressed in the particular form of what is described as the *marriage quaternio* of two linked couples than in more abstract forms.[30] The distinction can be seen in two contrasting novels by Patrick White: *Voss* and *Riders in the Chariot*. In the former, the two couples, Laura Trevelyan and Voss, and Belle Bonner and Tom Radclyffe, constitute a *marriage quaternio*, whereas in the latter the four 'riders' – Miss Hare, Mrs Godbold, Himmelfarb, and Alf Dubbo – with the chariot itself as the midpoint, constitute a mandala.[31] It is in the latter way that the characters in *Fifth Business* form a mandala. In the group as Liesl describes it, the principals and fifth business represent the four elements of the quaternity plus the midpoint; they are symmetrically arranged by sex (hero and heroine, villain and 'other woman') in pairs round the singleton midpoint 'who has no opposite of the other sex' (FB 267). Technically, also, they conform to the demand that a mandala be more or less abstract in its symbolism, because they are presented as human functions, rather than actual human beings, and constitute a forward-looking vision of psychic wholeness.

Not unexpectedly, this simplicity conceals a superbly poised ambivalence. The fifth business mandala can be interpreted in two ways, depending on who is at the midpoint, the centre of energy and the centre of attention. The choice is between placing the hero or heroine at the midpoint, with the other three principals and fifth business as the four symmetrically arranged elements surrounding him or her, or placing fifth business in the centre with the paired principals arranged symmetrically round him. The epigraph leaves the choice open.

The first interpretation is plainly Ramsay's own, in that he sees fifth business as a 'vital though never glorious role' (FB 9): Boy is at the centre and Ramsay himself is on the periphery – a planet circling the sun. The same arrangement is suggested by Liesl's description of the 'cabal' which killed Boy Staunton: 'He was killed by the usual cabal: by himself, first of all; by the woman he knew; by the woman he did not know; by the man who granted his inmost wish; and by the inevitable fifth, who was keeper of his conscience and keeper of the stone' (FB 313). Here Boy Staunton is clearly the midpoint, each of the other four acting specifically in relation to him rather than in relation to the remaining three. Part of the effect of the ambivalence is created by the fact that this interpretation, although suggested earlier, is not stated fully until the closing pages of the narrative.

The opposite interpretation is suggested when the idea of fifth business is first introduced. Whereas in the description of the cabal fifth business becomes merely the 'inevitable' fifth, in Liesl's original description to Ramsay she says that 'you cannot manage the plot without Fifth Business' (FB 267). Thus fifth business becomes the fulcrum, giving the principals their leverage for action and interaction. In this interpretation it is Ramsay who occupies the midpoint, with the other four on the periphery.

The full implications of the ambiguity, however, emerge only in a consideration of the identity of each of the other members of the cabal. If we consider it with Boy Staunton as the midpoint, then 'the woman he knew' is his wife (first Leola, then Denyse) and 'the woman he did not know' is Mary Dempster; Paul Dempster is 'the man who granted his inmost wish,' and Ramsay is 'the keeper of his conscience and keeper of the stone.' If, however, the positions of Boy Staunton and Ramsay are reversed so that Ramsay becomes the midpoint an interesting correspondence becomes visible.[32] Although the functions of the people involved change, their identities do not – that is, the people involved are the same, but their relation to the midpoint changes. For Ramsay, Mary Dempster is the woman he knew, and Leola is the woman he did not know; Paul Dempster remains the man who granted his inmost wish, and Boy Staunton becomes the inevitable fifth.[33] The correspondence between the two patterns suggests that such a reversal is not merely arbitrary but of some significance within the thematic structure of the novel.

The key to that significance is clearly the exact relationship, in terms of the Jungian archetypes, between Boy Staunton and Dunstan Ramsay. Boy Staunton is an important part of the past on which Ramsay reflects in his quest for self-knowledge. Staunton is his 'lifelong friend and enemy' (FB 1) and, in terms of the psychological revision of good and evil, the enemy who is also a friend is the 'devil within' – the shadow. Equally, Ramsay is shown as both enemy and friend of Staunton: 'he must have liked me. But ... I was jealous of him ... Later, when I had something to give and could have helped him, he did not want it' (FB 128). This is a clear picture of a reciprocal ego/shadow relationship.

If, however, fifth business is a mandala of the self, then, in terms of the archetypes of the psyche, the ego, because it is the centre of consciousness, must be at the centre. The archetypes of the unconscious (the shadow and the anima/animus of the personal unconscious, and the magus and sybil of the collective or transpersonal unconscious) then arrange themselves symmetrically, in pairs by sex and magnitude, around the midpoint in a balanced quaternity. This arrangement demonstrates in symbolic terms the status of the ego: it must be central (because the archetypes relate to it, not to each other), singular (unmatched by an opposite), and differentiated (to indicate that it is part of the consciousness, in contrast to the unconscious nature of the others). The midpoint of a tetradic mandala fulfils all these qualifications.

The duality of the mandala (as cabal with Boy Staunton at the midpoint, or as fifth business with Ramsay at the midpoint) therefore reveals a complex thematic pattern in terms of the archetypes. Ramsay and Boy Staunton form a reciprocal ego/shadow relationship, so that either may represent the ego, with the other as his shadow. The other three principal characters represent the other three archetypes, their identity remaining constant although their functions change. Leola is the anima figure: Boy knows her in the form of mundane love, and Ramsay avoids her.[34] Mary Dempster is the sybil figure: Ramsay understands her and has a strong and strange lifelong involvement with her, but Boy never understands her and forgets her quickly. Paul Dempster is the magus figure: again he is one with whom Ramsay is deeply involved over a long period, but of whom Boy is hardly aware.

Understanding is the key to an important change when Boy Staunton replaces Ramsay as the midpoint of the mandala: all the archetypes, the members of the cabal, then change their aspect towards the midpoint. In the cabal which surrounds Boy Staunton, all the members are to some degree inimical because his failure to understand them provokes varying degrees of hostility. He does not care about Leola, provoking as a result her resentment and lack of support. He does not understand Mary Dempster or acknowledge his responsibility for her plight, thus losing a source of spiritual enlightenment for which he later feels a need. More obviously, he does not understand Paul's true genius (he thinks of him as a mere entertainer), virtually inviting death by placing himself in Paul's power. Ironically, Paul is the one person capable of granting 'his inmost wish,' and also the one person willing to grant it, because it is a death-wish. Nor does Boy understand Ramsay; all the accumulated wisdom Ramsay finally can offer him is lost, and the stone for which Ramsay has been responsible becomes not the instrument of Boy's salvation (by awakening his sense of responsibility), but the symbol of his death. As Jung points out, 'when we leave things to the shadow they get done, but they are done against us instead of for us.'[35]

If Ramsay is the ego figure, however, the same people are friendly guides to autonomy. He understands Leola's weakness, so that she cannot sap his spirit. He understands Mary Dempster and acknowledges his share in her plight, so that he receives from her his initiation into his psychic world. He understands and befriends Paul and does not underestimate his power, so that Paul grants his 'inmost wish' by bringing him into contact with Liesl – thus opening the way for Ramsay to assimilate all that Liesl can offer him in his search for self-knowledge. Finally, Ramsay understands Boy, so that he is able to accept what is of value in Boy's friendship (the opportunity of financial security) without allowing himself to be manipulated to his disadvantage (in the affair of 'Gyges and Candaules,' or the Headship of Colborne College, for example).

A further paradox is that the attitude of the cabal appears as the opposite of what it is. Leola is not overtly inimical to Boy – she marries him, bears his children, and does her best to make his home comfortable. After he leaves Deptford, Mary Dempster fades completely out of Boy's life without affecting him at all. When Paul Dempster meets Boy again at Colborne College his behaviour is perfectly civilized and he makes no accusations. And Ramsay, acting as 'keeper of his conscience,' is apparently acting for Boy's own good. On the other hand, these same people appear inimical to Ramsay: Leola jilts him; Mary Dempster makes continuous and exhausting demands on his love and ability to provide for her; and Paul, in granting his wish for self-knowledge, does so in the context of the magic-show which brings humiliation and psychic disequilibrium at the same time. But through the suffering they cause him, they also bring him wisdom.

The difference in aspect of the archetypes in the lives of the two men is essentially a question of awareness of possible modes of reality. Ramsay comments that: 'to him [Boy] the reality of life lay in external things, whereas for me the only reality was of the spirit' (FB 128). Because Boy believes only in 'external' reality, his internal life remains unconscious: the archetypes develop autonomously, and go unrecognized when he meets their image-bearers in external reality. They are among the people who are objects of what Ramsay describes as Boy's 'naked wish to dominate' (FB 285); his relationships with Ramsay and Leola are left unexamined, his relationships with Mary Dempster and Paul are forgotten. But to ignore the existence of the inner reality does not eliminate it: 'called or not called, the god will come.'[36] Uncontrolled by the ego, the unconscious archetypes become uncontrollable, and the final section of the book shows Boy being steered irresistibly to his death by the powers whose existence he has persistently ignored.

For Ramsay the opposite is true, and the 'reality of the spirit' for him is the only reality. During his childhood and adolescence in Deptford he is obviously an isolated and somewhat unpopular figure. The same is true of his army service; he has no real friend among the men, and his hope of finding one among the Jesuits is unrealized. In Boy Staunton's financial world too, Ramsay is conscious of being a misfit, although he is not particularly disturbed by it. His surprise and anger at the article in the school quarterly also reveal a rather naïve expectation that people will recognize his true self behind the 'meagre figure' he appears. It is clear that Ramsay is not at home in the external world: his ignorance of it, except in a very limited sense, is nearly as complete as Boy's ignorance of the inner reality. The fifth business mandala makes a pattern of this external reality which finally enables him to see how he relates to it. For him, fifth business is a role in the sense of a persona – an individual's mask in relation to the rest of the social group. It is not quite a persona in Jungian terms, however, for the function of fifth business as Ramsay sees it is not the function which is visible to the school which is his social group. Fifth business relates Ramsay to his external world only from his own point of view.

The 'reality of the spirit' is the world in which he is fully at home. He is aware of his inner life and it is raised as much as possible to consciousness. He constantly analyzes and examines his relationships with other people, and in particular (although he cannot be said to deal with his inner reality in Jungian terms) with the image-bearers of his archetypes: Boy, Leola, Mary Dempster, and, to a lesser extent, Paul. As a result of this inward vision, the close of his life finds him on good terms with the archetypes of his inward life and peacefully assembling the totality of his life in the construction of his narrative. This totality is governed by his concept of fifth business, as Liesl hints by her reference to 'The Five' in her invitation to join Paul and herself in Switzerland (FB 314).

The fifth business mandala, then, is itself ambivalent. To Ramsay it reveals the pattern of his external life of which he has been largely unconscious; to the reader it reveals the pattern of his inner life in terms of the Jungian archetypes. In either case, the mandala itself remains the same, but what it means depends on who is looking at it. Thus the ambivalence of the patterns of opposites which provide the symbolic structure of the book is reiterated in the ambivalence of the unifying symbol in which those opposites are subsumed.

Ambivalence pervades the whole of *Fifth Business*. Beginning from the original paradigm of illusion, Davies successively undercuts his previous distinctions between illusion and reality, and presents the paradoxical conclusion that illusion both conceals and reveals. Subjective reality and objective reality may be the same thing or, in Jungian terms, the polarities of a single reality which is both subjective and objective and yet neither: the superordinate reality. The process of opposition and synthesis is shown in the symbolic structures of the novel: fantasy and realism, truth and falsehood, good and evil, light and dark. Each pair must simultaneously be both recognized as a duality and comprehended as an identity. The totality of these patterns is represented symbolically by the mandala which Davies calls fifth business. Through the ambivalence of the mandala, Davies reminds us that, however comprehending and comprehensive our view of duality in identity may become, we never arrive at a final unity, or 'truth.' That, as Jung points out, is not in our nature as human beings:

The pairs of opposites are qualities of the pleroma which are not, because each balanceth each. As we are the pleroma itself, we also have all these qualities in us. Because the very ground of our nature is distinctiveness, therefore we have these qualities in the name and sign of distinctiveness, which meaneth ... these qualities are distinct and separate in us one from other; therefore they are not balanced and void, but are effective. Thus are we the victims of the pairs of opposites. The pleroma is rent in us. (MDR 381)

5 / A Country and Its Foreigners

The Manticore (1972), the middle book of Davies' Deptford trilogy, seems at first sight to be a very simple book, appearing to one reviewer as 'an engrossing primer on the precepts of Carl Jung' and to another as 'unabashedly all about Jung.'[1] But it is a delusive simplicity, because even more than in *Fifth Business*, Davies' characteristic ambivalence is at work in *The Manticore*. I am not merely suggesting that under the apparent simplicity of its structural framework and symbolic texture the novel is in fact so complex that the paradoxes and convolutions of structural and symbolic patterns almost defy logical and linear analysis. At this stage of Davies' development as a writer, such complexity is no more than might be expected. What is startling about *The Manticore* is the scale of the ambivalence; it is of a different order of magnitude from anything previously encountered. For although the Jungian frame of reference is firmly established in the narrative of David Staunton's progress through the Jung Institute in Zürich and his analysis with Dr von Haller, it is immediately – somewhat surreptitiously to begin with, but after Liesl's reappearance, thoroughly and unmistakably – undercut. Davies, far from committing himself to Jungian theory in this most Jungian of his novels, reveals in fact a profound resistance to it.

The central themes of *The Manticore* – the nature of reality and the definition of human identity – are unchanged from those of *Fifth Business*. But the emphasis is considerably different, because Davies has abandoned the elaborate structure of the paradigm of illusion. The discussion of truth, falsehood, and reality, left as the unresolved paradox of subjective and objective reality at the end of *Fifth Business*, appears in *The Manticore* explicitly only as part of a discussion of other problems (the distinction between truth and meaning, for example), and is subordinate to the detailed tracing of David's progress towards becoming a full human being, in the course of which a concept of what that means is presented to us, for *The Manticore*, like *Fifth Business*, is a psychography. The inner life is that of David Staunton, and, like Ramsay's, it is narrated in the first person. The voice is that of David himself, Boy Staunton's son, whom we have last met in *Fifth Business* at his father's funeral, and who is at that time, according to Ramsay's trenchant description, 'forty, a barrister and a drunk' (FB 297). *The Manticore* is divided into three sections ('Why I went to Zürich,' 'David against the Trolls,' and 'My Sorgenfrei Diary'), each section narrating a different stage in David's self-exploration and each using a different narrative style. Each section is further distinguished by a different dominant symbol: the brazen head in 'Why I Went to Zürich,' the manticore in 'David against the Trolls,' and the bear in 'My Sorgenfrei Diary.' The end of the novel leaves David on the brink of a decision whether or not to return to Dr von Haller for further analysis.

Because *The Manticore* is so clearly parallel in form to *Fifth Business*, the presence of other parallels and of divergences between the two novels is strongly implied. Upon investigation, parallels and divergences between the narrators' personalities, the narrative structures, the implied audiences, and the narrative stances emerge as the most significant. A comparison of each of these features in *The Manticore* with its counterpart in *Fifth Business* reveals the extent and direction of Davies' shift of interest between the two novels.

In comparing the personalities of the two narrators, the parallels suggest themselves immediately, and far outweigh the differences. Both Dunstan Ramsay and David Staunton are parent-dominated, Ramsay by his mother and David by his father, and each of them tries to escape by acquiring a skill which will enable him to be independent. Ramsay sees his escape in terms of magic whereas David's attempt is made through his career as a lawyer: 'something in which I would know where I stood and which would not be open to the whims and preconceptions of people like ... Father' (M 193). In choosing law, moreover, David is not only trying to escape from his father, but also expressing (like Ramsay) a desire for knowledge, which he sees as being available to him through the study of law: 'I wanted a body of knowledge that would go as far as possible to explain people ... that would give me some insight into the spirit that I had seen at work in Bill Unsworth.' Even the terms of his definition are similar to those of Ramsay's (FB 196). Even more like Ramsay, who confesses to being close-mouthed since childhood and to enjoying 'the costive pleasure of being a repository of secrets' (FB 253), David sees knowledge as something to be accumulated but not shared: 'my nature is a retentive, secretive one, and all this revelation went against the grain' (M 38). Confronted with Liesl, David and Ramsay both find themselves giving up information more readily than usual. To a certain extent, their inability to confide easily is due to a lack of practice, because both men grow up isolated within their groups, having no close friendships in childhood or adolescence. This isolation further accounts for their naïveté in social relationships, which lasts through Ramsay's life but which is corrected in David's by older friends – Father Knopwood, for example, correcting David's understanding of the term 'swordsman' (M 182) – and by the experience of his practice in criminal law, which teaches him that the people with whom he is now involved are 'not to be trusted, or at least not taken literally' (M 218). Both David and Ramsay, moreover, show a considerable ruthlessness in getting what they want: Ramsay is willing to stomach 'blasphemy in a good cause'; David turns everything to good account in planning his career: 'I bent everything that came my way to my single purpose' (M 192). Such ruthlessness signals a certain lack of feeling in both men, and it is not surprising that two such similar characters share the same fundamental psychic deficiency: just as Liesl diagnoses Ramsay's problem as the 'revenge' of his unlived life and the bursting out of his bottled-up feelings, so Dr von Haller shows David that he has the same problem: he 'cannot feel, except like a primitive' (M 90).[2]

The only significant difference between the personalities of the two narrators arises in their respective definitions of what Ramsay calls a good cause. For Ramsay, it is his own cause, determined by him, and without reference to other people: 'I wanted my life to be my own; I would live henceforth for my own satisfaction' (FB 98); this ambition is to be realized alone and in some way through the quest for the little Madonna. David, however, with an equally clear idea of what he wants for himself and what he does not want, makes his definition in terms of other people. What he does not want, he defines in terms of the person who has tried to define him as a child and adolescent: 'I wanted to get away from Father and save my soul ... I did not mean to be a man who could be manipulated' (M 193). What he wants he defines in terms of the Oxford don, Pargetter, under whom he learns the profession which is to be his way of independence from his father and his father's world: 'I wanted to be like Pargetter ... to know, to see, to sift, and not to be moved' (M 195). But, by allowing his plan for himself to be shaped by his reactions to other people, David shows himself to be just as much manipulated as if he were directly controlled. Consequently it is possible to say of him, as Ramsay says of Boy, that for him the reality of life lay in external things. In this respect, David and Ramsay are opposites, just as Ramsay and Boy are opposites.

In the narrative structures the differences overshadow the parallels. Although each narrative is the account of a life, Ramsay's is a final paper, David's an interim report. From the perspective of old age, Ramsay's narrative moves confidently over the total surface of his life, anticipating and recalling events; transitions are smooth, sections appear as phases or stages in a continuum, and roughly equal time is given to the important periods of his life. David's narrative is without perspective: the time-shifts are sudden and the time given to events in the different sections is unequal. The lack of perspective and the elaborate narrative technique, which mixes retrospective narrative, current narrative, past conversation, and present dialogue, combine to present a narrative produced *in medias res*. In both novels, Davies' own skill as a narrator is demonstrated, but, in allowing us to see some of the skill by assigning it to his fictitious narrator in *Fifth Business*, he inserts a significant distance between the reader and the events narrated. Ramsay's narrative is reflective in tone also and there is less of the choppy sea of dialogue: Father Blazon, Liesl, and others deliver set-pieces, and Ramsay is allowed to admit that he has 'boiled down what she [Liesl] said' (FB 267) and is not presenting a verbatim report. The same is true of David's account: 'Without being a verbatim report, this is the essence of what passed between us' (M 67), but the dramatic dialogue is much closer to verbatim reporting than anything in Ramsay's narrative.

The question of audience arises at this point, for the audience implied for each narrative affects its shape and style. Ramsay is presenting a vindication of his life: his narrative is therefore shaped and styled to persuade his audience in the novel, the headmaster of Colborne College. David's narrative is exploratory: he is explaining his life to himself, if to anyone, and has no audience within the novel (Dr von Haller is not the audience for his narrative but for the analysis which is in part the subject of his narrative). The barrister's 'brief' which he prepares for her is not identified with the narrative, but affects the reader's response to the narrative by making the important point that David is concerned not to vindicate his life but to explain it. For in the English system in which David began his training, a 'brief' is not the case presented in court, but the material (documents) which a barrister receives from the client's solicitor and from which he formulates the case he will present in court. The notes which David inserts in the second section ('This is my Zürich Notebook ...' and 'The dream dossier I kept in another notebook ...') sufficiently resemble self-addressed memos attached to documents in files not to imply an audience.

His awareness of the presence of an audience underlies Ramsay's concern for the truth of his narrative which he intends as far as possible to be an accurate account of his life. David, however, is apparently concerned more with meaning than with truth. Dr von Haller requests him to speak 'honestly and with trust,' and sets up truth as an object of the work: 'That is what we are looking for. The truth, or some part of it' (M 116). In practice, however, she seems more interested in making sure that he understands the meaning of the facts and events he narrates. Early in his encounter with her, David claims that he does not intend merely to complain spitefully about his parents: 'So you must not imagine I have come here to whine and look for revenge on the dead' (M 70). Dr von Haller's response is not to say that he is lying (not giving a true account of his intentions), but that he does not understand the meaning of what he is saying. She also emphasizes understanding in her discussion of David's shadow: 'We are not working to banish your Shadow, you see, but only to understand it' (M 84). This distinction between truth and meaning can be related to the paradigm of illusion in the four earlier novels, and particularly to the paradox of illusion presented in *Fifth Business*. For if illusion functions as perception as well as deception, as metaphor as well as mask, then it might be said that truth is simply a form of illusion or, more straightforwardly perhaps, that truth is one form of whatever illusion is the other form of, and that is, possibly, meaning.

The final significant comparison between the two novels is the narrative stance of the two narrators in relation to the events they are describing. The essential difference between David's self-probing and Ramsay's is distance. Ramsay's account involves a thoroughgoing analysis of his life, but this is only possible because he is able to look back at it and see its problems in perspective. They are already solved, one way or the other, and in the past, and the issues involved can therefore be considered abstractly. Ramsay looks at who he has been; he is the subject of his life. David, on the other hand, is the object of his analysis: his attempt to understand who he is involves a series of bruising encounters with the same issues with no room for perspective or detachment. Ramsay's experience presents the conflicts or oppositions of his life (psychic and physical, transcendent and mundane, truth and falsehood, good and evil) generally and metaphorically; his encounter with the conflict between good and evil is his encounter with Liesl. David's experience presents the same conflicts in immediate, specific, and personal terms: his encounter with evil is his encounter with Jimmy Veale.

From the differences between the two narrators and between their respective narratives, a general conclusion can be drawn about the fundamental difference between *Fifth Business* and *The Manticore*. Ramsay's analysis of himself as subject – detached, finished (in both senses of the word), retrospective, and dealing with problems metaphorically and almost abstractly – provides a map of the interface between the psychic and the physical in the human psyche. But David, undergoing analysis as its object, records an individual's experience at the interface. *Fifth Business* is a novel of the nature of the psychic process; *The Manticore* is a novel of its operation.

It is, however, the same psychic process which is involved in both novels: they show different facets of the same crystal. Moreover, the pivot on which they both turn is not simply thematic. Structurally it is formed by the coincidence in time of the closing events of Ramsay's narrative and the opening events of David's, all of which are linked to the illusion called 'The Brazen Head of Friar Bacon,' which thereby asserts itself as far more than a mere conjuror's trick.

'The Brazen Head of Friar Bacon' is first introduced in *Fifth Business* at the time of Ramsay's encounter with the *Soirée of Illusions* in Mexico City when, on Ramsay's advice, it is substituted for an escape act. In instructing Eisengrim, who has never heard of it, about the brazen head, Ramsay also intructs the reader ' "It is unmistakably your thing," I said. "You can tell them about the great priest-magician and his Brazen Head that foretold the future and knew the past; I'll write the speech for you" ' (FB 249).[3] Ramsay emphasizes its quality of mystery which he considers appropriate for Eisengrim's personality as 'a poetic magician who took himself seriously' (FB 236), and there is no reason to suppose that his feeling that he has played some part in its success is unfounded. Ramsay describes the act technically as 'no more than a very good thought-reading act ... in a new guise' (FB 249). In spite of his recognition of the head's quality of mystery and in spite of the act's undoubted success, Ramsay considerably underestimates its power. This miscalculation recoils on him when David, two days after his father's funeral, encounters the brazen head for the second time: 'It began in darkness, and slowly the light came up inside a big human head that floated in the middle of the stage, so that it glowed. It spoke, in a rather foreign voice. "Time is," it said, and there was a tremble of violins; "Time was," it said, and there was a chord of horns; "Time's past," it said and there was a very quiet ruffle of drums, and the lights came up just enough for us to see Eisengrim ... who told us the legend of the Head that could tell all things' (M 53). Exhausted by misery and confused by drink, David regresses to an emotional state so primitive that he reacts to the head as though it were actually capable of divination: 'When ... Eisengrim was promising his answers to secret questions, I suddenly heard myself shouting, "Who killed Boy Staunton?" and I found I was on my feet' (M 54). The shock of hearing this question, elicited by the power of an illusion he himself has helped to create, precipitates Ramsay's heart attack.[4] But the shock of hearing his own question has an equally profound effect on David himself; metaphorically speaking, its impetus carries him all the way to the Jung Institute in Zürich 'to go mad under the best obtainable auspices' (M 58). On this level, the brazen head marks the end of Ramsay's narrated experience of the psychic process and the beginning of David's.

In David's narrative in *The Manticore*, however, it also fulfils a much more important function as the dominant symbol of the whole first section. In terms of Jacobi's description of the symbol in Jungian theory as a *meaning-picture* (from the German *Sinnbild*),[5] the brazen head is an extremely appropriate symbol for David's psychic situation at this time: it gathers all the elements in a single image. To begin with, the symbolism of the head indicates what David is doing wrong on a psychic level. In the jargon of popular psychology 'living in your head' means living according to your intellect and reason only, for the head is the seat of the intellect, reason, logic, and consciousness. 'I have lived by reason,' David tells Dr von Haller in defending himself against what he thinks of as a threat to reason, confessing unwittingly, in the language of reason and intellect: 'I have lived in my head' (M 161).

Equally significantly, however, the brazen head is a disembodied head – in the *Soirée* it floats apparently unsupported in mid-air – and its incompleteness indicates not only the incompleteness of David's personality, but also the nature of the missing element. The conscious mind, according to Jung, is a late development, differentiated from the primitive unconscious, but built upon it: 'our modern attitude looks back arrogantly upon the mists of superstition and of medieval or primitive credulity, entirely forgetting that we carry the whole living past in the lower storeys of the skyscraper of rational consciousness. Without the lower storeys our mind is suspended in mid-air. No wonder it gets nervous' (CW 11:56:35). This is exactly what happens to David: he gets nervous (or in clinical terms, neurotic), because his conscious mind (head) has lost contact with his unconscious (body). What is missing from his psyche is the feeling, instinctual element which his unconscious would normally supply.

The composition of the head adds further to this symbolic picture by indicating the effect of the psychic deficiency on David as a human being. The head is described as 'brazen,' indicating an alloy of base metals, and therefore of less value than gold (which for an alchemist like Bacon was the goal of the alchemical opus on the physical level and represented rebirth on the spiritual level).[6] Jung points out that the brazen head made by Bacon was not the only oracular head believed to have been made: 'According to legend, Pope Sylvester II (d.1003), famed as the transmitter of Arabian science, possessed a golden head that imparted oracles' (CW 14:626:434). Significantly, this head was said to have been made of gold, not base metal. Just as an oracular head made of bronze is inferior to one made of gold, the personality which exists on the conscious level only is inferior (of *base* quality), and therefore not fully human. David is losing his humanity by losing touch with his unconscious.

Even the minor detail of the head's hollowness contributes to the symbolic pattern. As the head is hollow, so are its words. The message given in reply to David's question leads Denyse on a wild-goose-chase ending in failure and humiliation when she tries to persuade the police that Eisengrim and his company were responsible for her husband's death in some physical and legally culpable way. Even David, who knows better than to take the words literally, is misled into taking them evidentially and hence into trying to get an explanation from Ramsay at Sorgenfrei. Liesl tells David quite frankly that the message from the head is totally without literal significance, a stock answer for getting out of an awkward situation: 'I gave a perfectly ordinary answer, like any experienced fortune-teller' (M 256). The head's message, therefore, is not legal evidence but, because "legal evidence and psychological evidence are quite different things" (M 59), it can be taken as psychological evidence. As such, it is both perfectly accurate and completely impossible to translate into legal evidence (as the conflicting interpretations reveal). In this way, the answer to David's question (which springs from his need to distinguish between meaning and truth) is both true and false, ambivalent, pointing forward not only to the ambivalence which David will discover within his own life, but also to the ambivalence in the presentation of Jungian theory in the novel.

In addition to symbolizing the various elements of David's psycho-

logical problem, the brazen head also symbolizes a particular danger
which David faces, and to which at one point he almost succumbs.
This danger is the loss of his soul. In discussing the autonomy of
the unconscious, Jung observes: 'Consciousness must have been a very
precarious thing in its beginnings. In relatively primitive societies we can
still observe how easily consciousness gets lost. One of the "perils of
the soul," for instance, is the loss of a soul. This is what happens when
part of the psyche becomes unconscious again ... Even a quite ordinary emotion can cause considerable loss of consciousness' (CW 11:29:17).
Dr von Haller refers indirectly to these same perils of the soul, after
hearing about David's question to the brazen head and consequent flight
in panic: 'I don't think there can be any doubt that it was a wise
decision' (M 55). She describes David's decision to come to Zürich as wise
because, as this part of his narrative reveals, he has already experienced a temporary loss of soul, a momentary loss of consciousness, in the
theatre: 'I suddenly heard myself shouting ... and I found I was on my
feet.' His flight is typical: an instinctive reaction to the 'peril' which has
overtaken him, a response felt but not understood as he runs from the
theatre without even knowing if anyone is chasing him. He describes his
state in rational, medico-legal terms to Dr Tschudi as being 'no longer
in command of my actions' (M 1); for him this means insanity, his only
choice being, 'to go mad unattended or to go mad under the best
obtainable auspices' (M 58). According to Jung's theory, David's fear is a
common one, but should be described in terms of the numinosum
rather than in terms of psychosis: 'In most people there is a sort of
primitive δεισιδαιμονία with regard to the possible contents of the
unconscious. Beneath all natural shyness, shame, and tact, there is a
secret fear of the unknown "perils of the soul." Of course one is
reluctant to admit such a ridiculous fear. But one should realize that this
fear is by no means unjustified; on the contrary, it is only too well
founded' (CW 11:23:14).[7] The brazen head has a numinous power and
can arouse this primitive δεισιδαιμονία in David when his conscious
mind is at very low ebb. The contact with the numinosum causes his
unconscious to erupt, as it were, and temporarily his whole psyche is
engulfed in the unconscious; when the eruption is over his re-emerging
conscious mind has been roughly alerted to the fact that something
very dangerous is going on in the psyche which requires attention and
help. Awareness of danger from the psychic realm produces fear but
a specific element increases the fear: the threat of the dark or demonic
side of the unconscious. The brazen head in itself does not refer to
this psychic darkness: it is 'light' or 'celestial' in the sense that no evil is

involved in producing it. But its existence implies its shadow counterpart, which is described by Jung:

We learn from the 'Ghaya [al-hakim]' that a fair-haired man with dark-blue eyes
was lured into a chamber of the temple, where he was immersed in a great jar
filled with sesame oil. Only his head was left sticking out. There he remained for
forty days, and during this time was fed on nothing but figs soaked in sesame
oil. He was not given a drop of water to drink. As a result of this treatment his
body became as soft as wax. The prisoner was repeatedly fumigated with
incense, and magical formulae were pronounced over him. Eventually his head
was torn off at the neck, the body remaining in the oil. The head was then
placed in a niche on the ashes of burnt olives, and was packed round with cotton
wool. More incense was burned before it, and the head would thereupon
predict famines or good harvests, changes of dynasty, and other future events.
Its eyes could see, though the lids did not move. It also revealed to people
their inmost thoughts, and scientific and technical questions were likewise
addressed to it.

   Even though it is possible that the real head was, in later times, replaced by a
dummy, the whole idea of this ceremony ... seems to point to an original
human sacrifice.[8]

Through the brazen head and its implied shadow or dark counterpart,
therefore, David learns experientially of the reality and dangers of
the psychic realm. Symbolically, the brazen head sums up the initial
stage of David's story. It diagnoses his present condition and points
forward to the possible outcome, exactly as Eisengrim persuades his
audiences that its hollow, plastic, electrically illuminated, wire-hung
counterpart can 'tell all things' (M 53). It dominates David's account of
the events immediately preceding his arrival at the Jung Institute.
From this point it is less important, although it is never entirely forgotten.

   The second section of the novel, 'David against the Trolls,' is the
narrative of David's analysis with Dr Johanna von Haller in the course
of which the dominant symbol of the section (the eponymous manticore)
emerges. But just as the events David narrates in the first section
coincide with the final events of *Fifth Business*, so the preliminaries to the
actual analysis are woven in and out of David's account of what has
brought him first to Dr Tschudi and then to Dr von Haller herself, so
that it is necessary to discuss them before discussing the analysis itself.
The preliminaries function in several ways: they introduce the Jung
Institute as a key to and setting for Jungian psychology, they distin-

guish Jungian psychology from Freudian, and they provide the framework for David's analysis by introducing specifically the theory of the analytic process, of dream interpretation, and of the function-types.

The emphasis in the introduction to the Jung Institute is on solid, down-to-earth realism of the same kind that characterizes the presentation of Ramsay's Deptford background in *Fifth Business*. David finds the Institute in 'one of those tall Zürich houses with a look that is neither domestic nor professional, but has a smack of both,' and is vaguely disconcerted by it: 'I think I expected something that would combine the feeling of a clinic with the spookiness of a madhouse in a bad film. But this was – well, it was Swiss. Very Swiss, for ... it had a sort of domesticity shorn of coziness, a matter-of-factness within which one could not be quite sure of its facts, that put me at a disadvantage' (M 4). The realism is emphasized by David's disappointment at the ordinariness. Dr Tschudi's office has 'no couch – nothing but a desk and two chairs and a lamp or two and some pictures' (M 4), and Dr von Haller's study is equally ordinary: 'rather dark and filled with books, and a few pieces of modern statuary' (M 17). The emphasis on the real and ordinary in the setting is reinforced by the portrait of Dr von Haller herself as a thoroughly average and rather attractive professional woman. Nevertheless, that emphasis throws into sharp relief two 'extraordinary' things which David notices: the 'matter-of-factness within which one could not be quite sure of its facts' of the house where the Jung Institute is situated, and the presence of Dr Tschudi's Alsatian: 'But I received the impression – I am rather good at receiving impressions – that the doctor met some queer customers in that very Swiss little room, and the dog might be useful as more than a companion' (M 4). These ominous notes in the realism are linked with the shadow counterpart of the brazen head and with the warning about the dangers of analysis, 'lions in the way,' which Dr von Haller gives David. Thus, ironically, there seems to be an undercurrent of danger precisely where David might expect to be safest – with his analyst.

David's ignorance of Jung when he arrives at the Institute – 'of the Jungians I knew nothing' (M 7) – is used to bring out the difference between Jungian and Freudian psychology, and in this part of the discussion there is little or no ambivalence. David's instruction begins abruptly when he finds himself faced with a woman as his analyst. Had he known anything about Jung, he might have been prepared for the possibility that Dr von Haller could be a woman, because in the Jungian school a large proportion of analysts are women.[9] Furthermore, 'I rather thought I would be put on a couch and asked about sex' David notes (M 3); but

Dr von Haller has no couch because Jung neither used nor encouraged the use of one by analysts he trained. He considered that it made his patients lazy and more inclined to think of themselves as sick 'passive' patients to be cured by an 'active' doctor, whereas one of the basic principles of his analytical theory was that analysis is a two-way, dialectical process: 'The crucial point is that I confront the patient as one human being to another. Analysis is a dialogue demanding two partners. Analyst and patient sit facing one another, eye to eye; the doctor has something to say, but so has the patient' (MDR 131). This is why Dr von Haller tells David, 'You will hear me express many opinions as we get deeper in. It is the Freudians who are so reserved' (M 38). David is not asked about sex in isolation because, as Dr von Haller explains, 'We have no quarrel with the Freudians, but we do not put the same stress on sexual matters as they do. Sex is very important, but if it were the single most important thing in life it would all be much simpler ... We want all kinds of things ... a very long list. So here in Zürich we try to give proper attention to these other things, as well' (M 62–3). The refusal to reduce everything to the question of sex and sexuality is because 'we do not work on the reductive plan, we of the Zürich school' (M 61). Jung's fundamental objection to the reductive plan is made on complex clinical grounds, but in its simplest form it is that 'the reductive standpoint ... always leads back to the primitive and elementary. The constructive standpoint, on the other hand, tries to synthesize, build up, to direct one's gaze forwards.'[10] Characteristically, the constructive method begins in the present, only going back to the past if it proves necessary. As Jacobi explains: 'An individual may be unable to adapt to his situation because he has not yet achieved a "natural" bond with his instincts, his unconscious, or else has lost it. Sometimes the roots of this state of affairs are to be sought in childhood, but sometimes they reside wholly in the actual situation. In this case the images and symbols which rise up to broaden the psyche and further the psychic process should be considered from the prospective, finalistic view, which starting from the actual situation sets out to create a new equilibrium in the patient's psyche.'[11] Dr Johanna's first demand is 'to hear about your trouble now,' for it is only after hearing David's account of his present situation that she can decide whether the roots of his problem lie there or in his childhood and must be sought there: 'from what you have told me I think we would be best to stick to the usual course and begin at the beginning' (M 62). The existence of optional alternatives to the 'usual course' is stressed in Dr von Haller's remarks as a way of emphasizing the greater flexibility of the Jungian analytical process in comparison with the Freudian.

David's ignorance of Jung also provides opportunity, of course, not merely for an exposition of the differences between Jungian and Freudian theory, but also for an exposition of Jungian theory. It is in this exposition that the undercurrent of ambivalence becomes more marked. Dr von Haller explains the principles and processes to him as they arise, and her explanations concern three major topics, of which the first is the analytic process itself.

The Jungian analyst's role can be defined in terms of listening and helping. 'My job is to listen to people say things they very badly want to tell but are afraid nobody else will understand,' is Dr von Haller's explanation (M 10). Her job as listener involves multiple roles; in David's legal terms she describes them as 'interested spectator ... Prisoner's Friend ... an authority on precedents ... custodian of that constant and perpetual wish to render to everyone his due' (M 65); in terms of the Jungian analytic process she must bear in turn each of the archetypal projections as they are raised to consciousness in David's mind: 'the treatment would be ineffective without these projections, and I am the one who is nearest and best equipped to carry them' (M 163–4). Role-playing by the analyst is not only one aspect of the dialectic principle in practice but also a specialized form of responsive listening. Even this is only half her task: she is also there, she tells David, 'to try to help you in the process of becoming yourself' (M 62). There are, however, limits to the help which an analyst can provide: 'But if the dangers are inescapable and possibly destructive, don't think that I can help you fly over them. There will be lions in the way. I cannot pull their teeth or tell them to make paddy-paws; I can only give you some useful tips about lion-taming' (M 62). The dialectic in practice does not translate into the 'dogfight' of their first encounter but into a partnership which will include not only mutual respect, but also honesty and trust on the part of the patient. Consequently, David as patient must adopt a responsible attitude towards the analysis. He must be prepared for difficulties as well as dangers: 'it is always difficult in the beginning' (M 11). He must be ready to make decisions: 'The decisions must be entirely yours' (M 59); and he must agree to follow a simple regimen (M 61). In addition, he will be expected to do a great deal of work himself on his analysis. This again is characteristic of the dialectic of analysis, because

it is most important that persons undertaking the difficult journey of the soul by the analytic way work on their analysis; otherwise they will not progress very far. For instance Jungian analysts usually require those undergoing analysis to write out their dreams, with all the relevant associations they can collect, and

in addition to make a full and careful record of the whole of the interview
with the analyst, noting down any points which they did not understand or which
had not been mentioned during the hour. It is also valuable if they will keep a
daily diary of the inner life, making a record of anything and everything that
had emotional significance during the day so that it can be correlated to the
unconscious material. Most patients have to be reminded of this obligation a
good many times, for it is very hard work. But the individual who persists in
this work soon discovers that he can do more and more for himself, so saving
much time in the analytic hour for deeper interpretation.[12]

'The doctor gave me plenty of homework,' David records (M 153), and
this homework, represented by the 'Zürich Notebook' (M 67), appears as
'David against the Trolls.' A patient is expected to present his material
in a way suggested by the analyst as best suited to his individual personality; from David, Dr von Haller demands a 'brief' of his case. She is at
hand to provide David with a technical vocabulary when required in the
course of his presentation; when he fumbles in his account of something that 'isn't love, usually; it's a kind of abject surrender, an abdica-
tion of common sense,' to which he cannot put a name, Dr von Haller
is quick to provide the term: 'Excuse me – yes, it has a name. We call it
projection' (M 52). Dr von Haller is also responsible for a description
of the route analysis will take: 'We generally begin with what we call
anamnesis ... We look at your history, and meet some people there
whom you may know or perhaps you don't, but who are portions of
yourself. We take a look at what you remember, and at some things
you thought you had forgotten. As that goes on we find we are going
much deeper. And when that is satisfactorily explored, we decide
whether to go deeper still, to that part of you which is beyond the
unique, to the common heritage of mankind' (M 63). This outlines the
structure of the section, with its swift changes from David's narrative to
the dialogue of the interjected discussions, and also points forward
beyond it. The whole explanation of analytic theory is designed, apart
from informing the reader, to use David's intellect or intelligence as
much as possible, for intelligent co-operation makes the analysis easier.
    The second major topic which Dr von Haller must introduce to
David and to the reader is the Jungian theory of dream interpretation.
David finds that difficult to accept: 'Nor did I like the dream-interpreta-
tion game, which contradicted every rule of evidence known to me'
(M 17). But legal evidence and psychological evidence are quite different
and the value of dreams to the analyst is that 'the dream comes in as
the expression of an involuntary, unconscious psychic process beyond

the control of the conscious mind. It shows the inner truth and reality of the patient as it really is: not as I conjecture it to be, and not as he would like to be, but *as it is*. I have therefore made it a rule to regard dreams as I regard physiological facts.'[13] Jung writes that one of his own dreams was 'symbolic, for it did not state the situation directly but expressed the point indirectly by means of a metaphor that I could not at first understand. When this happens ... it is not a deliberate "disguise" by a dream; it simply reflects the deficiencies in our understanding of emotionally charged pictorial language' (MHS 43). The dream which most clearly reveals Davies' artistic understanding of this emotionally charged pictorial language is the one in which David finds himself again at the scene of the discovery of his father's body: 'I had a dream, or a vision between waking and sleeping one night, that I was once again on that pier, and was wiping filth and oil from the face of a drowned figure; but as I worked I saw that it was not my father, but a child who lay there, and that the child was myself' (M 88). The function of emotion or feeling is where David is weakest, and consequently he needs firm reassurance from Dr von Haller that 'All dreams mean something' (M 14), and that dreams are not fanciful: 'They always mean exactly what they say' (M 159). Meaningless dreams, Jung asserts, are simply those which have not been understood: 'No amount of scepticism and criticism has yet enabled me to regard dreams as negligible occurrences. Often enough they appear senseless, but it is obviously we who lack the sense and ingenuity to read to enigmatic message from the nocturnal realm of the psyche' (CW 16:325:151). In particular, David must be prevented from confusing dreams with parapsychological phenomena: 'Dreams do not foretell the future. They reveal states of mind in which the future may be implicit' (M 15). In other words, dreams are not a form of second sight, clairvoyance, or precognition; where they appear to predict the future, the explanation is quite matter-of-fact: 'Many crises in our lives have a long unconscious history. We move toward them step by step, unaware of the dangers that are accumulating. But what we consciously fail to see is frequently perceived by our unconscious, which can pass the information on through dreams' (MHS 51). Dr von Haller's reassurance is particularly necessary in view of David's 'initial dream' and the mysterious figure of the gypsy, who returns to him at the end of the novel in a slightly altered form. Dr von Haller's explanation of dream interpretation is intended to educate David's weak emotional side, just as her explanation of the theory of analytic process was designed to take advantage of his highly-developed thinking function in order to facilitate the work of the analysis. What she gives David, however, is not an exposition of the whole theory, but a primer of its fundamentals to help him, and through him the reader, understand what is going on.

The theory of functions has to be introduced for the same reason: to help David to make the best of his analysis and to inform the reader through David. In simple terms, the theory is that:

the four functions – thinking, feeling, sensation, and intuition – correspond to the four aspects of reality to which the human being must make an adaptation. Each individual has one superior function which is his preferred way of approach to life. This is augmented by a second auxiliary function which is less conscious and therefore less developed than the first. The other two are generally little developed and function unconsciously and autonomously; this is especially true of the most inferior function, which is therefore closely connected with, and contaminated by, elements from the collective unconscious.[14]

David's response demonstrates how the function-types operate in his life on an everyday level. His first reaction is intellectual: 'Yes, I recalled Plato's theory of our fourfold means of apprehension' (M 91). This, together with his use of the term 'a rational man' to indicate his idea of the cultural norm, indicates that his superior function is thinking, as Dr von Haller confirms. But his behaviour also confirms and illustrates Dr von Haller's comment on his undeveloped feeling. One of the things that happens when the superior function is as highly developed as David's is that the operations of the other functions tend to be disguised as though they were operations of the superior one; David insists that he made his decision to go to Zürich on a rational basis, but Dr von Haller disallows this: 'your decision to come here was a cry for help, however carefully you may have disguised it as a decision based on reason' (M 92). It is typical of an overdeveloped 'thinker' to react to the operation of feeling in his life, when it is pointed out to him, as though it were a threat to his whole way of life; David's response to the idea that he uttered 'a cry for help' illustrates this reaction perfectly: 'So I am to dethrone my Intellect and set Emotion in its place' (M 92). This response in itself is an emotional response, as Dr von Haller is quick to point out: 'There it is, you see! When your unsophisticated Feeling is aroused you talk like that' (M 92). Harding explains the imbalance between superior and inferior function in terms of adaptation: the behaviour produced by the inferior function will be 'rather ill-adapted and compulsive.'[15] Part of David's work with Dr von Haller is to correct this imbalance, so that the behaviour governed by his inferior feeling can

become better adapted for, 'even though a function is lacking in consciousness, it is not for that reason nonexistent, nor is it hard to come
by.'[16] Consequently he must understand the operation of the functions
in his personality. Beyond this, Dr von Haller's explanation serves not
only to facilitate other aspects of his work, especially by showing him
where his strong superior function is useful and where his weak inferior function is a drawback, but also to instruct the reader on the theory
of the function-types.

In all of this instruction on the various aspects of Jungian theory, the
author's strategy is to make sure that the reader is learning as David
learns. But the ambivalence of Davies' attitude is seen in the constant
undercutting of the analytic process by means of the narrator's responses to and criticisms of it which are offered to his analyst as he listens
to her exposition of the theory and undergoes its practice. David is
shown distrusting psychotherapy from the beginning and his reasons for
choosing a Jungian rather than a Freudian analyst are purely pragmatic:
'The Jungians had two negative recommendations: the Freudians hated
them, and Zürich was a long way from Toronto' (M 7). His continued
resistance is shown in his response to key concepts: he distrusts dream
interpretation: 'I ... swallowed that [part of one such interpretation]
and admitted with reluctance that it might be true' (M 89); and he has
reservations about the concept of the unconscious: 'I haven't completely swallowed the idea of the Unconscious' (M 161). Dr von Haller
meets all his criticisms with reasoned argument which often involves the
introduction of new and important information. In this way David's
resistance supports the introduction of information necessary to the
reader, while at the same time forming an undercurrent of criticism
which is the other aspect of the novel's ambivalence but which only
comes into focus in the last section.

This ambivalence is further maintained in the presentation of the
characteristic figures of David's anamnesis which constitutes the whole
of the second section of the novel. It is not a typical Jungian analysis,
for no Jungian analysis can be typical: 'It is ... useless to cast furtive
glances at the way someone else is developing, because each of us has
a unique task of self-realization. Although many human problems are
similar, they are never identical.'[17] Because David is unique (as Dr von
Haller reassures him he is), so his self-realization will be unique. But she
also adds that because he is human his self-realization will include
those elements which make self-realization a human process: 'we are
members of the human race, as well, and our unique quality has
limits' (M 61). The principal elements of the self-realization process are,

in Dr von Haller's phrase, 'the Comedy Company of the Psyche': 'In my profession we call them archetypes, which means that they represent and body forth patterns toward which human behaviour seems to be disposed; patterns which repeat themselves endlessly, but never in precisely the same way' (M 207). They are the shadow, the anima (because David is a man, his soul is feminine), and the magus; the figure of the sybil is absent in the sense that she is not actually discussed (David's use of the word in describing his dream of Dr von Haller is not relevant because the discussion makes it quite clear that the archetype in the dream is the anima). What is of most interest in the account of these figures as they appear in David's life is the unusual features which they present, and it is by this device that Davies suggests that David does not quite fit into the standard pattern of the analysand.

The shadow is the first to be dealt with, because it lies between the conscious and the rest of the unconscious. David's encounter with his shadow, both internally and externally as projected onto Maitland Quelch, is dealt with very briefly in the narrative. He breaks off at the point where he is talking about his Cruikshank grandparents, and this break is followed by a concise and non-specific report of what Dr von Haller said about the shadow: 'Slowly, as we talked, a new concept of Staunton-as-Son-of-a-Bitch emerged, and for a few days he gave me the shivers. But there he was. He had to be faced, not only in this, but in a thousand instances, for if he were not understood, none of his good qualities could be redeemed' (M 83). Such brief treatment may be due in part to the absence of guidelines for dealing with the shadow:

It is a very difficult and important question, what you call the technique of dealing with the shadow. There is, as a matter of fact, no technique at all, inasmuch as technique means that there is a known and perhaps even prescribable way to deal with a certain difficulty or task ... If one can speak of a technique at all, it consists solely in an attitude. First of all one has to accept and to take seriously into account the existence of the shadow. Secondly, it is necessary to be informed about its qualities and intentions. Thirdly, long and difficult negotiations will be unavoidable.[18]

Jung was under no illusions about human nature: 'man is not fundamentally good, almost half of him is a devil,'[19] but that 'almost half' cannot be ignored because 'mere suppression of the shadow is as little of a remedy as beheading would be for a headache' (CW 11:133:77) – a point which Dr von Haller is careful to make to David: 'To banish your Shadow would be of no psychological service to you ... your Shadow is one of the things that keeps you in balance. But you must recognize him' (M 84). Understanding will develop as the shadow is recognized: 'Gradually ... a certain reconciliation with the shadow takes place. The sense of blackness and guilt which comes from contamination with the shadow is washed away.'[20] Although we are led to assume that David has recognized and reconciled himself to his shadow, the bearer of his projection still creates in him a certain irritation, not only in his later discussions with Dr von Haller, but also in the third section of the narrative where Matey has got himself into precisely the trouble which David forecast (M 239). This lingering irritation may be due not only to the inherent difficulties of the encounter with the shadow, but also, in part, to the prospective demands of the novel arising from its position as the middle of a trilogy. Although for the purposes of the analysis David's shadow may have been dealt with to Dr von Haller's satisfaction, David may still have to face him again.

The next figure to emerge from the unconscious is not one of the four major archetypes, but a figure complementary to the shadow, the friend or, in Harding's term, the companion: 'After the shadowy, even shady, elements of the personal unconscious have been brought to light and dealt with, a more definite figure usually appears, which is also the shadow or alter ego, but it now carries those qualities that are compensatory to the ego personality and in addition it frequently brings the promise of completeness. In this form it is known as the companion. There are many examples of this figure to be found in myths, where it is usually represented as semidivine, being more than human. It is in fact a forerunner of the Self.'[21] The encounter with the friend is presented in more detail than the encounter with the shadow. He is a positive (and rather appealing) figure, and David has no difficulty in accepting his presence or his significance, although he is at first surprised: 'I was astonished when one night Felix came to me in a dream' (M 96). There is a great deal of warmth in his recollection of Felix and, characteristically, David associates Felix's reappearance with a return to the state when emotion was acceptable: 'Does his appearance now mean some sort of reversion to childhood?' (M 123). Instead, as Dr von Haller explains, the reappearance indicates an awakening of that part of David's psyche which has been dormant since childhood: 'Only to an emotion you felt in childhood, and which does not seem to have been very common with you since.' But Felix is not wholly explicable: he is described as an 'Animal-Friend, and because an animal, related to the rather undeveloped instinctual side of your nature' (M 160). A parallel can be discerned, however, between Felix and the 'helpful animals' of

European folk-tales who assist the hero on his quest (cw 9(i):421:231). He is one of the unusual features of David's analysis because 'the Friend often appears as an animal, but rarely as a savage animal' (M 124), and he therefore reinforces to some extent the ambivalent undercurrent in the novel. The question of why David's animal-friend should be a savage animal is not answered, but is clearly related to the appearance of the bear as the dominant symbol of the third section of the novel, and appears to be its forerunner in the same way that the companion is the forerunner of the self.

After the friend has been recognized and the resolution is complete, the next figure to emerge from the unconscious for a confrontation with the ego is the anima. The anima, Dr von Haller explains to David, is 'the feminine part of your nature ... all that you are able to see, and experience, in woman' (M 162). Having encountered the shadow and the friend, David is prepared to accept the idea of an inner figure representing his idea of a woman. His difficulty comes in recognizing the projection of his anima onto Dr von Haller: 'If the Anima is my essential image, or pattern of woman, why does she look like you?' (M 163). His question suggests that by the word 'pattern' he means a concept in his mind which has a living external counterpart whom he will one day meet. What happens in fact is that he projects his pattern like a disguise onto any woman who attracts him in some way: 'the Anima must look like somebody ... But you can never see the Anima pure and simple, because she has no such existence; you will always see her in terms of something or somebody else' (M 163). Part of the analyst's role, as she has already indicated to him, is to accept his projections, and to play the parts assigned until he can understand the situation and recover the projection: 'now we have reached the Anima, and I am she; I am as satisfactory casting for the role as I was for the Shadow or the Friend' (M 164). The particular feature of interest in David's encounter with his anima is the dream in which Dr von Haller appears as a sybil with a smile of 'calm beauty,' leading a manticore on a golden chain (M 159). The manticore, as I have noted, is the dominant symbol of this section of the narrative. That it should make its appearance under the control of the anima is significant in two ways. First, it places the symbol in the realm of the feminine in David's psyche, which is curious in view of the fact that it is in the feminine realm that David's weakness lies: although his life has been rich in anima-figures, as Dr von Haller points out (M 206), he has not achieved a good relationship with any of them. For example, Judy Wolff has also been an anima figure for David, and he has not yet recovered this projection; he must learn to see Judy as she is before he can be in a proper relationship to his anima: 'You will see her as she is now ... and you will be delivered forever. So far as possible, lay your ghosts' (M 190). Second, the anima is the ego's guide to the transpersonal or collective unconscious which lies beyond her for, according to Jung, the anima is both '*the ligamentum corporis et spiritus,*'[22] and 'the personification of the collective unconscious' (CW 5:500:324). The implication is that David will achieve the proper relationship with his unconscious through the resolution of the anima.

Following the encounter with the anima comes the encounter with the magus. In David's life, the magus appears as his Oxford law tutor, Pargetter: 'a personal history like yours must include a few people whom it would be stupid to call stock characters, even though they appear in almost all complete personal histories ... And you have just been telling me about one of the most powerful of all, which we may call the Magus, or the Wizard, or the Guru, or anything that signifies a powerful formative influence toward the development of the total personality. Pargetter appears to have been a very fine Magus indeed: a blind genius who accepts you as an apprentice in his art!' (M 205–7). He illustrates another of the unusual features of David's analysis because, according to Dr von Haller, he appears quite late in David's development: 'But he has just turned up, which is unusual though not seriously so. I had expected him earlier' (M 207). With a collector's enthusiasm, she describes him as 'a very fine Magus indeed,' and emphasizes that Pargetter embodies the attributes of the magus very distinctly: he is a genius, blind, and David's instructor in law, which is for David his 'art' or 'mystery.' The combination inspired David and he came 'almost to worship Pargetter' (M 195). The natural respect and admiration which such a teacher might evoke from any student is particularly strengthened in David's case by Pargetter's acknowledgment of him as a disciple. Furthermore, Pargetter is a bachelor with apparently little use for women; David admits that Pargetter may have had something to do with his rejection of sex, and it is interesting to contrast this with Paul Dempster's experience with his 'father in art': 'One always learns one's mystery at the price of one's innocence, though my case was spectacular' (FB 305). It must be pointed out that Pargetter probably only completes a process already begun in David, because all of the older male figures in David's life – his father, Knopwood, Ramsay – are badly adjusted in their relationship to women. David, however, pays the price for his art not with his innocence, but with a part of his life.

In his misogyny and his blindness Pargetter suggests Tiresias, one of the most powerful magus figures in European mythology. It is partly because of this suggestion of the mythic in the way he is portrayed, and partly because, at least in Dr von Haller's view, he deliberately affects the role of magus in emphasizing his blindness, the teacher-pupil relationship, and the avoidance of women, that David is so powerfully affected. He never sees the real man: only his idea of the magus projected onto Pargetter. Moreover, it is because David is so powerfully affected that he gets so much out of the relationship, as Dr von Haller admits: 'you might not have learned so much from him if you had seen him more fully; young people love such absolutes' (M 227). Although the price is high, David apparently finds it worth paying; he leaves Oxford an initiate in his art, and without regret at what that initiation cost.

The magus, one of the most powerful of the archetypes of the unconscious, is the last to be encountered, but David has one more figure, not of the unconscious, to confront. Just as Pargetter the man apparently adopted the role of magus in which David cast him, so David himself adopts a role; 'Until the volcano claims me I live, in a sense, heroically' (M 226). Dr von Haller identifies 'this man on the edge of the volcano, this saturnine lawyer-wizard who snatches people out of the jaws of destruction' as David's persona (M 226), and explains that a persona is necessary for everyone: 'Everybody needs his mask, and the only intentional imposters are those whose mask is one of a man with nothing to conceal. We all have much to conceal, and we must conceal it for our soul's good' (M 227). In this way the persona is protective of the ego, but it can remain protective only if it is not recognized as a mask by others. The ego must, however, recognize the persona as something distinct from itself. If the persona is not recognized and the ego identifies with it, the persona's function is reversed: it destroys instead of protecting the ego: 'the mask freezes and behind it the individual wastes away.'[23] David has so far escaped permanent identification with his persona; he would not be in analysis if he had become identified with the protective mask from behind which he faces the world. But even as a protective device the persona is an ambivalent form of illusion: the mask both conceals and reveals. It conceals the ego's timidity and weakness, for example, by a show of compensatory aggression and strength. Because it is always constructed in terms of compensatory opposites, however, the timidity is always visible in the aggression, the weakness in the strength. David develops as his persona, his professional, public self, the mask of the 'saturnine lawyer-wizard.' Earlier in the analysis Dr von Haller points out how aptly his professional self is figured by the manticore in his dream: 'Not a bad picture of you in court, would you say? Head of a man, brave and dangerous as a lion, capable of wounding with barbs? But not a whole man, or a whole lion, or a merely barbed opponent. A manticore' (M 161). The complex ambivalence of the concept of the persona is reflected by the ambivalence of the figurative elements of the manticore. The forceful presentation of the image, moreover, suggests that, although David has not yet succumbed to identification with his persona, it nevertheless draws on elements deep-rooted in his psyche.

The acknowledgment of the persona as such, as 'a self with which to face the world,' is the last encounter in David's anamnesis. It has been a successful one, in Dr von Haller's view. David is 'drinking quite moderately now,' and he has reached the end of a 'reassessment of some personal, profound experience,' which has made him 'a much pleasanter, easier person' (M 235). All that can be done on this level has been done, and David has to decide whether or not to go on to a deeper stage in self-exploration. Yet David's anamnesis, his life explored in terms of the archetypes and within the framework of the analytic encounter, raises but does not resolve two closely interrelated problems in his life: his relationship with his father and his relationship with women (the latter appearing to be, at least in part, a consequence of the former). On the narrative level, these problems are allowed to become visible, but are left unprobed, and Dr von Haller suggests that the examination of David's whole complex of feelings and responses to the 'idea of a father' has to be postponed until a later stage of analysis, if David chooses to go on: 'your real father, your historical father ... is by no means the same thing as the archetype of fatherhood you carry in the depths of your being, and which comes from – well, for the present we won't attempt to say where' (M 238). The fact that the problem is not discussed creates a slight catch in the narrative, however: the constant presence of Boy Staunton, virtually unregarded, creates an expectancy that is left unsatisfied.

To the series of unusual features in David's analytical encounter (that his animal-friend is a savage animal, that the magus figure appears comparatively late in his analysis, and that David, in spite of his unsatisfactory relationships with women, is rich in anima figures) must be added that of the unresolved 'father problem.' All of these anomalies are deliberately drawn to the reader's attention by Dr von Haller's comments on them, and the cumulative effect is to create an expectancy of something out of the ordinary about David, an expectation both denied and confirmed by Dr von Haller. When David claims to have been having 'remarkable spiritual – well, anyhow, psychological – adventures,' Dr von Haller contradicts him: 'By no means, Mr Staunton. Remarkable in your personal experience, which is what counts, but – forgive me – not at all remarkable in mine' (M 235). Earlier, however, she has used the phrase 'a personal history like yours,' immediately after telling David how fortunate he has been because 'not everybody encounters a Pargetter' (M 205), implying that David is exceptional in at least one respect.

One result of the expectancy created by these anomalies is to focus attention on yet another anomaly – the treatment of the manticore. On the narrative level it is treated rather summarily as a figure in one of David's dreams, and as such it is interpreted to him briefly in terms of his undeveloped feeling and of his professional manner in court. The only overt indications of its importance are that it is the eponymous figure of the novel as a whole, and that we are told explicitly that the unconscious 'chooses its symbolism with breath-taking artistic virtuosity' (M 161). Investigation of the manticore, however, demonstrates not only that it is the dominant symbol of the section, occupying much the same position as the brazen head in the first section, but also that the choice of it as such reveals a certain artistic virtuosity on the part of Davies himself. It derives a certain advantage from its position in the narrative because it appears in company with the anima at the turning-point of David's analysis. As Dr von Haller points out, it is here that the first signs that the 'eclipse' of the anima, and therefore of all that is under her tutelage in David's psyche, is almost over (M 206). It is also a dream-figure in a very clear and impressive dream, which lends it a certain numinosity of the sort ascribed to the archetypes themselves and particularly to the anima. Perhaps more than from either of these factors, it draws power from being so little known; it is unblurred by familiarity and careless use because, as Dr von Haller emphasizes, the manticore is 'not common, even in myths' (M 158).

David's dream provides a simple picture of the manticore under Dr von Haller's control: 'On a chain you held a lion, which was staring out of the picture. The lion had a man's face. My face ... The lion's tail ended in a kind of spike, or barb' (M 158). The description corresponds closely to the definition in the *Oxford English Dictionary*: 'a fabulous monster having the body of a lion, the head of a man, porcupine's quills, and the tail or sting of a scorpion.' The word *manticore* is derived, according to the OED from Latin (*manticora*) and Greek (μαντιχωρας) and from the Old Persian word for 'man-eater,' transliterated by McCulloch as *martijaqâra*. According to McCulloch,

The manticore is born in India. It has a triple row of teeth which fit alternately, a man's face, bluish eyes, a lion's body the colour of blood, and a tail like the sting of a scorpion. Its whistling voice resembles the melody of pipes. It seeks human flesh, is active, and leaps so that neither large spaces nor broad obstacles delay it ...

Most early writers name Ctesias as their source for this fabulous animal. Aristotle ... speaks of the spines in the animal's tail which it shoots off arrow-wise, but Pliny omits this detail ...

Artists varied in their portrayal of the head of this beast, in one case giving it a woman's head ... but more usual is its depiction as a heavily maned beast having a man's face topped by a Phrygian cap ... How to depict a scorpion-like tail concerned none of the artists except the literal minded illustrator of BM Harl.3244, f.43v., where an oddly pointed tail is attached to a sharp-toothed monster clawing a human body.[24]

All the early accounts stress that the manticore is a 'man-eater,' and as late as 1607 Topsell's account records that 'his appetite is especially to the flesh of man.'[25] Even when human beings have progressed a long way from the days when they could as easily be the prey as the predators, the idea of a 'man-eating' animal seems able to inspire a particular terror (as the reputation of man-eating tigers suggests). Furthermore, although the idea of one's body being eaten by an animal is terrible, that of having one's soul eaten by a supernatural animal is even more terrible. On the symbolic level the manticore consumes souls, and in David Staunton's life this symbolic function operates in three ways: the manticore is man-eating persona, man-eating phallus, and man-eating devil.

As man-eating persona the manticore reveals the destructive effect of David's professional mask on his ego. David's persona is constructed as part of his devotion to law and justice. He is willing to admit that the art of law cannot have a single master, and even to acknowledge that the law is his master; moreover, although he points out that 'the law ... works in the cause of justice' and that 'justice is the constant and perpetual wish to render to everyone his due' (M 55), it is quite clear that he sees the law as something greater than the individual. He admires its power and his admiration is legitimate, but he fails to recognize the potential destructiveness of that power if turned against the individual. He is contemptuous, in fact, of those who are frightened by it: 'What if all this silk and bombazine and horsehair awed and even frightened the simple people who came to court for justice? It would do them no harm to be a little frightened' (M 204). Paradoxically, he is right. The power of the law is not dangerous to those who fear it, because they will always be aware of its potential danger. But David himself has lost the proper fear and, because he no longer fears it, the law is destroying him: as its servant he sees himself as being above the 'simple people' who are afraid of it and he no longer has any feeling for them. In a very sophisticated way he is repeating his childhood attitude to 'the people down by the crick.' His feeling is totally undeveloped – so much so that it is symbolically represented not wholly by an animal, but at least in part by an insect: 'Do not forget that stinging tail. The undeveloped feelings are touchy – very defensive' (M 161). The manticore in David's dream, however, is not hurling darts from his tail like a porcupine; it has merely the stinging tail of a scorpion. Significantly, however, the scorpion was reputed to sting itself to death with its own tail, so that David's undeveloped feeling could, in the right circumstances, be the cause of his death.

As man-eating phallus the manticore is less easy to recognize because a three-way rather than a two-way symbolic relationship is involved. The concept of the man-eating phallus is one which Jung describes as having occurred to him in a dream when he was three years old. In his account of the dream he describes finding an underground passage, with a doorway 'closed off by a green curtain':

Curious ... I pushed it aside. I saw before me in the dim light a rectangular chamber about thirty feet long. The ceiling was arched and of hewn stone. The floor was laid with flagstones, and in the center a red carpet ran from the entrance to a low platform. On this platform stood a wonderfully rich golden throne ... Something was standing on it which I thought at first was a tree trunk twelve to fifteen feet high and about one and a half to two feet thick. It was a huge thing, reaching almost to the ceiling. But it was of a curious composition: it was made of skin and naked flesh, and on top there was something like a rounded head with no face and no hair. On the very top of the head was a single eye, gazing motionlessly upward ...

At that moment I heard from outside and above me my mother's voice. She called out, 'Yes, just look at him. That is the man-eater!' That intensified my terror still more, and I awoke sweating ... Only much later did I realize that what I had seen was a phallus. (MDR 11–12)

Normally the phallus is regarded as the 'source of life and libido' (CW 5:146:97); it 'represents the libido, or psychic energy in its creative aspect' (CW 5:180:124), and it 'stands for the creative divinity' (CW 5:183:126). The phallus becomes destructive of the ego (man-eating) if this libido is inverted or turned back into the unconscious and becomes trapped there: 'Whenever some great work is to be accomplished, before which a man recoils, doubtful of his strength, his libido streams back to the fountainhead – and that is the dangerous moment when the issue hangs between annihilation and new life. For if the libido gets stuck in the wonderland of this inner world, then for the upper world man is nothing but a shadow, he is already moribund or at least seriously ill' (CW 5:449:292–3). David faces such a crisis in trying to make himself truly independent of his father by taking a woman for the first time. The normal process of regression of the libido into the unconscious to gain reinforcement and its subsequent return to consciousness is, however, brutally disrupted by Boy Staunton's possessive interference with his son's life in steering him into Myrrha Martindale's bed. David is simultaneously presented with the fact that his father has not only foiled his attempt at sexual, and therefore total personal independence, but that his controlling influence offers him only an inadequate concept of sexuality as he discovers during Knopwood's exposition of the 'swordsman' ethic. Although David is unwilling to admit it even to Dr von Haller, his father has made a fool and a child of him at a crisis point in his life, and the result is a psychic wound which keeps his libido firmly retracted into the safety of the unconscious. The other older male figures in his environment (Ramsay, Pargetter), who should be able to support a renewed bid for independence by showing him a more psychologically adequate sexuality, are themselves sexually inadequate and therefore offer only negative reinforcement of his father's example.

Pargetter's influence is strongest because it is through him that David still hopes to become independent of his father, not realizing that to follow Pargetter's advice will leave him as psychologically dependent on his father as ever. Independence must be won by a fight, and to follow Pargetter's advice to put his emotions in cold storage is merely to evade the issue. By doing so, David unwittingly takes the decision that emotions are the least valuable (or even the valueless) part of his personality in the career he has chosen and, because least valuable, dispensable. He still places some value on his intuition and his sensation, because they can both to some extent be useful to him. But he does not realize the extent to which excluding emotion or feeling from his conscious mind will imprison the corresponding psychic energy in his unconscious. Jung's assessment of those who undervalue sexuality and feeling will be applied to David:

Where there is an undervaluation of sexuality the self is symbolized as a phallus. Undervaluation can consist in an ordinary repression or in overt devaluation. In certain differentiated persons a purely biological interpretation and evaluation of sexuality can also have this effect. Any such conception overlooks the spiritual and 'mystical' implications of the sexual instinct. These have existed from time immemorial as psychic facts, but are repressed on rationalistic and philosophical grounds. In all such cases one can expect an unconscious phallicism by way of compensation. (cw 9(ii):357:226)

The implication is that the manticore symbolizes the self (for if the self is symbolized by the phallus and the phallus by the manticore, then the manticore can equally symbolize the self). Dr von Haller's remark to David that his 'real self may be something very disagreeable and unpleasant' (M 62) is thus true, although she is not necessarily referring specifically to his Jungian self at this point. Since the manticore, in its physical appearance a teratological composite of human, animal, and insect parts, symbolically represents an equally ill-matched assortment of fierce, self-destructive, unconscious feeling and cold, over-differentiated, conscious thinking, it clearly represents the dark or demonic self. The demonic quality of the manticore is in keeping with traditional symbology according to which such teratological creatures are symbols of complex evil.[26]

The medieval Christians, who knew about the manticore from the bestiaries, understood this and they made the manticore a symbol of the man-eating devil,[27] presumably associating it (because of its lion body) with the lion in the New Testament: 'Be sober, be vigilant; because your adversary the devil, as a roaring lion, walketh about seeking whom he may devour.'[28] Davies, as we have seen, considers the devil to be 'not the commonplace symbol of evil but the symbol of unconsciousness, of unknowing, of acting without knowledge of what you're intending to do.'[29] David Staunton leads an unexamined life, in spite of the elaborate ritual he goes through to account for his actions: 'I put myself through the usual examination afterward to be quite sure ... the sort of examination one always makes to determine the nature of anyone's conduct, his degree of responsibility, and all that' (M 1). This takes place in the court of 'Mr Justice Staunton' and the case 'hung, in the end, on the McNaghton Rule ... It is a formula for determining responsibility. It takes its name from a nineteenth-century murderer called McNaghton whose defence was insanity. He said he did it when he was not himself. This was the defence put forward for Staunton. The prosecution kept hammering away at Staunton to find out whether, when he shouted in the theatre, he fully understood the nature and quality of his act, and if he did, did he know it was wrong?' (M 57). It is not possible to act with real knowledge of what you intend to do, however, unless you have examined the alternatives. David has examined one reality – the conscious, physical, rational, mundane reality – and has assumed that it is the only one that exists. His remark that Ramsay 'treated the spirit as an ever-present reality' (M 107) implies that he himself does not consider it a reality and, moreover, he admits that he 'gave up the idea of a soul many years ago' (M 162). This attitude assumes that the other reality (the irrational, unconscious, psychic reality) does not exist, as if the unconscious were simply the absence of consciousness and the irrational the absence of rationality, and so the other reality remains unrecognized. When this other reality breaks through, as it does when he encounters the oracular brazen head in the theatre, the effect is sufficiently violent to force him to take account of the other reality by putting himself into Jungian analysis. In so far as he has acted up to this point without really knowing what he was doing (in spite of his attempts at self-examination), David has been guilty of the evil of unknowing or unconscious action.

David, however, is not the only person in *The Manticore* who is guilty of this kind of evil. Davies chooses, in addition, to examine such evil (and its concomitant good) in three other people: Bill Unsworth, Jimmy Veale, and the farmer's wife who murders her husband. When Bill Unsworth concludes the wrecking of the empty summer cottage by defecating on the owner's photographs, David examines the possible reasons for it: Bill acts neither from spite (feeling, passion) nor from principle (reason, morality), nor from any other purpose or cause. So far as David can judge at the time, Bill is 'simply being as evil as his strong will and deficient imagination will permit. He is possessed, and what possesses him is Evil' (M 151). David himself recognizes the nature of the act, without being aware of the implications of his choice of the word, when he describes it as 'animal.' In the sense of being purely unconscious, without any human consciousness involved, 'animal' precisely characterizes the action in Jungian terms. In the case of Jimmy Veale, however, the issue is more complex. We are told that when Jimmy tortured the old woman to find out where her money was, he knew what he was doing and he knew it was wrong, in the sense at least that he knew it was criminal. To this extent he acted consciously. But because he does not repent it seems unlikely that he understands his actions as morally wrong, and in this sense he acts unconsciously. Evil, moreover, marks him outwardly: according to David, Jimmy has 'the look of one who has laid himself open to a force that is inimical to man' (M 225). On the one hand, both Unsworth and Veale have acted unconsciously and consequently indefensibly because evil, being the abrogation of human responsibility (whether to the point of acting like an animal or to that of being no more than the tool of an abstract force) is that for which no defence is possible. On the other hand, the farmer's wife, with whom the two men are contrasted, knows what she is doing and knows that it is wrong; she offers no denial and David introduces extenuating circumstances (M 219), implying that she pleads guilty. Her action is presented as having been taken consciously in the knowledge that such an action is both criminally and morally wrong. But because it is conscious, it becomes defensible; it is her own human action and not that 'force ... inimical to man' acting through her, and it is, therefore, free of evil.

Evil, the devil of unknowing or unconscious action, emerges in David's dream as a manticore, therefore, because it has only the 'face' of human consciousness (Bill Unsworth and Jimmy Veale look like human beings but act like animals), whereas its 'body' is not only as powerfully animal as the lion, but also as senselessly destructive (of others and of itself) as the scorpion. This is the 'devil within,' the shadow in its internal and infernal form of a force inimical to man. David admits to liking the danger: 'I was always aware that I stood very near to the power of evil ... and I had better admit that I like the moral danger' (M 226). But the manticore is the man-eater, more dangerous than the volcano David describes so glibly because it draws on the unlimited power of the unconscious psyche at the very roots of his existence.

As man-eating persona, man-eating phallus, and man-eating devil, the manticore is a manifestation of the darkness in David's psyche and of his demonic self. Nevertheless, although every demonic manifestation has its celestial counterpart, the celestial counterpart of the manticore does not appear in the novel. The potential for its emergence in David's experience exists, however, and it is marked by the fact that in his dream the manticore is under the guidance and control of the anima, in spite of the fact that David's relationship to women and to his own feminine side has been thrown badly out of kilter by his relationship with his father. It is true that his sexual maturation has been disrupted to the extent that he has given up sex without much of a struggle, that he is thoroughly disconcerted by the thought of a woman analyst, and that he prides himself on understanding women. But below all this masculine confusion his anima image is essentially wise and loving: she controls the destructive manticore by a golden chain and, the dream implies, she can convert him to his light or celestial counterpart. Indeed, on the dust-jacket of the first edition she is shown with her right hand raised in blessing.

The manticore, however, has another function in the novel besides its symbolic one as David's dark self. Quite literally the manticore is a monster, and the most obvious accompaniment of a monster is the hero who kills it (as in the myths of Perseus, Bellerophon, and Beowulf). The killing of the monster is part of the hero's life-pattern, 'the way to life [which] passes through death.'[30] The emergence of the manticore, so thoroughly and respectably Jungian, is in fact a further sign of Davies' ambivalence about Jungian analytical psychology. Parallels between the hero-journey and the analytic process of self-exploration have been drawn elsewhere, notably by Harding: 'In dreams and myths, as well as in parable and allegory, man's inner life and the process of his inner development is almost constantly represented as a journey, a progress from one stage to the next. On the way persons and adventures are encountered and a goal is envisioned which may or may not be reached, but whose attainment is thought of as the climax and fulfillment of life's effort.'[31] Moreover, running through David's analysis there is a consistent series of hints about his own mythologem, the hero-journey. His recurrent dream is of himself guarding an immensely valuable treasure; Dr von Haller raises but leaves unanswered the significant question about this dream: 'why are you a prince, and a child?' (M 237). The answer is suggested in her earlier comment on David's ritual of self-interrogation: 'It is the heroic way, and you have found it without help from anyone else. That suggests that heroic measures appeal to you, and that you are not really afraid of them' (M 65). The implication of the mythic references is that David has the potential to become a hero. Davies offers us, not the hero-journey as a symbolic analogue of analysis, but analysis as a symbolic analogue of the hero-journey, ironically revealing that analytical psychology is not a truly heroic mode and thus repeating the suggestion of ambivalence.

Yet another suggestion of ambivalence concerns the relationship between psychology and common sense. Because 'David Against the Trolls' is only the first stage of a full analysis, as Dr Von Haller makes clear, then it is natural to suppose that David could fulfil his potential as a hero through the second and deeper stage of his analysis. But at the end of the anamnesis, David suddenly suffers an uprush of dislike for 'more mystification': 'I thought we had got past all that. For weeks it seems to me that we have been talking nothing but common sense' (M 236). Dr von Haller's response is to stress the link between common sense and psychology: 'Are you still scampering back to that primitive state of mind where you suppose psychology must be divorced from common sense?' Her response implies that psychology is indeed linked to common sense. She has, however, already unambiguously limited the potential of common sense to the non-heroic, saying that 'everything that makes man a great, as opposed to a merely sentient creature, is fanciful when tested by what people call common sense' (M 160). Common sense is, moreover, an attribute of the conscious mind, in that it is a form of cognitive mentation. In an individual whose thinking is the strongly differentiated superior function, as David's is, common sense is an ego-resource. But, as Harding points out, 'anyone who wishes to embark on the journey of the soul, or on the quest for individuation, must resign all ego resources and face the ordeal stripped.'[32] David must be stripped of his common sense before he can really begin his hero-journey, for common sense is not a quality of heroes, and he cannot achieve his status as a hero within a system linked to it as psychology is.

The problem can be expressed in slightly different terms by saying that, as Dr von Haller points out, David must be educated to feel. But feeling is not part of the intellect or thinking function, even when it is differentiated, and education is an intellectual process even when it takes account of the irrational or psychic reality. Dr von Haller can educate David to allow himself to feel and to understand his feeling, but she cannot educate him to feel; to use the metaphor she uses, she can teach him about martyrdom, but he can experience the fire only by jumping into the flames. The only way that he can really learn to feel is to be so overwhelmed by an emotion that he is willing to abandon thought and common sense altogether and trust his feeling as a mode of functioning. What he needs for this is something quite other than common sense – a sense of the numinous.

With this final paradoxical assertion of the limits of Jungian psychology the second section of the book closes. In this section, however, the various ironies (of the treatment of the manticore itself, of David's questioning of Jungian theory, and of the anomalies of his analysis) all leave the author's ambivalence only indirectly apparent. The ironies occur within the context of the analysis and in the presence of the analyst, and are outweighed by orthodox Jungian theory as presented by so forceful and vivid a character as Dr von Haller. With the irruption of Liesl into David's life, however, the balance of power swings to the other side, and he leaves behind the symbolic analogue in order to undertake the hero-journey itself.

Liesl appears at the beginning of the third section of the book in which David takes a Christmas vacation at St Gall. There he meets Ramsay, accompanied by 'the nearest thing to an ogress I have ever beheld' (M 245), who is introduced to him as 'Fraulein Doktor Liselotte

Naegeli.'[33] David is confused and when Liesl 'asked me to join them at her country home for Christmas, I had said yes before I knew what I was doing. The woman is a spellbinder' (M 246). Liesl brings into David's life all those elements which Dr von Haller set aside, for she is the demonic counterpart of the analyst, as she ironically acknowledges: 'Jo von Haller! ... Not friends, really, but we know each other' (M 246), adding later that 'Jo von Haller ... is really excellent, though not at all my style' (M 256). The only feature they have in common is that each has a low voice, but whereas Dr von Haller's is pleasant, Liesl's is positively beautiful; Dr von Haller has a fine face, whereas Liesl is an ogress; Dr von Haller's clothes are unremarkable, neither fashionable nor dowdy, where Liesl is very smartly and expensively dressed; Dr von Haller is altogether a person to inspire confidence, whereas Liesl has a distinguished femininity. The contrast is not only physical. David's relationship with Dr von Haller is one of confidence and she requires his trust; Liesl, on the other hand, is confessedly dangerous: 'It's my métier. You thinkers drive me to shake you up' (M 268). With Dr von Haller, David's relationship is strictly within professional limits, but Liesl promises him love, 'the love that gives all and takes all and knows no bargains' (M 276).

Liesl's function as a counter to the orthodox Jungian theory expounded by Dr von Haller is made further explicit by her criticism of the analytic process. From the demonic side, she confirms David's mistrust of the analytic way as the route for his hero-journey. Analysis, she points out, is limited because it is a system: 'Analysis with a great analyst is an adventure in self-exploration ... But one must remember that they were all [Freud, Adler, Jung] men with systems ... All men of extraordinary character, and they devised systems that are forever stamped with that character' (M 264). The true hero-journey is taken alone, and the men who made these systems were heroes themselves in the true sense because they 'did not go trustingly to some doctor and follow his lead ... they went into the unknown absolutely alone' (M 264). What is to be followed is the example, not the system, and what he has been shown by Dr von Haller is only the way to begin: 'Jo has set you on your path' (M 263). He has yet to take the journey – after Liesl has shaken him out of his habits as a thinker.

The evidence of the 'Sorgenfrei Diary,' however, is that by the time Liesl intervenes it is almost certainly already too late for David to have any choice in the matter of whether or not he will undertake his hero-journey. 'A good many persons ... find themselves thrust out upon the road to individuation,' writes Jung (MDR 346), and David seems to be among them: his hero-journey begins in the bookshop in St Gall with his encounter with Liesl and Ramsay. When David describes the meeting as 'a coincidence,' Ramsay contradicts him: 'As an historian, I simply don't believe in coincidence ... I suppose you had to meet us, for some reason. A good one I hope' (M 252). There is no causal connection, within the narrative, between Liesl and Ramsay's presence in a bookshop in St Gall and David's. But it is clearly not accidental. It is rather an example of what is described in Jungian theory as *synchronicity*: 'a psychically conditioned relativity of space and time' (CW 8:840:435) or, more simply, 'the simultaneous occurrence of two meaningfully but not causally connected events' (CW 8:849:441). Von Franz points out that 'synchronistic events ... almost invariably accompany the crucial phases of the process of individuation.'[34] In this case the crucial phase of David's hero-journey which the synchronistic event accompanies is the opening phase; its occurrence indicates that David is already beginning his hero-journey.

Almost immediately David is faced with the appearance of the hostile spirit or adversary (who in the Jungian scheme that Davies appears to be discarding is called the shadow). His adversary is no longer on the human scale (Matey and his peculations), but appropriately on the heroic scale, on the inner scale of the monstrous destructive dream-image of the manticore, in the person of Magnus Eisengrim. David has instantly detested him the previous year on first seeing the *Soirée of Illusions*: 'he was making fools of us all ... exploiting just that element in human credulity that most arouses me – I mean the *desire* to be deceived' (M 52). Yet David's hostility at that encounter is tinged with respect for Eisengrim's ability to deceive on such a scale: 'I didn't want Eisengrim to be as good as he was. I thought him dangerous and I grudged him the admiration the audience plainly felt for him' (M 54). At Sorgenfrei he is at first irritated by Eisengrim's 'royal airs' but he cannot help admiring his arrogance: Eisengrim 'is superb, and knows it.' Finally he even begins to like him. There is an affinity between them, as there has been between David and his other shadow, Matey, which he describes as a 'covert spiritual kinship' (M 241). David recognizes the similarity between himself and Eisengrim: 'He wants people to be in awe of him, and at a distance: so do I' (M 257). And Eisengrim's declaration of indifference, 'But you see I don't care about being understood, and I don't ask to be forgiven,' echoes David's remark about the people of Pittstown in the lonely period when he was building up his career as a lawyer and drinking heavily: 'I didn't care whether they understood or not' (M 232). But Eisengrim, explaining to David the difference between Paul Dempster's life-story and Magnus Eisengrim's 'autobiography,' takes care to ask David if *he* understands (M 259), because it is important that the hero and his adversary understand each other. Significantly, when David first meets Eisengrim at Sorgenfrei, he not only recognizes him as an adversary, but also shakes hands with him, unwittingly following Liesl's advice to Ramsay to 'shake hands with your devil.' In so doing, and in avoiding the hostile reaction which Eisengrim's opening remarks seem designed to provoke, he achieves a standard of behaviour which he sees as 'a credit to Dr Johanna, and to Pargetter,' and which the approval of Ramsay and Liesl signifies to be appropriate to his status as hero as well (M 251).

If Eisengrim emerges as the hero's adversary, Ramsay begins to emerge in the mythic role corresponding to that of the magus: the hero's tutor (as Chiron the Centaur was tutor to Jason, and Merlin to King Arthur). He has already completed a journey of his own and can, therefore, understand David's need to complete a similar one, but his ability to help David lies chiefly in the way in which he can correct some of David's misunderstanding of his father. Like Liesl and Eisengrim, Ramsay comes back into David's life as a potential conductor for the numinous element, a role suggested by his concern for and disposal of the pink stone (M 279).

With the introduction of the major characters of his mythologem, David is well started on his hero-journey. Its route, which all heroes follow, is described by Joseph Campbell: 'The standard path of the mythological adventure of the hero is a magnification of the formula represented in the rites of passage: separation – initiation – return: which might be named the nuclear unit of the monomyth.'[35] On the purely psychological level the journey represents the regression of the libido into the unconscious in order to accumulate before a crisis is faced, yet in so doing to place itself at risk, 'for the unconscious is both the mother of all life and also it is death, the devourer.'[36] David's life after the failure of his bid to make himself independent of his father illustrates the consequences of the failure of the libido to return from its regression. In the normal pattern of events, regression is followed by return: 'If the libido manages to tear itself loose and force its way up again, something like a miracle happens: the journey to the underworld was a plunge into the fountain of youth, and the libido, apparently dead, wakes to renewed frutifulness' (CW 5:449:293). This renewal is what David will experience if he continues as he has started.

At a second level, the journey represents a second birth into a higher stage of development. In primitive societies it is visible as the rite of initiation in which the child or adolescent is acknowledged as an adult member of the group. Such rites, like all rites in Campbell's view, 'together with the mythologies that support them, constitute the second womb.'[37] In symbolic form it is presented as pseudo-death or a death-analogue, and in mythic and literary material often inaugurates the full hero-journey. In *Fifth Business*, Ramsay's long coma (after being wounded at Passchendaele) and return to consciousness constitute a second birth which forms the prologue to the quest for a whole self that takes him almost the rest of his life. David, whether as analysand seeking individuation, or as hero seeking apotheosis, must pass through a pseudo-death 'for the way to life passes through death, and no one who avoids it can reach the desired goal.'[38]

Liesl explains the concept of rebirth to David in response to a question about the second part of his self-exploration: 'It's a thing one experiences – feels, if you like. It's learning to know oneself as fully human' (M 267). It involves something quite different from the Christian concept: 'it's more a re-entry and return from the womb of mankind' (M 268). Those who have undergone rebirth are the 'twice-born,' among whom, as Liesl has already pointed out to Ramsay in *Fifth Business*, are Ramsay, Eisengrim, and herself (FB 266).[39]

David's hero-journey will, if successful, put him among the twice-born whose state or nature Campbell describes in terms of Eastern religious philosophy: 'In India the objective is to be *born* from the womb of myth, not to remain in it, and the one who has attained to this "second birth" is truly the "twice-born," freed from the pedagogical devices of society, the lures and threats of myth, the local *mores*, the usual hopes of benefits and rewards. He is truly "free" ... "released from living" ... that reposeful "superman" who is man perfected – though in our kindergarten of libidinous misapprehensions he moves like a being from another sphere.'[40] The state Campbell describes has been imagined by David; he calls it a state of *esse in anima*: 'I am beginning to recognize the objectivity of the world, while knowing also that because I am who and what I am, I both perceive the world in terms of who and what I am and project onto the world a great deal of who and what I am. If I know this, I ought to be able to escape the stupider kinds of illusion. The absolute nature of things is independent of my senses (which are all I have to perceive with), and what I perceive is an image in my own psyche' (M 242–3). But, although David can imagine this state of being, he is still imagining it from within a rational framework of thought; it is clear that he is far from experiencing it. At the same time, his experiences as a child, adolescent, and adult, as he records them, include many incidents which show a spontaneous responsiveness to psychic events beneath the conscious level of his over-developed rationality. As a boy he is sensitive to the strange quality in Ramsay: 'there was always something about him that held the imagination ' (M 207); he has a fondness for poetry which is not common among rationalists (M 215); and he records, in terms which almost suggest some vision of the twice-born life, a theatre visit which impressed him: '"Have you ever seen the Habima Players do *The Dybbuk?* I did long ago, and this had something of that quality about it, as if you were looking into a stranger and more splendid world than the one you know – almost a solemn joy"' (M 54). His responsiveness is particularly evident during periods when his conscious personality is disturbed, as it is during the days immediately after his father's death. He is particularly 'aware' on the occasion of Denyse's attempt to get a death-mask of her husband, when he feels the room is 'alive with unusual currents' (M 35). His awareness is sharpened, too, by his visits to Sorgenfrei; he calls it a 'dream castle,' but at the same time it troubles him (M 248). He responds to something exhilarating which he cannot identify: 'Is it the air, or Liesl's company?' In his first few days at Sorgenfrei, David is 'high' in both the literal and the metaphorical senses of the word. His death-analogue takes him down to the depths in space and time and spirit, deep in a mountain cave among relics of a palaeolithic bear-cult.

Unlike Dr von Haller, Liesl has no use for common sense. When David confesses that 'I can't remember ever feeling what I suppose you mean by awe' (M 267), she immediately proceeds to confront him with something which should inspire awe. The expedition is planned so that David is at the disadvantage of not knowing even where they are going, let alone why; in the outer cave, 'apparently quite famous since somebody ... proved conclusively in the nineties that primitive men had lived here ' (M 269), all evidence has been removed and he is further bewildered. Liesl leads him into the entrance to the inner cave and they begin 'a horrible descent' which, combined with cold, discomfort, constriction, and Liesl's determined silence, reduces him to a state of terror.

For Liesl herself, the bear-cult cave is obviously a numinous place: 'Liesl was in a mood that I had never seen in her before; all her irony and amusement were gone and her eyes were wide with awe' (M 271). She tries to convey this sense to David by showing him the careful arrangements of bones and skulls: 'They are bears. The ancestors worshipped bears. Look, in this one bones have been pushed into the eye-holes. And here, you see, the leg-bones have been carefully piled under the chin of the skull ... No cave-bear could come through the passage. No; they brought the bones here, and the skins, and set up this place of worship. Perhaps someone pulled on the bear skin, and there was a ceremony of killing' (M 272).[41] She is angry and disappointed at his failure to respond, but he does not 'feel enough for it to mean anything' (M 272). The parallels she draws between the act of worship in primitive and in modern man merely arouse his rational faculty. Her impromptu act of worship before they leave does alarm him: 'This was worse – much worse – than Dr Johanna's Comedy Company of the Psyche' (M 273). But the emotion it inspires is not the proper fear of the numinous, the awe of what she is worshipping, but revulsion.

Liesl's attempt to initiate David into the company of the twice-born has failed, and they start on the outward journey. At this moment when the failure of human effort to affect David is complete, something else intervenes: 'Suddenly, out of the darkness just before me, came a roar so loud, so immediate, so fearful in suggestion that I knew in that instant the sharpness of death' (M 275). Here the numinosum itself breaks through David's conscious barriers; the sound is fearful because it suggests a presence – the presence of a deity. This 'proper fear,' awe, leaves him terrified far beyond the point of revulsion or panic; he is paralyzed and helpless; 'I was at the lowest ebb, frightened, filthy, seemingly powerless, because when I heard Liesl's voice ... I couldn't go on' (M 275). Ironically, when he does not move in response to her demand, Liesl fails to realize what has happened: 'It's only a trick of the wind. Did you think it was the bear-god coming to claim you?' But the bear-spirit has claimed him, and he acknowledges his 'death': 'I'm done.' Again, ironically, she demands, 'What gives you strength? ... Have you no ancestors?' and unknowingly gives David the necessary clue to his way back: 'I thought of Maria Dymock ... would Maria Dymock see me through? In my weakened, terrified, humiliated condition I suppose I must have called upon Maria Dymock and something ... gave me the power I needed' (M 275). His rationalism puts up an automatic objection, but it is without any real conviction: David recognizes exactly what has happened to him. By the end of the day he can even put into words his understanding, that he is 'renewed – yes, and ... reborn, by the terror of the cave' and by the promise Liesl makes to him (M 276) which constitutes the reward of his first experience of awe.

Even the fact that Liesl was only indirectly an instrument in awakening David's dormant sense of awe and the numinous is part of the confirmation of her function as a counter to orthodox Jungian theory. It was not her activity, free of common sense though it was, which 'scared the shit out of him,' but the direct intervention of something other than human. Her attempts were made on a human level and, because of David's implied potential, they interfered rather than assisted. Jung himself experienced a similar phenomenon in his efforts to help his friend Richard Wilhelm in an 'inner conflict,' and records his failure in Wilhelm's response, 'a drawing back, an inward shutting himself off' (MDR 377). Liesl's arguments and her prayer before the bear-skulls produce exactly the same response in David: he suddenly creates a gap between himself and the Sorgenfrei group; they become the 'sort of people' he does not recognize (M 273). Significantly, Jung adds to the record of his experience with Wilhelm: 'This is a phenomenon I have observed in many men of importance. There is, as Goethe puts it in *Faust*, an "untrodden, untreadable" region whose precincts cannot and should not be entered by force; a destiny which will brook no human intervention' (MDR 377). The prompt response of the bear-spirit, whom Liesl wittingly or unwittingly invoked in praying before the skulls, and of Maria Dymock, whom David invoked in his desperate need, strongly suggest such a destiny for David Staunton, and remove him even further from the realm of clinical psychology.

The visit to the cave is the narrative climax of both the section and the novel as a whole, and the symbol which dominates this final section is the bear. The function of this dominant symbol can best be expressed, not like the symbols of the brazen head and the manticore in terms of meaning-pictures, but in terms of the *coincidentia oppositorum*,[42] for it holds within a single image all the ambivalences which refer to David as hero. For, Jung writes, 'he who stems from two mothers is the hero: the first birth makes him a mortal man, the second an immortal half-god' (CW 5:496:322). The mythic example he cites is Heracles, who 'had two mothers, the helpful Alcmene and the vengeful Hera, from whose breast he drank the milk of immortality' (CW 5:295n). For David, the dual mother – the source of life and death, light and darkness – is the bear.

The bear as animal symbolizes the forces of the unconscious: 'theriomorphic symbols always refer to unconscious manifestations of libido' (CW 5:261:180). Libido which remains trapped in the unconscious is a negative force, a 'man-eater,' which can destroy the whole psyche. On the other hand, libido which, having been allowed to regress temporarily into the unconscious, is then raised to consciousness and integrated with the ego, is a source of energy to the psyche. David is forty, an age which Jung regarded as the beginning of the second half of life, and he faces the task of the second half of life, individuation: 'At this stage the mother-symbol no longer connects back to the beginnings, but points towards the unconscious as the creative matrix of the future. "Entry into the mother" then means establishing a relationship between the ego and the unconscious' (CW 5:459:301). In David's life the bear represents the energy of the libido in the creation of the rest of his life, potentially either a positive or a negative force.

The bear as animal also represents the instinctual side of the psyche, as Dr von Haller points out to David in their discussion of Felix. In particular, David records, Felix represents 'some rather kind impulses and some bewilderment' (M 160), which are attributes of the instinctual, feeling function. The instinctual side of the psyche, if left undeveloped (undifferentiated) and unintegrated with the rest of the conscious personality, will produce moody, probably rather ill-adapted and compulsive behaviour.[43] Raised to the conscious level and integrated, the instinctual side of the psyche will assist the conscious personality to 'know what is of value to himself, and what is of value to others ... [and] be at home in personal contacts.'[44]

The bear as bear (rather than just as animal) 'is associated with Artemis and is thus a "feminine" animal' (CW 5, 322n). It represents the feminine element in David, the eros principle at work, and is another manifestation of his anima. Again, it can be either positive or negative. On the negative side, the bear could be 'the old maternal beast that can crush a man to death with her great hugging arms;'[45] the implication of 'maternal' being that the powerful female impulse to hold (most clearly manifest in the hugging of the child) will crush the rest of the personality if it is allowed to operate uncontrolled. In the bear, therefore, resides a power which can hug David's psyche to death or, properly controlled, integrate it powerfully. On the positive side, the bear, as a 'lunar' animal (also by association with Artemis) characterized by receptivity,[46] represents the ability to form relationships available to David through his feminine element: the ability to perceive and function synthetistically. This aspect of the feminine we have already encountered in the sybil leading and controlling the manticore. A further manifestation of the same aspect, more closely associated with the bear, is Maria Dymock, whose fierce maternal love reaches out through time to her great-grandson in response to his cry for help and puts at his disposal the feminine strength that was her own and is, therefore, the inheritance of her descendants if they choose to avail themselves of it.

Finally, however, the bear represents more than individual psychic elements; it represents the psychic totality. For in this final section, the bear manifests the self. Because the self is a complex entity, its symbolism can never be straightforward, as Jung admits: 'Anything that a man postulates as being a greater totality than himself can become a symbol of the Self' (cw 11:232:156). Hence, in *Fifth Business* the concept of fifth business is a symbol of the self in the quaternary, circular, and abstract form of a mandala; and in the previous section of *The Manticore*, the manticore is a symbol of the self as a teratomorphic being. Jung also makes clear that the self can be manifest in animal form: 'It goes without saying that the self also has its theriomorphic symbolism. The commonest of these images in modern dreams are, in my experience, the elephant, horse, bull, bear ...'[47] The bear as symbol of the self unites all the polarities within itself as the dual mother. Unlike the manticore, however, which is a dark manifestation of the self of which the light counterpart was merely implied by the appearance of the anima with the manticore, the bear contains both the light and the dark self as potentials within it. For this symbol of the self is essentially prospective: David's rebirth among the company of the twice-born after his symbolic death in the cave is only the beginning of a longer hero-journey still to be taken.[48]

Davies is more ambivalent than ever in *The Manticore*, and his ambivalence is made abundantly clear when, in the third section of the novel, Liesl articulates the counter-theory to Jung, which has been present up to this point only as an ironic undercurrent. Through her Davies presents the notion that Jungian theory does not offer the final answer, or even the best answer, to the question of human identity, and that such an answer must rather be sought in the heroic mode of romance. During his anamnesis David has recounted to Dr von Haller a statement made by Father Knopwood, that 'all formulas for meeting life – even many philosophies – are illusion' (M 184). The analyst allows it to pass unchallenged, but Liesl's discussion of the inadequacy of all systems makes it clear that all formulas include not only Father Knopwood's Christianity (in David's view) but also Jungian psychology. What has hitherto been implicit in the novel, Liesl makes explicit: Jungian psychology is itself illusion. So, ironically, Davies' 'engrossing primer' of Jungian psychology undercuts the value of that psychology as a way of comprehending and living life to its fullest human extent. The final irony of *The Manticore*, however, is that its ambivalence about the Jungian formula or system is, as Jung's own words make clear, unexceptionably Jungian: 'I have not the faintest idea what "psyche" is in itself, yet, when I come to think and speak of it, I must speak of my abstractions, concepts, views, figures, knowing that they are our specific illusions ... All things are *as if* they were. *Real* things are *effects* of something unknown ... We have no idea of absolute reality, because "reality" is always something "observed." '[49]

6 / The Naked Magician

> I am destitute of pleasure
> Knowing that knowledge tricks us beyond measure

says Goethe's Faust,[1] and it is tempting to see in this statement an image of Davies' position at the end of *The Manticore*. He has apparently reached the point where the Jungian psychology which has fascinated him for so long will no longer serve as an instrument in his attempt to define human identity in his fiction. In a sense, this development was inevitable. Jung himself, as I have pointed out, was aware that his archetypes were 'specific illusions.'[2] His discussion of the nature of the unconscious mind and the self in 'Psychology and Religion,' furthermore, helps to elucidate more precisely the nature of Davies' predicament at the end of *The Manticore*; in it he points out that the nature of the unconscious is such that 'there is bound to be an illimitable and indefinable addition to every personality' (cw 11:66:40), and it is implied that this addition may lie beyond the reach of psychology. Davies is, therefore, still in agreement with Jung's thought when he appears to abandon Jungian theory for what might be described as simple heroic romance.

In *World of Wonders* (1975), in which he continues his attempt to define human identity, he is too canny to abandon Jungianism altogether, and, although he seems to have dispensed with Jungian trappings, he has not dispensed with the central idea of the Jungian self. The specific Jungian self presented here is that of Magnus Eisengrim, whom we have previously met only in secondary roles in *Fifth Business* and *The Manticore*, but who returns in *World of Wonders* as the hero in more than one sense of the word. What Davies has chosen to do is to explore as fully as possible the idea that myth and Jungian psychology are not mutually exclusive: the Jungian process of individuation and the mythic hero-journey coexist within the same human frame of reference and even within the same events. Davies achieves this congruence by showing Eisengrim as an individual moving in terms of Jungian psychological theory towards individuation even as he moves in terms of the romance mode through the phases of the hero-journey. Some lingering hint of Davies' ambivalence about Jungianism remains: he signals this ironic approach clearly (but humorously) when in Eisengrim's life a counterpart to Dr von Haller and her Jungian dream-analysis appears in the person of Mrs Constantinescu and *Zadkiel's Dream Book*. Within this double framework of myth and psychology, Davies explores not only what each can offer towards a definition of human identity, but also what differences in such a definition arise from the fact that although myth and psychology coexist, they are not necessarily coextensive. The discrepancy, which perhaps may correspond to Jung's 'illimitable and indefinable addition,' is discussed in terms of Spengler's Magian world view, and includes the still unresolved paradoxes of truth and falsehood, good and evil, and subjective and objective reality. Davies' final position demonstrates, if not a complete rejection of Jung's theories as a basis for defining human identity at least a reduced confidence in their capacity to provide such a definition.

Because Eisengrim's most recent previous appearance in the trilogy, at the close of *The Manticore*, coincides with Davies' most obviously ambivalent view of the Jungian mythos he has so carefully developed up to this point in his work, the reader might well expect that Eisengrim's development, if it is to be in terms of Jungian individuation, would be in some way exceptional. Contrary to expectation, however, Eisengrim's development towards the individuated self is perfectly straightforward. The method of presentation is equally straightforward for Davies returns to the rather simplified mode he employed in the Salterton trilogy, showing Eisengrim's successive encounters with the archetypes as a series of personal encounters with people in his environment. All the major archetypes of the unconscious (shadow, anima, magus, sybil) are present, although the persona is ignored, and the only unusual feature is that they do not appear in the usual order. The order in which they do appear (magus, sybil, anima, shadow) is dictated by Davies' decision to organize the events of Eisengrim's life to conform closely with the mythologem of the hero-journey through the underworld and back again. From the Jungian point of view, Eisengrim's progress towards individuation is therefore perfectly normal, in spite of his bizarre environment.

Eisengrim's first archetypal encounter is with the magus. In his personal history, the first bearer of this archetype is Willard the Wizard, who later gives place to Sir John Tresize. The encounter with Willard is classically straightforward. As soon as Eisengrim meets Willard he is aware of 'a dark and enchantingly wizard-like gaze' (ww 27), which entrances him and which indicates Willard's power or mana as an archetypal manifestation. His rape and subsequent abduction represent the psychological shock and withdrawal through which he must pass in order to enter the inner world of his own spirit to begin the development of his personality, represented externally by his initiation into the art of illusion of his magus figure. Willard as magus, moreover, is fully as powerful as Pargetter is for David Staunton: the acquisition of the art of illusion is as serious and demanding as the acquisition of the art of law, and Willard is no more easy to please than Pargetter: 'Willard never laughed ... never praised ... he was sharp about mistakes, and demanded more and more refinement of success' (ww 57). He is a more reluctant teacher than Pargetter but, even so, Eisengrim acknowledges, ' he taught me all there is to know about ... cards' and 'all the basic work' with coins (ww 80). Eisengrim therefore emerges from his 'apprenticeship' with the complete technique of his art. The mana exerted by the magus is not, however, lessened by Eisengrim's mastery of technique; it does not even wane as Willard's physical domination of Eisengrim wanes. In their last few years together, as Willard's physical condition deteriorates, Eisengrim is as strongly bound to Willard by hatred and revenge as he ever was by fear and awe in the earlier years. Only Willard's death sets him free, and enables him to move on to a second apprenticeship to a 'great master,' Sir John Tresize. What Eisengrim learns from Tresize is not the technique of illusion, but something more intangible. Eisengrim himself speaks later of this stage of apprenticeship as 'trying to learn the ropes of another mode of life' (ww 235). Most of it is devoted to the development of 'a new style' and to being 'born again' (ww 202). A significant difference between the two apprenticeships is that with Willard Eisengrim seems to be living only half consciously (he acquires his mastery of illusion obsessively and without really thinking about what he is doing or why he is doing it), whereas with Sir John he is conscious of some purpose: 'I possessed a few hard-won facts, but he had artistic imagination. My job was somehow to find my way into his world, and take a humble, responsible part in it' (ww 207). As a result of Tresize's responsibility towards his apprentice (a responsibility either obliterated by heroin or simply lacking in Willard), Eisengrim not only finds his way into Tresize's world but also finds that he shares the older actor's artistic imagination,

as is evident in his portrayal of Robert-Houdin. Again the death of his
master frees him from his apprenticeship, this time to go his own way
and to develop his own mastery.

It is during his apprenticeship with Willard that Eisengrim encounters
the bearer of the corresponding feminine archetype, the sybil, in the
person of Mrs Constantinescu. The sybil is probably the least known of
the Jungian archetypes, and Martin comments that the sybil 'is by far
the most difficult of all the archetypal images to describe adequately,
since it is at one and the same time immensely powerful but impalpa-
ble and diffuse.'[3] As the bearer of the sybil archetype in Eisengrim's
individuation, Mrs Constantinescu manifests both the power and the
impalpability of the archetype. Eisengrim immediately recognizes her
mana: for him she is ' a strange old girl' (ww 124), and he acknowledges
something mysterious about her, admitting that she 'may have been
a real gypsy, as she claimed' (ww 125); her occupation of keeping 'a
mitt-camp' clearly is designed to support her strangeness, and she is
even gently ambiguous about her profession: 'don't put your faith
in sideshow gypsies' (ww 128). In keeping with the generally creative
and synthetistic function of the sybil,[4] Mrs Constantinescu offers
Eisengrim kindness, to which he responds in part gratefully and
in part sceptically: 'I was inclined to think ... Mrs Constantinescu was a
nut' (ww 131). Nevertheless, in spite of his scepticism, he makes good
use of her judgment and follows her advice about his life with Willard:
'it's not good, but it could be worse ... But if you don't like it, do
something about it' (ww 129). His response (to clean himself up) is the
first step on the road to regaining self-respect. The full importance of
the encounter, however, is seen in his comment: 'Almost everything of
great value I have learned in life has been taught me by women'
(ww 124). His relationship with Mrs Constantinescu is the first
demonstration of the truth of this in his life and, at the same time,
because of her archetypal mana, the reason for it. In establishing a
good relationship with her, Eisengrim establishes a good relationship
with his own feminine side at a very deep level, which enables him
to benefit from other women whom he encounters and who have
something to offer him. As he says simply, 'she liked me,' and from
this good relationship stem all his subsequent good relationships with
women in general.

The second feminine archetype, the anima, comes into his life at the
same time as the second bearer of his magus image. The relationship
of the anima to the sybil is not easy to define. Martin points out that 'the
fact that the Great Mother is also the Virgin, Persephone no less than

Demeter, links this figure with the anima in a man's psychology,'5 and the absence of the sybil, *per se*, in David Staunton's life indicates that often the relationship with the anima is sufficient for a man's relationship with the feminine within himself. Hence the difference between the sybil and the anima in Eisengrim's life essentially seems to be that the strangeness or *mana* of the sybil is sufficiently muted in the anima to enable Eisengrim to establish a more personal, although classically patterned relationship with the bearer of the anima.

The bearer of the anima is also a woman who likes Eisengrim. She is Milady, the wife of Sir John Tresize, and 'professionally known as Miss Annette de la Borderie' (ww 177), of whom Eisengrim says: 'Except for old Zingara [Mrs Constantinescu] ... she was the only woman I had ever known who seemed to like me, and think I was of any interest or value' (ww 273). The impact of Milady on Eisengrim's life clearly follows the pattern of an anima encounter. Years later, when he narrates the story of his life, he remembers the first time he saw her and that he 'had a feeling something important had happened' to him (ww 176). She has the characteristic ability of the anima to illuminate an individual's entire life: 'I was constantly aware of her, and what I believed to be her spirit transfigured everything around me. I held wonderful mental conversations with her ... and they gave me a new attitude toward myself' (ww 177). In the days between his audition (his first meeting with Milady) and the start of rehearsals, he feels 'cut off from Paradise' (ww 178). The numinosity of the anima, muted though it is by comparison with the mana of the sybil, is also apparent when he admits that he was 'beglamoured' by Milady (ww 210). Anima enchantments do not, in the normal course of events, last very long, and usually they come to an abrupt and painful end, leaving the enchanted not only thoroughly disenchanted but also thoroughly vulnerable to a new enchantment. But Eisengrim is not typical: as a result of the previous favourable relationship with the sybil, and of the favourable relationship with the anima herself, he has established a sufficiently good relationship with the feminine in himself to be able to avoid disenchantment and to withdraw the projection without psychological trauma. His fierce loyalty to Milady remains unimpaired by his new ability to see her as she really is: 'She had a beauty all her own ... I saw all of that, and felt it through and through me like the conviction of religion, but still, alas, I saw that she was old, and eccentric, and there was a courageous pathos about what she was doing' (ww 218). Consequently he is able to become 'a friend of Milady's, and rather less of an adorer' (ww 273), with benefits not only to himself, but also to Milady. It is a friend, therefore, that he loses at her death a few weeks after that of Sir John, and it is because of what he has learned from her of friendship with women that he, in turn, is able to befriend the friendless Liesl when he meets her.

The bearer of the shadow archetype in Eisengrim's life emerges shortly after his meeting with Sir John and Milady in the person of Roland Ingestree – 'the Cantab,' as Eisengrim refers to him. The hostile relationship between shadow and ego can be traced throughout the relationship between Ingestree and Eisengrim in the period when they are both members of Tresize's company. The hostility begins because Eisengrim instinctively recognizes that for Ingestree the theatre is 'a kind of crude extension of Eng. Lit. at Cambridge' (ww 253), and this recognition arouses Eisengrim's fiercest and deepest loyalties to his profession (for him the theatre 'refreshes dry places in the spirit'). As a result, he projects onto Ingestree all the qualities which he cannot afford to admit in himself: Ingestree's social climbing, intellectual pretension, desire to impress, and vindictiveness are all qualities Eisengrim himself possesses. Even looking back on the period, he can admit to them only by offering superior motives: 'I thirsted for something better' (ww 253). Nevertheless it is clear from Eisengrim's narrative that he does eventually retrieve the projection, for he takes, at Liesl's suggestion, the name Eisengrim, which means 'the sinister hardness, the cruelty of iron itself': 'I took the name, and recognized the fact, and thereby got it up out of my depths so that at least I could be aware of it and take a look at it, now and then. I won't say I domesticated the wolf, but I knew where his lair was, and what he might do' (ww 347).[6] Thus he solves what Jung describes as one of the most important problems facing the individual at this point: 'how he is to reconcile himself with his own nature – how he is to love the enemy in his own heart and call the wolf his brother.'[7] With the recognition of the shadow-wolf, moreover, comes a clear-headed attitude to evil: 'We can't know the quality or the results of our actions except in the most limited way. All we can do is to try to be as sure as we can of what we are doing so far as it relates to ourselves' (ww 269). This strongly resembles a formula for the practical application of a concept of good and evil which has undergone Jung's psychological revision (cw 11:291:197). Consequently, Eisengrim can later admit that he 'toyed' with Ingestree to punish him for his act of vindictive cruelty towards Sir John, but he distinguishes this from the harboured grudge or desire for vengeance of which Ramsay accuses him. Yet some form of reconciliation clearly takes place between Eisengrim and his shadow for, as the group are making their final farewells, Ramsay notices 'a rather curious exchange of friendly words and handshakes' between the two men (ww 332). With this action Eisengrim, like David Staunton in *The Manticore* and Ramsay himself in *Fifth Business*, carries out Liesl's advice to Ramsay to shake hands with his devil.

The second person in Eisengrim's life to represent his shadow, although he is not a bearer of the archetype, is David Staunton. In their encounter, as related in the final chapters of *The Manticore*, it could be said that Eisengrim appears rather as David's shadow than the other way round. An immediate affinity of the sort characteristic of an archetypal encounter is evident between them, in spite of the fact that their minds work in completely opposite ways. The most important difference between them is that of function-type, and it is by comparing Eisengrim with David that it becomes possible to discover Eisengrim's function-type. David is a 'thinker,' and diametrically opposed in the Jungian scheme to the thinker is the person whose function-type is feeling. This is Eisengrim's function-type, demonstrated in his narrative of his childhood and adult life which is presented from the viewpoint of a man who relates to the world through his feelings. Indeed, Ingestree suggests that Eisengrim's feelings have so coloured his universe that they are all that his narrative offers: 'so far as his story is concerned, we might as well make up our minds that all we are going to get is his feeling' (ww 63). Ingestree's remark supports Ramsay's earlier remark that Eisengrim, is 'a man of strong feeling,' whose feelings 'take concrete shapes' (ww 40). As a man of 'feeling,' Eisengrim is shown to be acutely sensitive to every element of his environment (including people) in terms of liking or disliking them. He understands this characteristic in himself and has accepted it, as he reveals when describing his first meeting with Gus: 'I have always had a quick response to people, and though it is sometimes wrong it is more often right. If I like them on sight they are lucky people for me, and that's all I really care about' (ww 47). In contrast with his ability to feel, Eisengrim's capacity as a thinker is shown to be weak. Liesl says he has 'no brains at all' (ww 325), obviously an exaggeration for, as Ramsay notes over the business of the subtext, he can on occasion be a remarkably quick learner. Nevertheless, he admits his weakness: 'I don't suppose I've ever had more than half a dozen ideas in my life, and even those wouldn't have much appeal for a philosopher' (ww 261). But, as he immediately points out, ideas are of very little use in the kind of theatre which has been his life: 'Sir John's theatre didn't deal in ideas, but in feelings. Chivalry, and loyalty and selfless love don't rank as ideas' (ww 261). Since we are locked firmly into Eisengrim's perspective by the first-person narration of his reminiscences, and released only temporarily for the conversations and comments which follow each episode, we are consequently locked into Eisengrim's feelings about what has happened to him. His judgments on this may be unreliable, as Ramsay suggests, but his feelings about it are trustworthy. The strength of his feeling is also an important feature in his presentation as a mythic hero.

The emergence of Eisengrim as hero (in the sense of central character) should hardly surprise any reader who has followed Davies this far through the trilogy. For, although Davies' primary interest seems to be in thematic patterning, he is an exceptionally careful and economic craftsman in the contruction of plot and character. And Eisengrim is too magnificent a character to be relegated permanently to the secondary roles he takes in *Fifth Business* and *The Manticore*. In addition, Eisengrim is presented as the mythic hero in the sense used to describe the heroes of folktale and romance. Davies' technique of presenting Eisengrim as such a hero is simple without being obvious. To begin with, Eisengrim is given the status of mythic hero by what the other characters say about him; moreover, in the course of their remarks he is associated both directly and indirectly with two great mythic heroes of Western culture, Merlin and Faust. His life-history, too, follows very closely the journey of the mythic hero as traced by Campbell in his examination of the monomyth of the hero. These two strands are woven into a tightly-ordered pattern and each alone, as well as the total pattern, requires careful attention.

The most positive identification of Eisengrim as a mythic hero lies, as it happens, outside *World of Wonders* itself. In discussing the Deptford trilogy, Davies explains his own view of it: 'One man becomes a speculative scholar with a touch of the saint about him: one man lives a sensual, self-serving life and dies, at the age of seventy, because he is suddenly faced with the reality – or one of the realities – of what he is: the third man lives heroically, in the sense that his life is a struggle against severe odds, and achieves a queer kind of fame ... All three are, in various ways, liars. All three do some good in the world and some evil. But it is in the inner life that one is almost a saint, one a failure, and one a hero.'[8] The three men are obviously Ramsay, Boy Staunton, and Magnus Eisengrim. Davies does not use the word 'hero' to describe Eisengrim explicitly, but the discussion which follows Eisengrim's account of his attendance at Willard's deathbed makes the identification indirectly. In the course of this discussion, Ingestree defines an autobiography as 'a romance of which one is oneself the hero' (ww 289). Liesl says that, 'Everybody's life is his Passion' (ww 151) and, because the inner narrative of the novel is clearly Eisengrim's life and autobiography, it is also his passion. The analogy implied between Eisengrim and Christ, whose life, death, and resurrection form (from the mythographer's point of view) one of the clearest examples of the life of the mythic hero,[9] suggests Eisengrim's heroic status. Later Ramsay insists that the others 'look at his [Eisengrim's] history in the light of myth' (ww 153) and calls it 'simply the very old tale of the man who is in search of his soul, and who must struggle with a monster to secure it' (ww 155). By identifying Eisengrim as a mythic hero implicitly rather than explicitly, Davies not only avoids overemphasizing the idea, but also leaves himself room to exploit the ambiguity of Eisengrim's personality through the ambiguity of the two heroes whom he chooses to juxtapose with him, Faust and Merlin.

The association with Faust is made as far back in the trilogy as *Fifth Business* when Ramsay encounters Eisengrim under the name of Faustus Legrand in *Le grand Cirque forain de St Vite*. Later in the same book the association is reiterated, not only by the appearance of Eisengrim in 'The Vision of Dr Faustus' in his *Soirée of Illusions*, but also and more subtly by the appearance of Liesl as a clearly demonic figure. She is, as we have seen, Ramsay's devil in *Fifth Business*, but equally clearly her relationship to Eisengrim suggests a servant or at least a subordinate who is in fact the source of power of the one whom she 'serves,' as Mephistopheles serves Faust but controls the power which is nominally Faust's. In *World of Wonders* this Faust theme is made explicit when Liesl explains that she named herself Vitzlipützli from the German puppet play of Faust,[10] in which Vizibuzli (as it is there spelt) is, according to Liesl, 'the least of the demons attending the great magician' (but according to the play itself 'der Liebesteufel,' the love-demon), and that she did so as a 'delicate compliment to Magnus' (ww 332). The emphasis is on Eisengrim's stature as a great magician, for through his association with Faust he is also associated with Faust's 'numerous predecessors ... among them Solomon, Simon Magus, Virgil, Cyprian, Merlin, Roger Bacon, Robert the Devil, Zyto, various popes.'[11] But, although Liesl draws the parallel with an older version of Faust, we are not intended to rule out any further association of Eisengrim with the later Faust, the damned and redeemed tragic hero of Goethe's drama. In fact, Liesl's statement that Goethe is not the source from which she draws her demonic identity indirectly but effectively ensures that Goethe's hero is brought to mind. In particular, Eisengrim is to be associated with the

redeemed Faust of part ii, act v; Eisengrim is also redeemed and becomes a figure of light.

Liesl's emphasis on Eisengrim's stature as a great magician is repeated
when Ramsay associates him with Merlin in recognizing Eisengrim's
laugh as 'Merlin's Laugh' (ww 156). For most readers Merlin is both the
greatest and the most famous of all the great magicians because he was
King Arthur's tutor and counsellor (as interpreted with varying degrees
of sophistication or vulgarity by writers from Malory to the present). But
that is not, for Davies' purposes, all that is needed to understand Eisengrim. By introducing 'Merlin's laugh' from the original medieval
source – the various approaches to the Grail legend – Davies refers the
reader to the more sinister tradition of Merlin which underlies the
popular one. Le cri de Merlin, which Davies describes as 'a strange
laugh ... heard when nobody else was laughing ... because he knew what
was coming next' (ww 156), is in the Grail legend a manifestation of
Merlin's gifts of clairvoyance and prophecy which are of specifically demonic origin. In the older Grail legends the demonic element in Merlin (as well as its counterbalance for good) is the primary object of interest to the writers who deal with him. Merlin was said to be the son of
the devil himself, from whom he derived his power, and of an innocent virgin, under whose pious influence Merlin renounced evil and
turned his demonic power as far as possible to good ends. Within the
legend Merlin 'functions as a form of projected conscience, in that he
exposes the mistakes and crimes of the people. As the prophet of hell
put into the world by the Devil he is, moreover, clearly distinguishable as
the Antichrist.'[12] The association of Eisengrim with the prophet of
hell and the antichrist extends his demonic quality, and Eisengrim as
Merlin is a figure of darkness.

The association of Eisengrim with the demonic Merlin also provides a
context for the detailed exploration, principally in Eisengrim himself,
of the demonic egoism of the artist. Merlin as magician represents the
artist, and for Eisengrim magic is art on the same level as painting,
poetry, music, film, or any other creative activity. Davies has pointed out
elsewhere that art masters those who serve it,[13] but in the discussion in
World of Wonders his statement appears euphemistic: art does not
become 'master' of the artist, it becomes his inner god – his daimon in
the Greek sense and, in Eisengrim's own words, 'a mean old bitch'
(ww 18). As such it not only commands the artist to the point where his
sanity is destroyed, as Davies has demonstrated in the portrait of Giles
Revelstoke in A Mixture of Frailties,[14] but also subsumes the artist's ego so
thoroughly that little or no distinction can be made by the artist between

himself and his daimon. The latter, Eisengrim makes clear, is what happened to him: as the operator inside the card-playing automaton Abdullah he 'became the soul of Abdullah, and entered into a long servitude to the craft and art of magic' (ww 52).

In this situation the artist's personality becomes identified with the autocratic, tyrannical, jealous god within him, and this is what is termed egoism, although the reference is not to the personal ego of the individual artist but to the impersonal ego of the inner daimon. This egoism devours the artist's experience in order to feed itself, as Ingestree remarks of Eisengrim's close observation of Sir John Tresize: 'It had what I can only call a wolfish quality about it, as if you were devouring everything. Especially devouring Sir John' (ww 267). The metaphor of the artist as a devouring wolf is made explicit in Liesl's account of the original from which she has borrowed Eisengrim's stage name: it was, she explains, the 'great wolf Eisengrim' in the beast-legends of Europe (ww 331) and, as Eisengrim points out, the name also signifies the sinister hardness and cruelty of iron itself. The beginnings of Eisengrim's egoism lie in his childhood; when he is recounting his experiences he refers to the 'ravening desire' he felt to know the secrets of Willard's magic the moment he saw him on the platform outside the tent (ww 26). He accepts Ingestree's accusation of wolfishness without argument, taking up the metaphor and playing with it as if he had invented it: 'We wolves like to possess things, and especially people' (ww 347); he particularly acknowledges the truth of Ingestree's description of his attitude to Sir John Tresize: 'I loved him and served him faithfully right up to the end, but in my inmost self I wanted to eat him, to possess him, to make him mine' (ww 348).

Liesl, however, recognizes that this egoism carries with it a counterbalancing factor: 'with that wolfishness went an intensity of imagination and vision' (ww 323). It is because the wolfishness and the vision go together that Eisengrim's wolfishness becomes most evident in his relationship to Sir John Tresize, for it is in Sir John that Eisengrim recognizes the same intensity of vision. The hunger to devour Sir John is therefore the hunger to acquire everything Sir John is as well as everything he knows about his art – to assimilate, finally, Sir John's vision and imagination in his own.

Sir John, however, almost invites such assimilation by demonstrating to Eisengrim the very wolfishness that Eisengrim turns against him. He is not altogether an innocent victim: he has his share of the wolfish egoism of the artist as well as of the vision. Eisengrim says that he has 'never known anyone who came near him in the truly absorbing and

damning sin of egoism' (ww 192); it is 'absorbing' because it absorbs
all the artist's personality and attention, as well as the life of his victims,
and 'damning' because it is absorption with a false god. In Eisengrim's
relationship with Sir John, it is implied, the old wolf weakens and is
pulled down by the young one. This outcome is inevitable, however,
because it is necessary to the constantly self-renewing nature of art that
Sir John's skill and knowledge must pass, even by such a cruel process,
to a younger man. If it is not passed on, it will be lost. Even the cruelty is
necessary, for such an egoism as Sir John's or even Eisengrim's own, in
its turn, will not easily part with what has been won with so much effort.
Moreover, the pulling down is not, Eisengrim claims, something he
had 'greedily sought' (ww 272), for the wolf's hunger 'just exists, and
possesses' the wolf (ww 347), and must be satisfied. The process is
entirely impersonal.

Part of Eisengrim's heroic quality is his ability to deal with his own
wolfishness. He does not disclaim responsibility for it or try to pretend
that it does not exist, and consequently he achieves a considerable
measure of self-awareness. The implication is that Eisengrim has developed enough to be able to look at himself, and he shows himself to be
increasingly less identified with the inner daimon and hence more
capable of heroic action. As a mythic hero he is destined to acquire
wisdom, and his self-awareness and responsibility form a part of that
wisdom, making it similar to the wisdom of the redeemed Faust (the
knowledge of evil) as well as to that of the demonic Merlin (the knowledge of human behaviour and nature). As a result of his self-awareness
and self-responsibility, Eisengrim is able to recognize the demonic wolf
when he meets it in others and, particularly importantly, he identifies
Boy Staunton as a 'devourer' and a 'fellow-wolf' (ww 350). This portrait
of Boy as a wolfish egoist is in deliberate contrast to Eisengrim himself
and to Sir John. In them, wolfish egoism is accompanied and therefore
to some extent tempered by artistic vision: in associating Eisengrim with
Faust it is the redemptive element to which attention is drawn. Moreover,
Eisengrim comments that there was in Sir John at the end, even when he
recognized the wolf in Eisengrim, a 'gentleness and compassion' towards him (ww 348), suggesting that Sir John, having won through to a
self-awareness similar to that which Eisengrim later achieves, can also
be seen to have moved beyond a total identification with his daimon. It is
not surprising that Boy, who lacks imaginative vision of any kind, is also
lacking in self-awareness, as Eisengrim makes explicit: 'He set to work to
devour me. He went at it with the ease of long custom, and I don't
suppose he had an instant's real awareness of what he was doing'

(ww 348). Consequently, because Boy has 'no real comprehension of the shadow-wolf that loped after him' (ww 347), it destroys him. In this way, Boy Staunton seems to represent the hero who fails, in deliberate contrast to Eisengrim, the successful hero.

The discussion of egoism which continues through the book emphasizes Eisengrim's demonic side in that it is the shadow-wolf egoism of his Merlin aspect with which we are most directly confronted. Nevertheless, it is important that the association with Faust should not be underestimated and that both associations be maintained in equilibrium. Because Eisengrim is associated with both Faust (the figure of light) and Merlin (the figure of darkness), it is clear that he is not wholly either, and it is from the unreconciled presence of both within him that his essential ambiguity stems. It is the element of light which makes him both the fascinating entertainer in public and the equally fascinating charmer in private, but it is the element of darkness which finds its satisfaction in destroying Ingestree's peace of mind in revenge for Ingestree's original humiliation of Sir John. This ambiguity is sustained in the contribution of both Merlin and Faust to Eisengrim's life not as heroes but as magicians, possessors of great learning. Eisengrim ironically is presented as learned not academically, having little formal education and less use for it as he emphatically announces, but psychologically, in human nature or behaviour. As a result of his constant observation he has acquired a great deal of practical information which enables him not only to understand but also to manipulate people – even people like Ramsay who are aware that he is a manipulator – in a way that seems to them like 'magic.' The ambiguity of the two magician figures, and of all that they represent, makes Eisengrim not only a plausible character but a fascinating and realistic one as well, in spite of his somewhat oblique presentation as a mythic hero.

Eisengrim's life is no more obviously a heroic adventure than he is obviously a hero. Nevertheless, it corresponds closely to Campbell's pattern of separation, initiation, and return, and a discussion of Eisengrim as hero in terms of Campbell's exposition of the individual components of the prototypical hero-journey and the sequence in which they occur is rewarding.[15] Eisengrim's life approximates Campbell's pattern in a way which can be shown not only to reflect its basic structure, but also to interpret it imaginatively and, at times, even humorously.

To begin with the hero must leave home to reach 'the threshold of adventure.' For Eisengrim that threshold is the village fair in Deptford. In absolute terms, perhaps, a village fair does not seem particularly impressive as a threshold for heroic adventure, but compared to the drab, cramped environment of Deptford it seems to promise tremendous wonder and excitement. Eisengrim is 'fiercely' attracted to the fair and attributes his attraction to the wiles of Satan. The attraction lies in the promise of relief, however temporary, from the desolation of the life he leads in Deptford because the people of Deptford consider his mother a 'hoor,' a term which he does not even understand. Eisengrim identifies the carnival world with the spirit underworld of the heroic adventure when he remarks that at the fair he 'descended into hell' (ww 15). On the fairground he encounters the shadow presence guarding the passage to the underworld in the person of Willard, who is one of the attractions of Wanless's World of Wonders, which clearly represents that underworld of adventure. In this choice of a symbolic locale for hell, Davies' feeling for appropriate environment is obvious. The carnival world is unfamiliar and somewhat bizarre for most people, and it has a charged, hallucinatory atmosphere which can be very disturbing. Part of its strangeness derives from the sharp contrast between the carnival and the drabness of Deptford. But the fact that the World of Wonders is a 'freak' show is also responsible for a great deal of the strangeness, because there remains in many of the most sophisticated an atavistic awe of human deformity.[16] In this encounter, Campbell says, the hero may either defeat or conciliate the shadow guardian or be slain by him and descend in death. Davies treats this somewhat ambiguously, for Eisengrim's encounter partakes a little of both alternatives; the 'offering' with which he conciliates Willard is his sexual innocence, yet being raped by Willard is clearly a kind of death by crucifixion in Campbell's terms.

He does pass, however ambiguously, the threshold of adventure, and finds himself in the 'world of unfamiliar yet strangely intimate forces,' appropriate to the hero, as he becomes part of Wanless's World of Wonders; in this world he meets the necessary tests in the form of hostile powers and finds the equally necessary helpers in the form of friendly powers. The most severe test is his subjugation to Willard, emphasized by his confinement to the bowels of Abdullah. In a sense, however, he is tested continuously not only by the need to survive inadequate food, poor clothing, and sexual abuse, but also by the hostility of Happy Hannah (the Fat Woman) and other members of the carnival. But Eisengrim also meets the requisite 'helpers': Gus, who saves his life by preventing his probable murder at Willard's hands, Em Dark, who remembers to feed him when Willard forgets, the theatre property man who gives him the knowledge of clockwork and machinery which is to help him considerably later on, and Mrs Constantinescu who offers him not only sensible advice but also a certain kindness.

At the 'nadir of the mythological round' the hero undergoes a supreme ordeal, after which he is free to begin the return journey out of
the underworld. For Eisengrim, freedom does not come suddenly, and
his ordeal is his long struggle to free himself from Willard. It begins with
his first spurt of rebellion when, in a fit of temper, he breaks Abdullah
and threatens Willard, and it ends only with Willard's death from morphine addiction some three or four years later in Europe. It is at this
point that Ramsay identifies Eisengrim as 'the man who is in search of his
soul and who must struggle with a monster to secure it,' the monster
obviously being Willard.

The rise of the hero from the nadir to the threshold of the underworld is triumphant. In Campbell's terms 'the triumph may be represented as the hero's sexual union with the goddess-mother of the world
(sacred marriage), his recognition by the father-creator (father atonement), [or] his own divinization (apotheosis).' In Davies' terms, these
elements are worked out in Eisengrim's relationship with the Tresize
Theatre Company, and in particular with Sir John and Milady. The
accommodation of the mythological elements in the naturalistic terms of
the old-fashioned travelling theatre troupe proves a useful narrative
device for Davies. His own familiarity with the Old Vic gives a note of
authenticity to the narrative. It is, moreover, a milieu unfamiliar to
most of his readers, and consequently interesting. The theatrical setting
also maintains the 'strangeness' of atmosphere found in the world of
carnival and vaudeville, although the strangeness is now less clearly
demonic than it has been previously. But the theatre world is not entirely free of the demonic, and Davies exploits this by making Eisengrim
a mixture of good and bad in keeping with his environment but in
contrast to the traditional myth-hero who tends to be all bad or all good.
As a result of this ambiguity, the 'sacred marriage,' with Milady as the
'goddess-mother,' can be presented so that it is entirely free of the demonic element; what develops between Eisengrim and the elderly
actress is a strangely tender and intimate platonic love affair. Yet the
same ambiguity is manipulated to create out of Eisengrim's relationship with the 'father-creator,' in the person of Sir John Tresize, something which closely resembles psychic cannibalism – the 'terrible, vam-
pire-like feeding on his personality and his spirit' of which Ingestree
accuses Eisengrim (ww 237). This second phase of the hero's stay in the
lower world is, according to Campbell, 'intrinsically ... an expansion of
consciousness and therewith of being,' and is indicated in Lind's remark
to Eisengrim: 'So for you the Canadian tour was a time of spiritual
growth' (ww 253).

The return to the upper world is the final phase of the hero's adventure. 'If the powers have blessed the hero,' says Campbell, 'he now sets forth under their protection, although they remain in the lower world.' So after the deaths of Sir John and Milady, Eisengrim leaves their world and returns to the everyday world as a clockmender. But he does not return empty-handed for every successful hero brings with him from the underworld a 'boon that ... restores the world.' Eisengrim's learning from and experiences with the denizens of the lower world form, of course, the totality of wisdom which he brings with him. But the particular boon which he has wrested from his relationships with Willard and Sir John is the combination of skill and stage-craft as a magician which enable him, once returned to the upper world, to 'enchant, and humour, and make partners in their own deception' the audiences at his *Soirée of Illusions*.

Davies is not being flippant when he makes stage magic the boon that restores the world. On the contrary, because 'theatre is a metaphor of some dimensions,' Eisengrim's career is a serious and important contribution to society. For Davies the theatre is 'the element of illusion in life, the difference between appearance and reality. In the theatre you can be in the know about what makes the difference, and it is fascinating that you can know what creates the illusion, know everything about it, be part of it, and yet not despise the people who want the illusion, who cannot live without it.'[17] In creating the deliberate, self-proclaimed 'illusions,' which more than any other form of theatre suggest that the impossible may in fact be possible, the magician is responding to and providing for this deep need in his audience. Moreover, that this need for illusion is a need for something more than entertainment alone is made clear in Davies' insistence that 'the job of theatre is the illumination of the spirit.'[18] The magician, therefore, because he understands and is part of such a spiritual illumination, has a tremendous social responsibility to give his audience what it needs and not to despise it for that need. It is with some justification that Eisengrim claims that his *Soirée of Illusions* is 'an entertainment in which a hungry part of the spirit is fed' in an evening of 'visions and illusions' (FB 244, 236). Davies implies that Eisengrim in this way offers to the world what he won in his heroic adventure. Eisengrim's magic, the craft and art he has learned at such cost, is important to the world. Consequently, Eisengrim the fierce egoist is ironically much more involved in humanity than the lesser egoists with whom he is contrasted. (Ramsay, for example, as a teacher would seem to be necessarily more socially involved, but is in fact less so; he is less concerned with his teaching than with his hagiographical research and the saints whose deaths have put them beyond

the reach of involvement as well as beyond the need for illumination.)
Eisengrim's involvement is indicated in his response to children: as a
child himself he has experienced what he later describes as the 'primal
evil' and 'pure malignance' of children, yet one of his first acts on his
return to the upper world is to use his skill as a clockmender to help a
small girl who has broken the trick mechanism of her father's walking-
stick.

An important contribution to the clarity with which the mythic pattern
of the hero-journey is presented is made by characterizing Eisengrim
as a man of very strong feeling who lives in terms of his feeling. Emotion
is utilized, not only in the presentation of Eisengrim himself (for the
reader may identify more readily with a character whose feeling he
shares than with a character whose thoughts he shares), but also in the
presentation of what he experiences, his descent into a dark realm in
quest of his soul. Because Eisengrim is a person of strong feeling, the
original emotions of his childhood exist unchanged by time or later
experience, and they are conveyed to us in all their raw pungency by
Davies' finely-honed technique of understatement. Eisengrim's
narration clearly makes his audience within the novel suffer vicariously
all the isolation, terror, and mystery of each stage of his life in the
underworld (Lind, a fellow artist, perhaps most of all). They experience
not only the particulars of Eisengrim's quest, but also the pattern of the
quest itself. To a considerable extent the audience outside the novel also
participates vicariously in his life, and the claustrophobia of Eisengrim's life in the carnival and as Sir John's double is felt as strongly as the
sense of release and relief on his return to the everyday world.

The strength of the feeling for the pattern of the quest also contributes to the clarity with which the mythic pattern is exposed. The issues
involved in the quest are presented directly for Eisengrim never stops to
analyze abstract ideas. He does not, for example, analyze the nature
of evil (as both Ramsay and Staunton do), although it is an important
issue in his quest. Eisengrim merely experiences it, and in very concrete terms, in his relationship with Willard, beginning with their initial
encounter. Davies presents the rape of a child as the evil it is by examining it through the senses and sensitivities of its victim, and by employing a technique of sensuous detail. The accuracy of his observation of
detail and his skilful manipulation of it play a large part in convincing
the reader that evil is truly present in the dark, stinking latrine of an
Ontario fairground, truly manifest in the person of Willard, and truly
active in his rape of ten-year-old Paul Dempster.

Even Paul's age is important thematically, and Davies' fine control of his material is demonstrated by his placing of the first conscious experience of evil in Paul's life. Paul is rather young in some ways, perhaps because he is a minister's son, but older in others because of his mother's condition. He is the right age, however, for the meaning of what has happened to him to be clear to him. It is not merely that the psychology is right. It is right within the pattern of myth that the development of the hero should be precocious, and this detail serves to emphasize the mythic element in Paul Dempster's metamorphosis into Magnus Eisengrim.

The full extent of Eisengrim's metamorphosis into a hero is visible in the counterpoint suggested between the lives of Magnus Eisengrim and David Staunton. Both have undertaken the journey in search of self and faced the problem of evil. David has almost every material advantage that can be imagined, and has undertaken his journey under the beneficent auspices of Jungian analysis (the process designed to replace, for modern man, the lost pattern of initiation), only to discover finally that such analysis may be a poor substitute for the real hero-adventure of which he may be capable. Eisengrim starts from the very bottom, without any material advantages and with very little in the way of beneficence around him, and fights his way through a squalid and genuinely dangerous underworld to a triumphant return as a hero in the upper world of everyday. David's status as a hero is only potential at the end of *The Manticore*; but at the end of *World of Wonders* Eisengrim stands before us as a fully-fledged hero, the world-restoring boon (his magic) firmly in his grasp.

The congruence of Eisengrim's individuation (in the mode of Jungian psychology) with his hero-journey (in the mode of romance) demonstrates that the two modes are not as distinct as Davies has seemed to imply at the close of *The Manticore*. Campbell relates his own work to psychology: 'Dream is the personalized myth, myth the depersonalized dream; both myth and dream are symbolic in the same general way of the dynamics of the psyche.'[19] Moreover, in discussing the use of the term *archetype* he cites Jung's use of classical sources for the term and comments: 'The tradition of the "subjectively known forms" ... is, in fact, coextensive with the tradition of myth, and is the key to the understanding and use of mythological images.'[20] In this sense, myth objectifies what is subjective. Individuation is a subjectively known process; the hero-journey an objectively observed process; hence the myth of the hero-journey can be said to objectify the subjective state of the individual undergoing the process of individuation. Davies' apparent preference in *World of Wonders* for the hero-journey may indicate that he is, in his attempt to define human identity, if not abandoning the subjective frame of reference in favour of the objective, at least seeking confirmation or support for the subjective frame by adducing an objectification (objective parallel) of it. Indeed he may be said to be adducing two objective frames of reference to parallel the single subjective Jungian frame, for he also uses Spengler's theory of the Magian soul to explain Eisengrim and to expand the objectivity of the world in which Eisengrim's hero-journey occurs.

This expansion is produced by a number of thematic patterns which not only unite the upper and lower worlds of the hero myth into a single romance universe, but also establish the congruence of that unified romance universe with the universe outside the novel. As a hero of romance, Eisengrim clearly requires a romance world or universe as his setting. In the carnival and in Sir John's theatre company, he undoubtedly has it. But these two environments represent the under-world of the heroic adventure from which he eventually emerges into the everyday upper world of London museums and wartime Geneva. His activity as a hero is not limited to his sojourn in the underworld, but is continued in the upper world whenever he offers, through his *Soirée of Illusions*, the world-restoring boon of his 'enchanting' magic. The two worlds are, however, related. Because the upper world of Eisengrim's life is entirely congruent with the world outside the novel (the reader's world), the implication is that the underworld is also congruent with the reader's world, and that what Eisengrim experiences in the carnival and the theatre, however bizarre and exotic it may seem, is not entirely alien to us.

Davies begins to establish the necessary unity and congruence of the romance universe by drawing a series of parallels between the upper and the lower world, between the carnival and the theatre world and the world outside them. He suggests, to begin with, that the people outside Wanless's World of Wonders are nearly as bizarre as those inside it. Liesl, for example, describes herself as looking after her adolescent ill-ness 'like an ape' and calls herself 'The Herr Direktor's granddaugh-ter Fräulein Orang-Outang' (ww 327), establishing a parallel between her and Rango, the carnival monkey. The parallel also implies that only Liesl's gentle breeding and her grandfather's wealth separate her from a carnival freak.

Conversely, however, Davies also makes it clear that the carnival freaks, their respective talents set aside, are relatively normal in personality and behaviour. World War I creates among the Talent ex-actly the same kind and amount of bitterness as it would in any other group of mixed nationalities at that time, particularly because they lead a boring life, boredom being as Eisengrim says, 'a rich soil for every kind of rancour and ugliness' (ww 81). In becoming ill-tempered and quarrelsome the Talent behave exactly like anyone in a boring job. Moreover, like their counterparts in the outside world, the Talent readily attack genuine love and affection when it exists between two of its members, as it does between Em and Jim Dark. The Talent also share the conventional social attitudes of outsiders: 'Gus Wanless was a sentimentalist, American-style, and it never entered her head that a boy in my situation would be prepared to do anything rather than go home' (ww 49). Equally important, the Talent live by the same moral code as outsiders. 'As I grew to know these ... people,' Eisengrim says, 'I discovered that their deepest morality was precisely that of the people they amused; whatever freedom their travelling way of life might give them, it did not cut far into the rock of North American accepted custom and morality' (ww 49). The Talent who ostracize Eisengrim as Willard's 'bum boy' are not very different from the Deptford villagers who ostracize his mother as a 'hoor.'

Beyond this, however, Davies sets up a more subtle system for unifying the upper and lower worlds into a single universe. Certain preoccupations repeat themselves in both worlds and on all levels of the narrative. In both there is a preoccupation with the standards of the art its inhabitants practise. In Wanless's World of Wonders, there is a code which forbids Willard to reveal to the audience that Happy Hannah is 'gaffed,' even though she gives him the most outrageous provocation: such a betrayal would be 'unforgivable professional conduct' (ww 69). Similarly, Sir John's company is governed by a code of proper behaviour with 'a tariff of company fines for unprofessional conduct' (ww 280). Ramsay too, as a historian, is governed by the demands of the 'document,' the historical record on Magnus Eisengrim, about which he constantly searches his conscience: 'Was this a base ambition for an historian and a hagiologist? ... unless I falsified the record what could be dishonest, or artistic, about making a few notes?' (ww 20)

The parallel which Ramsay implies between dishonesty and artistry is the second of the shared preoccupations which help to unify the upper and lower world. All three groups of artists with whom Eisengrim is involved share a common concern about the morality of deception. In the carnival, the deception is 'gaff,' which is 'the element of deception in an exhibition,' and unavoidable, although there is 'a moral stigma attaching to it' (ww 66). 'Gaff' is the lowest form of deception in entertainment, because it is simply deception for the sake of gain, and the effect depends upon the audience remaining deceived.

The nature of deception and the question of its morality becomes more complex in the Tresize company. The deception here involves Sir John's use of Eisengrim as 'the Double' in *Scaramouche* (ww 180). The purpose of using a double for the stunts is not to deceive the audience into thinking that the elderly Tresize has learned to walk the tightrope, but to persuade them to decide to believe it because that is what they want to believe. Most of the audience 'will prefer to believe it's a reality' (ww 186), thus making a conscious choice to believe in something they know to be a trick – Coleridge's 'willing suspension of disbelief.' This level of deception is accepted by the theatre company and the question of morality is dealt with when Eisengrim, under the name of Mungo Fetch, becomes a part of the company. He is listed in a way which neither admits nor denies his role as Sir John's double. Deception at this level is a responsibility shared between the deceiver and the deceived.

Lind admits his use of deception quite frankly: 'these divergences between the acceptable romance of life and the clumsily fashioned, disproportioned reality are part of my stock-in-trade' (ww 288). Nonetheless, although the film-makers have a certain amount of latitude in interpreting the period of Louis-Philippe, it can be justified only in terms of 'artistic licence and necessity' (ww 6), that is, in terms of a departure from the morality of honesty for a specific and limited purpose. Furthermore, Lind as an experienced director, working with Kinghovn (an expert cameraman), can deceive people with the truth: by the use of light, for example, or by emphasizing one particular point of view (ww 152).

Beyond Lind's use of truth to deceive is Eisengrim's deception practised in the art of illusion. His audience have 'the sophistication that takes pleasure in being deceived' (ww 303), not by the complicated apparatus of Robert-Houdin, but by the naked magician himself (ww 4). For the essence of Eisengrim's art is to make the audience 'partners in their own deception' (ww 5), and this kind of deception is free from moral stigma in that it depends on the audience remaining undeceived about the deception. In terms of morality, 'gaff' and voluntary deception lie at opposite ends of the spectrum of deception. The concern of everybody, from the carnival Talent to Lind and Eisengrim, with the morality of deception helps to demonstrate that the universe inside and outside the carnival, the underworld and the upper world, are one.

Davies' second device is to make plain, dull, everyday Canada a place of romance. And like any place of romance it has both a dark and a light side. 'If I were going to hell,' says Ingestree, 'I don't think I'd start from Canada' (ww 21). There are many Canadians who would agree with him. Nevertheless, the effect of Eisengrim's tale of his years with the carnival is to make clear that hell is just under Canada's surface and that Canada is as near to hell as any other place one might start from. This presentation of the dark side of romance apparently misleads some of the critics into thinking that Canada is a part of the dark side only: Anne Montagnes, for example, in her review of the novel states that 'Canada is the inside of Abdullah. The Golden World is Liesl's castle, Sorgenfrei.'[21] Neufeld, however, correctly points out that 'the mystery that culminates in Sorgenfrei has its roots in Deptford.'[22] Davies' point is that the universe of romance is not a single place, or even a group of places, but a unity, and a unity with more than one aspect. To see Canada only as the inside of Abdullah is to miss not only the weirdness of the underworld around Abdullah (a weirdness which represents within the world of the novel the 'bizarre and passionate life of the Canadian people' to which Davies refers elsewhere),[23] but also the other aspect of Canada presented, for Canada includes part of the light aspect of romance. Eisengrim's escape from the Canada represented by Abdullah and the carnival is an escape from the dark side of the romance universe, but in returning with the theatre tour he is exposed to its light side. This is represented to some extent by the delights of the train and the Royal Alexandra theatre, but primarily by 'that piercing, enveloping, cleansing Canadian light' (ww 265). Certainly, Sorgenfrei – warm, luxurious, well-staffed Sorgenfrei – is part of the romance universe; but so equally is Canada with its 'dramatic shortening of the days which has such ominous beauty' (ww 290). As Eisengrim says: 'I thought a lot of Canada was romantic' (ww 263) and, because he recognizes the romance of Canada, the Canadian tour is for him 'a time of spiritual growth.' The romance universe, for Davies as for others, is essentially a universe of the spirit.[24]

To complete his presentation of the unity of the romance universe and its congruence with the world outside the novel, Davies introduces Spengler's theory of the Magian world view through Liesl's version of what appealed to her in *Der Untergäng des Abendlandes*. She has read Spengler in the period immediately following her disfiguring illness and, although it would seem to be heavy going for most adolescents, its rhetoric, which Frye describes as having 'little humour, though plenty of savage and sardonic wit, and a fine gift for gloomy eloquence,' being 'full of woo-woo noises and shivery Wagnerian whinnies about the "dark" goings-on of nature and destiny,'[25] is eminently attractive at that age. Her adult view of Spengler is introduced when she identifies the Magian world view in Eisengrim (ww 323–5). What she describes of the Magian world finds direct parallels in the nature of the romance universe. The Magian world is one informed by wonder, and Spengler's description of the manifestations of the element of wonder links the Magian world view directly with the romance form of the fairy-tale (itself a form of hero-myth), down to the inclusion of the hero's 'helpers' and the hostile forces: '*The world of Magian mankind is filled with a fairy-tale feeling. Devils and evil spirits threaten man; angels and fairies protect him.*'[26] The division of these spirits into good and bad, angel and devil, helper and enemy (Liesl's 'ambiguous gods,' perhaps) is a part of 'that ... dualism which, ever the same under its thousand forms, fills the Magian world,' and which includes 'polarities in the most primary sensations [which] mingle with those of the refined and critical understanding, like good and evil, God and Satan' (II 233–4). One of these polarities is that of light and dark. For the Magian 'quivering cavern-light that the spectral darkness ever threatens to swallow up' (II 237) corresponds to the light and dark elements of the romance universe which in *World of Wonders* is doubly represented in the romantic presentation of Canada. There thus exists a considerable correspondence of individual elements in the romance universe with those in the Magian world view. Beyond this, however, there is a corresponding unity in each. For although dualistic in its manifestations, the Magian world view is essentially holistic because there is always a comprehending consciousness: 'Magian waking-being is the *theatre* of a conflict between the two world-substances of light and darkness' (II 241). This unity reinforces the unity of the romance universe.

In addition, Davies employs the correspondence of the Magian world view and the romance universe to imply the latter's congruence with the world outside the novel. By insisting upon this congruence he makes the romance universe correspond with a 'real,' 'historical' equivalent outside the novel: the romance universe, he thus implies, is not something fictional created for the novel but a reality on which he has drawn for purposes of fiction. The extent of the congruence created is, of course, dependent to a certain degree on the reader's acceptance of Spengler's theories both outside the novel and within it. Given some degree of acceptance, however, it is clear that Davies is ultimately implying that his readers also inhabit a romance universe.

If the romance universe is set up not merely as a background for the career of Magnus Eisengrim, but has implications about the nature of the universe outside the novel, those implications, as they are made in the course of the novel, deserve some consideration. The introduction of Spengler's notions about the Magian soul and the Magian world view, in addition to making the unified romance world congruent with the world outside the novel, brings into play two other important facts: the dual universe and the nature of the invisible universe which is one part of that universe.

The dual universe does not involve the existence of alternate physical universes, but the simultaneous and collocal existence of two different modes of being. Davies, through Liesl, describes the latter as they were in the Magian culture: 'the invisible world that existed side by side with ... the tangible world' (WW 323), although clearly they are not side by side in any spatial sense. The invisible universe permeates the visible or tangible one, so that human beings inhabiting that part of the dual universe which we call the visible world also inhabit a coextensive invisible world, although most of them are unaware of its existence. The idea of the dual universe is not, of course, original with Spengler; it extends back in historical time even before the time of the Magian culture as he imagines it, and is manifest in many literatures and philosophies, where it is put to many different uses.[27] For Davies, however, it has a specifically Canadian application. He touches on this briefly in *The Manticore* (M 98–9), and at greater length in an interview when he discusses the Canadian habit of seeing the two sides of a conflict not only as aspects of the same thing but also as tending to run into one another. The irrational intrudes into or is manifest in the rational, and Canadians are, consequently, very near to an understanding of the dual universe. It is to this quality that Davies ascribes their potential as 'a very formidable people.'[28]

Consequently the nature of the invisible universe takes on considerable importance in *World of Wonders*. Having introduced the idea of the Magian world view, Davies uses the concepts which characterize Magian thought to amplify our knowledge of the invisible 'world of wonders.' Much of what is said at Sorgenfrei about Eisengrim's autobiographical narrative, as well as much that Eisengrim himself says in the course of the narrative, becomes more comprehensible once Liesl has introduced the concept of Magianism.

The principal issues raised by Eisengrim's narrative and the subsequent discussions of it are not altogether new in Davies' thinking. They include the problems of good and evil, God and the devil, light and darkness, truth and illusion, with which Davies has concerned himself before. But in *World of Wonders* new ramifications appear: the problem of divine intervention, the text and the subtext, history and the document, truth and art, and the nature of 'wonder.' The result is a structure of ideas in which, as Neufeld points out, 'the number of narrative filters and qualifiers threatens to obscure the story completely.'[29] This complex structure anticipates one of the theories which it introduces, for it clearly presents a verbal analogue of the type of culturally characteristic decoration in the arts which Spengler calls 'the Arabesque,' and about which he says: '*This* is the genuine Magian motive – antiplastic to the last degree, hostile to the pictorial and the bodily alike. Itself bodiless, it disembodies the object over which its endless richness of web is drawn' (I 215). 'Web' is the key term in Spengler's characterization of the decorative motif of the Magian culture, and it is also the most appropriate metaphor for Davies' use of Magian thought in the novel.

In a web there is no clearly defined starting-point, but, because a discussion of Davies' ideas must start somewhere, it is logical to begin with one of the basic tenets of Magian thought: the 'primary-dualism' that springs from 'the tension between Macrocosm and Microcosm (which is identical with the waking-consciousness)' and that leads to 'further oppositions of symbolic importance' (II 233). Spengler distinguishes between polarities of the most primary sensations, such as light and dark and up and down, and 'those of the refined and critical understanding, like good and evil, God and Satan' (II 233–4). It is the latter with which Davies is primarily concerned and which provide the background not only for Eisengrim as a 'Magian soul' but also for aspects of the other characters.

Spengler identifies Magian culture as co-extensive with a particular feeling for the nature of space or the spatial universe which is symbolized by the cavern: 'The world, as spread out for the Magian waking-consciousness, possesses a kind of extension that may be called cavern-like' (II 233). A certain symbol dominates every culture, defining or identifying it by its manifestations in all fields of human activity, including religion. The effect on Magian religion of the dominant Magian symbol is profound: 'The *single* world volume, be it conceived as cavern or as space, demands the *single* God of Magian or Western Christianity' (I 187). Magian religious thought, therefore, is basically monotheistic (Magian Christianity less so than Magian Judaism, more so than Manicheeism and the Persian religion which Spengler also classifies as Magian), but requires the existence of 'the Devil – the great adversary' (I 187), in order to account for the existence of evil in the world or, as Ingestree puts it: 'if the Devil had not existed, we should have had to invent him. He is the only explanation of the appalling ambiguities of life' (WW 93). The slight fuzziness of Magian monotheism is due to Spengler himself for, although his theory of Magian thought requires as a correlative of the singularity of the cavern symbol that the religions be monotheistic, he refers elsewhere to a 'duality of world powers' in

Magian thinking (1 187), and this wavering between monotheism and dualism is never satisfactorily resolved. Although the devil was important in earlier Christian thinking, since the Renaissance (the beginning of Spengler's 'Faustian' culture in whose decline we are now living) he, like the angels and the saints of the Magian hierarchy of heaven who have 'grown paler and paler, more and more disembodied,' has 'disappeared unnoticed from among the possibilities of the Faustian world-feeling,' and has been 'passed over in silence by perplexed Protestant theologians' (1 187).

In the character of Dunstan Ramsay, Davies presents one of the few Protestants to face his perplexity about the devil and to become, in essence, a 'diabologian' (ww 60). As such, he reflects on the devil, and attempts to 'discover the attributes of the Devil' which theologians have left unmapped and undefined. He finds that it is not an easy job, for it cannot be done 'simply by turning a fine definition of God inside out; he is something decidedly more subtle than just God's opposite' (ww 43). Davies also makes this point: 'So let me say crudely that I do not believe very much in the God of somebody who hasn't a first-class Devil as well. We have all seen during the past fifty years what happens to God when you try to pretend there is no Devil.'[30] Ramsay, in the course of his research, identifies some specific attributes of the devil, that the devil is, for example, 'a setter of prices, and a usurer, as well' (ww 60), and he also speculates that the devil may have 'invented numbers' and 'Time, with all the subtle terrors that Time comprises' (ww 60). Moreover, whereas God is 'above jokes,' as Eisengrim points out to Ramsay, 'the Devil isn't. That's one of his most endearing qualities' (ww 40). By making his characters (Ramsay specifically but Eisengrim and the others also) preoccupied with the devil, Davies gives the devil equal time, so to speak, and when Lind says, 'When I drink to the Devil I shall want to be quite serious' (ww 93), his seriousness is obvious not only to his listeners in the novel, but also to the readers outside it. The devil consequently becomes much more substantial than usual, and we are thus directed towards a dualistic position of the sort Spengler has suggested for the Magian culture.

That such a dualistic position is not entirely unacceptable to Davies emerges in his discussion of good and evil which, he says, form the evidence for the existence of both God and his substantial adversary found everywhere because, as Ramsay points out, 'both God and the Devil wish to intervene in the world' (ww 44), and do so through human agents. Consequently, Ramsay's investigation of the attributes of the devil leads him to the conclusion that 'if the Devil is the ruler and inspirer of evil, he is a serious adversary indeed,' for then he is also 'the origin and ruler of that great realm of manifestly dreadful and appalling things which are not, so far as we can determine, anybody's fault or the consequence of any sin ... cancer wards, and the wards for children born mis-shapen and mindless' in which he feels evil to be 'palpable ... in spite of whatever could be done to lessen it.' Ramsay concludes further that evil is so constant that 'one might almost conclude that such evils were necessities of our collective life' (ww 43). As Davies points out: 'Without Evil there is no tension, and without tension there is no drama ... Our conception of human life is of a varying degree of tension between opposites,'[31] and this very Spenglerian formulation implies that Evil is necessary for life: without it the tension between opposites is diminished or lost, and with it a part at least of the structure of the universe. In *World of Wonders*, Lind, who more than any other character represents the artist as seer, presents this dualism without the slightest trace of qualification or ambiguity: 'Evil is the reality of at least half the world' (ww 150).[32] Outside the novel, Davies seems to accept the implications of a dualist position for himself: 'If art makes me a Nestorian, a Manichee, a dualist, and probably a Gnostic – so be it.'[33] Noticeably, however, the dualism remains qualified by the conditional 'if.'

Whereas in his discussion of evil Davies appears to move towards a Magian dualism, in his discussion of the evidence of God's intervention he shifts his position. Although he begins by adopting a Magian position, he ends by transforming it into something which in Spengler's terms is not Magian at all. Spengler says that 'the Magian deity is the indefinite, enigmatic Power on high that pours out its Wrath or its Grace, descends itself into the dark or raises the soul into the light as it sees fit' (II 235). In Eisengrim's formulation of 'the Great Justice and the Great Mercy,' Davies begins to depart from Spengler, who contends that in the Magian world 'there is no place for individual causes and effects ... and consequently there is no *necessary* connexion between sin and punishment, no *claim* to reward' (II 240). The terms 'justice' and 'mercy,' however, have clear connotations of such a necessary connection between sin and its punishment or reward, for in their operation 'somehow, at some time, we get all that's coming to us. Everybody gets their lumps and their bouquets' (ww 355); this phrase carries a clear implication of cause and effect. Furthermore, as Ingestree says, 'no good action is ever wholly lost,' although according to Eisengrim, 'no evil action is ever wholly lost, either' (ww 268). This transformation of the Magian concept of unrelatedness into a wholly Faustian 'universally effective dynamic concatenation' of cause and effect forms the core of the structural organization of *World of Wonders*, and Ramsay's admission at the end of the novel that he kept the pink stone 'to be a continual reminder of the consequences that can follow a single action' represents what Davies calls 'the theme of the single action that bore results for sixty years.'[34] Most importantly for the thematic development of the trilogy however, this action is a 'responsible' action – that is, an action taken by someone capable of being morally responsible for it. In discussing the genesis of the trilogy, Davies says: 'I began it because for many years I had been troubled by a question: to what extent is a man responsible for the outcome of his actions, and how early in life does the responsibility begin? I concluded ... that it began with life itself, and that a child was as responsible as anyone else if it chose a course of action knowingly.'[35] On this point, Davies does not so much draw on Spengler as contradict him. Spengler makes it clear that for the Magian soul the question of personal responsibility does not arise; Magian piety is characterized by a '*will-less* resignation, to which the spiritual "I" is unknown' (II 240), so that 'every attempt to meet the operations of God with a personal purpose or even a personal opinion is "*masiga*" – that is, not an evil willing, but an evidence that the powers of darkness and evil have taken possession of a man and expelled the divine from him. The Magian waking-consciousness is merely the *theatre* of a battle between these two powers and not, so to say, a power in itself' (II 240). Spenglerian 'will-less resignation' may operate in *World of Wonders* in such things as Eisengrim's denial of any desire for vengeance (ww 341) and of any capacity for 'sweet reasonableness' in his treatment of Boy Staunton on the night of his death (ww 354). Both, he implies, result from the impersonal 'great Justice' which operates through him without his personal participation and which is itself an 'unapproachable' concept for modern Faustian thought (II 235). Elsewhere in the novel, however, this abnegation of personal moral or ethical responsibility, which Spengler sees as central to Magian thought, does not seem to be acceptable to Davies.

For although Eisengrim may be, as Liesl describes him, a Magian soul, and thus according to Spengler's formulation have no responsibility for the operations of good and evil within himself, being simply a vehicle for the 'great Justice,' elsewhere he is shown to be much more Jungian: 'If you're going to do something that looks evil, don't smear it with icing and pretend it's good; just bloody well do it and keep your eyes peeled' (ww 269). This formulation represents the psychologically revised concept of morality as the conscious responsibility for one's actions summed up in Jung's quotation of the Logion of the Codex

Bezae: 'Man, if thou knowest what thou doest, thou art blessed, but if thou knowest not, thou art accursed, and a transgressor of the law' (cw 11:291:197). It is Eisengrim, too, who modifies the statement that no good action is ever wholly lost by adding that 'no evil action is ever wholly lost, either,' implying that his is the Jungian attitude that evil has to be accounted for – an attitude quite alien to the Magian soul for whom, according to Spengler, evil must be wholly destroyed (II 253). The Jungian view is also expressed by Ramsay, for whom responsibility in action (moral decision) is the function of a 'will' which operates when God and the devil both intervene in the consciousness of a single individual: 'It's the moment of decision – of will – when those Two nab us, and as they both speak so compellingly it's tricky work to know who's talking' (ww 358).

Spengler's concept of will-less resignation depends upon a further Magian distinction. That is the distinction, and hence also the opposition, between spirit (Greek *pneuma*, Hebrew *ruach*) and soul (Greek *psyche*, Hebrew *nephesh*): 'The *nephesh* is always in one way or another related to the bodily and earthly, to the below, the evil, the darkness. Its effort is the "upward." The *ruach* belongs to the divine, to the above, to the light ... It is poured out' (II 234). The organ of personal moral responsibility is the 'soul,' but, because in Magian thought the soul is the *nephesh*, part of the lower, it cannot distinguish between good and evil; what is good in the individual is simply the 'divine spark' or that individual's share of the divine pneuma. The Magian soul in allowing the pneuma to act through it becomes not merely an agent but a manifestation of good in the world. Thus Eisengrim, who becomes a mythic hero in the romance tradition, also becomes, in Liesl's life, an agent of God: 'Magnus himself intervened in my life ... at a time when I needed an understanding friend even more than I needed a lover. It wasn't the Devil that sent him' (ww 358). Yet the devil also acts through Eisengrim (or through any soul passively resigned to supernatural possession), allowing the 'wolf' of his impersonal egoism to devour Sir John spiritually. The Magian soul is not required to suppress the wolf because the divine pneuma itself, not the human individual psyche, 'must rule, overcoming, suppressing, destroying the other' (II 253).

In addition to being the manifestation of good in the world, the pneuma is, for the Magian soul, light and truth because 'from the unattainable Godhead its Spirit, its "Word" is released as carrier of the light and bringer of the good' (II 236). The individual through whom the pneuma manifests itself corresponds to the mythic hero of romance, the saviour of his people, returning to them with his world-restoring

boon by which the imagination and the soul are fed. The 'Word' is
literally the last word because it is a direct manifestation of the pneuma
and hence of truth – truth in the absolute sense of Magian thought in
which 'truth is itself a substance, and lie (or error) [a] second substance'
(II 244). As opposed to absolute truth, our ideas of truth are imperfect
or partial because absolute truth, being manifest in a human vehicle,
becomes coloured or filtered by the human and evil nature of that
vehicle. Consequently the individual Magian consciousness itself can be
compared to the Magian symbolic 'expression-space' of the cavern
through which 'the light shines ... and battles against the darkness'
(II 233).

The concept of absolute truth in the Magian sense as opposed to
contemporary, non-Magian concepts dominates the discussion of art
and history in *World of Wonders*. Both are claimed to be or at least to
possess truth and yet are demonstrably imperfect in Magian terms.
No one in the novel, not even Kinghovn, is so naïve as to think that the
truth of Eisengrim's story is merely the sum of the facts: 'He's giving
us a mass of detail, and I don't doubt that every word he says is true in
itself, but to call that truth is ridiculous' (ww 288–9). Facts mean nothing
unless interpreted, and the artist and the historian are interpreters:
vision (in the artist) and judgment (in the historian) select and arrange
facts, and in the end they transcend them; Ramsay's ghosted and largely
fictional autobiography of Eisengrim is 'a poetic autobiography, far
more true to the man he has become than any merely factual account of
his experience could be' (ww 15). Thus truth becomes a variable,
subject to the choice of the artist. According to Kinghovn, to obtain truth
in film (or 'the appearance of truth') all that is needed is 'somebody
like Jurgen [Lind] to decide what truth is' (ww 152) and somebody like
Kinghovn himself to film it and record that decision. Even Kinghovn,
however, has doubts that such 'subjective' truth is in any way final.

Ramsay, as a historian, also resists allowing the artist supremacy in the
possession or revelation of the truth: 'You will never persuade me to
believe that truth is no more than what some artist, however gifted he
may be, thinks is truth ... Give me a document, every time' (ww 63).
The document, he suggests, is a fact which may be tested, weighed, and
judged objectively. But Lind himself immediately draws attention to
the flaw in his reasoning – the document has to be written by someone.
Historians, indeed, may be more prone to error than artists because
historians work not with their own visions but with other people's
records of their impressions of the truth; their material has, therefore,
already been filtered through and perhaps coloured by one human con-

sciousness, however much the writer may have striven for objective truth. The tenor of the discussion seems to indicate that both artist and historian are subjective in their recording of truth and that the revelations of both art and history are at best partial and imperfect.

To obtain objective truth, unfiltered through the subjective consciousness of artist or historian, it is necessary, in Liesl's words, to 'shoot the film from God's point of view and with God's point of focus' (ww 152). It is she who introduces the Magian concept of truth into the discussion, for her image of 'God's point of view' – with all its apparent absurdity – reflects Spengler's theory of truth. Spengler says that for the Magian soul 'truth is ... something other than for us. All our epistemological methods, resting upon the *individual* judgment, are for him madness and infatuation, and its scientific results a work of the Evil One, who has confused and deceived the spirit as to its true dispositions and purposes' (II 235). It is not an artist's subjectivity which prevents him from achieving truth but his individuality because, in Magian thought, even a completely objective individual would be as far from truth as anyone else. The Magian soul has no individuality on the spiritual level but is simply 'a *part of a pneumatic "We"* that, descending from above, is one and the same in all believers' (II 234). Truth for the Magian is 'something alien and higher [which] dwells in him, making him with all his glimpses and convictions just a member of a consensus which, as the emanation of God, excludes error, but excludes all possibility of the self-asserting Ego' (II 235). The artist in asserting the operation of personal vision and the historian in asserting the operation of personal judgment are both removed from truth in this sense, because both are equally operations of the 'self-asserting Ego,' which belongs to the lower realm of error in which the pneuma as truth can have no part. In the words of St John (whose gospel is in Spengler's terms a Magian scripture): 'the light shineth in darkness; and the darkness comprehended it not' (John 1.5), that is, the darkness cannot comprehend the light either metaphorically or literally because as equal substances light cannot mix with darkness any more than oil can mix with water.

For Magian humanity this immiscibility posed no problems. In that culture holiness was manifest in 'eremites, dervishes, and stylites, in whom nothing more is of the world, whose waking-consciousness now belongs only to the Pneuma' (II 254), and who existed, in fact, only as part of the 'We.' Towards this state the Magian soul is brought by 'glimpses and convictions' (II 235) of the upper light which is manifest in the lower as 'wonder.' Wonder might, therefore, be described as the interface between the upper and the lower, darkness and light, error and truth, death and life, the point at which the individual becomes aware of the oppositions and polarities in his present state and, to use a word of which Davies is particularly fond, is 'beglamoured' as Eisengrim is 'beglamoured' first by the carnival and later by Milady.

In contrast to the Magian soul, however, Spengler places the Faustian soul, who is 'an "I" that in the last resort draws its own conclusions about the Infinite' (II 235). The Faustian soul, therefore, by rejecting participation in the 'We,' is identified with the 'self-asserting Ego.' Consequently it is confined to knowledge of the lower world and has lost the faculty of wonder. This is the modern state of mankind, Davies suggests, where education encourages the self-asserting ego and the epistemology of individual judgment. Ultimately we have 'educated ourselves into a world from which wonder, and the fear and dread and splendour and freedom of wonder have been banished' (WW 324).

Wonder, moreover, is the 'antithesis of ... security' (WW 324). It may, therefore, be associated with that 'uneasy sense that something is laughing at us which is one of the paths to faith' (WW 152), and which Lind sees as distinguishing the artist from the technician. To Kinghovn's statement that there is no God and that he has never felt the necessity of inventing one, Lind replies, 'Probably that is why you have spent your life as a technician' (WW 152). Wonder or the uneasy sense of being laughed at is a path not only to faith but to art, and the artist is somebody who possesses such a sense of wonder and unease and is, consequently, a Magian soul in comparison with the wonderless Faustian souls of the surrounding society.

In presenting Magianism, Davies does not, however, present it with complete accuracy. Liesl's discussions of Magianism do not always present the facts of Spengler's theory precisely. She says, for example, that Magianism 'was a religion, but a religion with a thousand gods, none of them all-powerful and most of them ambiguous in their attitude toward man' (WW 323). According to Spengler, the Magian world view is not a religion, but a culture (in his own specific sense of the word), which gave rise to a number of religions: 'the sacraments and scriptures of the Persian, Jewish, Christian, "post-classical" and Manichean religions' (I 183). Moreover, each of these religions was either dualistic or monotheistic; none had anything like an extended pantheon. It is possible that Liesl's phrase 'a thousand gods' is intended to express the multiplicity of religions which arose in the Magian culture, but if so it is a rather misleading phrasing and, because Davies does not normally permit his characters to express themselves ambiguously where clarity is required on important points, we may legitimately question the intent of the misdirection implicit in Liesl's words. There is perhaps a clue in what she says about her earlier attitude to Spengler's work: 'from it I had drawn a mishmash of notions which tended to support whatever I felt like doing' (ww 320). Like her, Davies too refers to Magian thought 'to support' his concept of the world of wonder, not to define it. At key points in this particular use of Magianism, moreover, Davies not only modifies it, but modifies it in the direction of Jungianism.

Nevertheless, Magianism has not been introduced into *World of Wonders* merely to explain by implication something of the world outside the novel by amplifying and adding to our understanding of it reached through our knowledge of the world of romance. Magianism and romance both offer visions or interpretations of the universe. Magianism interprets the universe in terms of opposed dualities of force operating at every level from the highest to the lowest; romance interprets it in terms of social relationships. They also, however, have common factors: each takes into account the existence of the other world beyond the physical, and each provides a subtext for experience, 'a reality running like a subterranean river under the surface; an enriching, but not necessarily edifying, background to what is seen' which must be fished up 'out of your own guts' (ww 14). As alternate interpretations of the universe, both Magianism and romance can also be identified as 'myth' for 'myth explains much that is otherwise inexplicable, just because myth is a boiling down of universal experience' (ww 153–4). In this sense, myth is the core of *World of Wonders*.

The two myths, romance and Magianism, coincide in the novel in the person of Magnus Eisengrim, and the correspondence between them ensures that they shed light on each other as well as on Eisengrim. Because their frames of reference are different, however, they do not both identify him (in the sense of giving him an identity) in the same way. Romance identifies him as the hero; Magianism identifies him as the artist. The latter sets him in relationship to something above and other than the human – art; the former sets him in relationship to the human – the society in which he lives. Neither of these two external relationships, however, identifies him completely; neither identifies him in relation to himself – as a person. It is left to Jungianism to do this by identifying him as an individuated self. Hence the basic Jungian concept of individuation is as essential to *World of Wonders* as it is to *The Manticore*, although in quite a different way.

Beyond this the juxtaposition of Jungianism, romance, and Spenglerian thought suggests a further shift in Davies' approach to the problem of human identity. Clearly, Davies has not resolved his ambivalence about Jungianism. On the one hand, the use of the Jungian psychologem of individuation in the life of Magnus Eisengrim and the way in which Jungian concepts are used to modify Spenglerian thought both demonstrate not only that Davies is unable or unwilling (or perhaps both) to abandon it entirely, but also that it still has considerable vitality and fascination for him. On the other hand, his doubts are considerable. To begin with, by juxtaposing Jungianism with the two myths, Davies implies that Jungianism itself functions as a myth: the myth of the individuated self. He does not necessarily imply that the process of individuation does not happen as Jung says it happens, but that what Jung calls individuation is simply a pattern derived from 'a boiling down of universal experience' (ww 155); the process of becoming an adult goes on within each individual, and individuation is one way of describing it. Moreover, Davies recognizes that Jungianism, or the Jungian myth, is a way of describing the pattern as it is manifest as a 'subjectively known form' (whereas the hero myth and the Spenglerian myth are ways of describing it as it is manifest in objective forms), but he seems reluctant to grant it any priority because of this. In sum, the thrust of what he does with Jungianism in *World of Wonders* is to suggest, not that Jungianism is the way of defining human identity, but that it is a partial way, defining the individual in relation to himself or herself only. To describe an individual completely, the hero myth and the Spenglerian myth must also be used. Thus all three myths are necessary to describe any individual, for each individual must function as an integrated human being (an individuated self), as an individual in relation to other individuals (a hero in society), and as an individual human being in relation to something other than and above the human (an artist).

All the myths in *World of Wonders*, moreover, are public myths: ways of looking at the universe which are shared by large numbers of people. The romance myth, for example, has been popularly understood for centuries and in many countries; Magianism is an individual reshaping of generally known theories which have become assimilated in popular thinking; Jungianism is an individual articulation of a theory which although private is widely known. Yet myth need not always be fixed in its public form, as Davies demonstrates in his reshaping of detail in the romance myth and the Magian myth to make each more relevant to his intent. By associating myth with subtext he suggests that myth must have a personal dimension – it must be fished up 'out of your own guts.' Myth, in fact, may be considered as Philip Toynbee considers language: 'By the time a man has acquired his maximum power over language, there is hardly a word left which hasn't acquired a whole complex of transparent meanings which are inextricably bound to its literal sense ... Every word is a private possession of each speaker, as well as a means of communication: a great writer can somehow make others half-hear these private reverberations of his; and the "effect" of a word is that of two echo systems meeting and reverberating together.'[36] Myth is infinitely variable and, as Davies demonstrates by his juxtaposition of three public myths and his private modification of them, it must be reshaped by each individual to match his or her own understanding.

Finally, Davies' use of myth in *World of Wonders* refutes Faust's complaint that 'knowledge tricks us beyond measure.' By placing the Jungian myth alongside the Magian and the romance myths, Davies declares himself outside all of them. Yet the artistic form of the novel, shaping the three myths into a unified form, itself provides another way of looking at the universe: the triple (romantic, Magian, and Jungian) myth. Davies thus demonstrates that myths are merely myths – ways of knowing, and not knowledge. Unlike Faust, Davies insists that we are tricked only when we confuse the myth with its subject, and think that the way of knowing is the thing known. If we remain clear in our minds that myths are only ways of knowing then, far from deceiving us, they become sources of enrichment in our lives. We are then in the position of Eisengrim's audience – co-operating in the illusion that deceives us and willing partners in our own deception. Davies himself, moreover, stands revealed as the supreme artist, the naked magician who fascinates us with his sheer skill. From the apparent impasse at the end of *The Manticore*, Davies ecapes to triumph at the end of *World of Wonders*.

Epilogue: Untreadable Ground

In the foregoing chapters I have demonstrated that Davies' work
reveals a progressive attempt to define human identity in the fullest
possible sense. In the development of his work from *Shakespeare's Boy
Actors* to *World of Wonders*, he can be seen to examine the possibilities of
role-playing, the second self, the autonomous personality of the artist,
the Jungian self, the romance hero, and the Magian soul, and to assess
each as a possible mythologem of the completed human identity. His
exploration of these possibilities is rooted in his deep and long-lasting
affinity with Jung, and, for the most part, is carried out within a frame
of reference firmly based on Jung's ideas. Nevertheless, Davies eventually moves beyond his affinity with Jung to a more impartial assessment of Jungianism as simply one way of looking at the universe, one
myth among a number of others, and finally he is able to present the
Jungian self as only one among several concepts of complete human
identity.

Each step of his exploration of human identity involves incursions into
what Jung calls 'the smaller infinity' (MDR 389), for a definition of
human identity can be formulated only in terms of the inner reality of
human beings. It is this inner reality which Davies describes as the
'enchanted landscape.' His inner world is not, however, 'the cosy nursery
retreat of Winnie-the-Pooh. It is a tough world, and it only seems
irrational or unreal to those who have not grasped some hints of its
remorseless, irreversible, and often cruel logic. It is a world in which
God is not mocked, and in which a man reaps – only too obviously –
what he has sown.'[1] It is clear that his concept of the 'enchanted landscape' is broad enough to include not only Jungianism but also the
romance myth of the hero and the concept of the Magian soul. It is also
easy to see in it a specific analogue of Jung's view of the inner reality, the

'indefinitely large hinterland of unconscious psyche' (cw 11:66:40). Consequently, Jungianism provides an interpretative approach to his enchanted landscape and to Davies' experience of it.

What Jung says of those who undertake the long process of individuation by exploration of their inner landscapes may equally be applied to the writer in search of a myth: 'Nevertheless it may be that for sufficient reasons a man feels that he must set out on his own feet along the road to wider realms. It may be that in all the garbs, shapes, forms, modes, and manners of life offered to him he does not find what is peculiarly necessary for him' (MDR 343). Clearly, what is 'peculiarly necessary' for a writer is the myth which produces the psychosymbolic structures of his or her work. Elsewhere, Jung defines what is peculiarly necessary for the individual as his or her 'treasure,' which is the individual's self, 'new-born from the dark maternal cave of the unconscious' (cw 5:580:374). This is to be found in the wider realms of the inner reality, through personal experience of the unconscious within, and because every individual is unique that experience of the inner reality and the symbolic embodiment of it will also be unique. To remain unique, however, the self must emerge from one individual's experience only, uncontaminated by another's vision. Although Jung speaks of observing an 'untrodden, untreadable' region in many men of importance, both *The Manticore* and *World of Wonders* suggest that such a region exists in every human being. Consequently, with the exception of one particular group of people, experience of the inner reality is private to the individual and 'untreadable' ground to outsiders. The exception is, of course, the group of those we call artists, all of whom have in one way or another the particular gift of being able to share their experiences of the private inner reality with others through the medium of their art. Like myth, literature is an objectification of subjectively known forms, but, whereas myth, including such general theories as Jungian psychology and Spenglerian history, expresses these subjective forms impersonally, literature expresses them personally. Considered as an objectification of subjectively known forms, moreover, literature lies half way between myth and dream. Davies as a writer is an individual who objectifies his own individual experience of the inner reality by relating it to general Jungian psychological theory. He can do this because, although each individual human being is unique, all human beings are members of the human race, and hence to a very large extent similar: their inner reality consequently will have common features. Any objectification of that inner reality by a writer in which the common features are described may, therefore, provide a map of the territory by which anyone who enters his or her own reality may roughly be guided.

It is this role of literary art as a map of inner reality, and the corresponding role of a writer as a map-maker, which prompt Davies, I believe, to describe himself as a moralist: 'I seem to have emerged as a moralist; my novels are a moralist's novels.'[2] He seems to be using the term in a sense which includes, among other elements, a great deal of the Jungian psychological revision of good and evil: personal responsibility for the examination of human conduct (self-examination, it is implied, being the prerequisite for the examination of others), and a Jungian respect for the integrity of the self in others (demonstrated by the refusal to instruct or judge). Hence, the moralist is a map-maker: 'A moralist is one who looks at human conduct with as clear an eye as he can manage, and says what he sees, drawing, now and then, a few tentative conclusions. He is not necessarily someone who beats the drum for a particular code of conduct, someone who rebukes what he believes to be sin, someone who looks down on people who are driven by passion, craving or fear. But if passion, craving, or fear are what ail them, he will not pretend that it is otherwise. He is compassionate but he strives not to be deluded.'[3] His work, therefore, is not prescriptive but descriptive – just as a map is descriptive.

It is as a moralist, however, that Davies issues a warning about maps of the inner reality. The map, he insists, is not the territory: Davies' personal experience, however illuminating and significant for his readers in its form of 'a moralist's novels,' remains his personal experience. Just as, in *World of Wonders*, he refuses to substitute Jung's ideas for his own, his readers also must refuse to substitute Davies' experience of inner reality for their own. In moving beyond Jungianism so decisively in this novel, therefore, Davies unambiguously declares that it is the territory we must concern ourselves with, not the map.

The exploration of the 'smaller infinity' which Davies began in his earliest work has, by the end of the Deptford trilogy, reached maturity. It is not finished, and it cannot be finished, precisely because it is the exploration of infinity. Davies has not defined human identity because it is indefinable; he has divined it, because it is, in its true form, that which Jung calls the *imago Dei*, divine.

Notes

All publishing information for works by Robertson Davies is given at first mention. In discussing the major works, page references refer to the edition given and are given in parentheses in the text. Individual titles are abbreviated as follows:

AMF   *A Mixture of Frailties*
FB   *Fifth Business*
LM   *Leaven of Malice*
M   *The Manticore*
SBA   *Shakespeare's Boy Actors*
TT   *Tempest-Tost*
WW   *World of Wonders*

Publishing information for the *Collected Works* of C.G. Jung is given below. In the text, the title of the individual work cited and the title of the volume in which it appears (if it is different) are given in the notes at first mention; subsequent references to the same work are given in parentheses in the text. References to the *Collected Works* are to the edition given (other editions may have different paging, but the same paragraph numbers will apply), and are cited as cw, followed by volume, paragraph, and page numbers, e.g., cw 15:129:82. A comprehensive general index is found in volume 20.)

The Collected Works of C.G. Jung, ed. Sir Herbert Read, Michael Fordham, and Gerhard Adler, trans. (except vol. 2) by R.F.C. Hull, Bollingen Series xx (London: Routledge and Kegan Paul; Princeton: Princeton University Press). See especially:

  5 *Symbols of Transformation: An Analysis of the Prelude to a Case of Schizophrenia* (1956; 2d ed. 1967)

6 *Psychological Types* (1971)
7 *Two Essays on Analytical Psychology* (1953; 2d ed. 1966)
8 *The Structure and Dynamics of the Psyche* (1960; 2d ed. 1969)
9 (i) *The Archetypes and the Collective Unconscious* (1959; 2d ed. 1968)
   (ii) *Aion: Researches into the Phenomenology of the Self* (1959; 2d ed. 1968)
10 *Civilization in Transition* (1964; 2d ed. 1970)
11 *Psychology and Religion: West and East* (1958; 2d ed. 1969)
12 *Psychology and Alchemy* (1953; 2d ed., rev. 1968)
13 *Alchemical Studies* (1967)
14 *Mysterium Coniunctionis: An Inquiry into the Separation and Synthesis of Psychic Opposites in Alchemy* (1963; 2d ed. 1970)
15 *The Spirit in Man, Art, and Literature* (1966)
16 *The Practice of Psychotherapy* (1954; 2d ed., rev. and aug. 1966)
17 *The Development of Personality* (1954)
18 *The Symbolic Life* (1976)

Publishing information for other works by Jung is given at first mention; subsequent citations are given in parentheses in the text abbreviated as follows:

L   *Letters*
MDR *Memories, Dreams, Reflections*
MHS *Man and His Symbols*

PROLOGUE

1 Liliane Frey-Rohn, *From Freud to Jung: A Comparative Study of the Psychology of the Unconscious* (New York: Putnam 1974), 3.
2 C.G. Jung, 'Seven Sermons to the Dead,' *Memories, Dreams, Reflections*, ed. Aniela Jaffé, final rev. ed. (New York: Pantheon Books 1973), 389.

CHAPTER ONE

1 Donald Cameron, 'Robertson Davies,' *Conversations with Canadian Novelists* (Toronto: Macmillan 1973), 35.
2 Robertson Davies, 'Great Hoax from Little Acorns,' *Sat. Night* 56:14 (28 December 1940), 14.
3 Robertson Davies, 'A Paradise of Dainty Devices,' *Sat. Night* 56:42 (28 June 1941), 21.
4 Robertson Davies, 'A Broader Concept of Masochism,' *Sat. Night* 57:12 (29 November 1941), 24.

5 Robertson Davies, 'Good and Bad Psychology,' *Sat. Night* 57:4 (4 October 1941), 21.

6 Ernest Jones, *Sigmund Freud: Life and Work*, 3 vols. (London: Hogarth Press): 1. *The Young Freud 1856–1900* (1953); 2. *The Years of Maturity 1901 – 1919* (1955); 3. *The Last Phase 1919–1939* (1957).

7 Robertson Davies, 'The Explorer of the Unconscious,' *Sat. Night* 69:20 (20 February 1954), 19.

8 Robertson Davies, 'The Incorruptible Savant,' *Sat. Night* 73:4 (15 February 1958), 20–1.

9 Robertson Davies, 'A Forward Look,' *Sat. Night* 70:49 (21 January 1957), 21.

10 C.G. Jung, *The Undiscovered Self* (London: Routledge and Kegan Paul 1958; reprinted in *Civilization in Transition*, CW 10).

11 C.G. Jung, *Psyche and Symbol: A Selection from the Writings of C.G. Jung*, ed. Violet de Laszlo (Garden City, NY: Doubleday 1955); P.W. Martin, *Experiment in Depth* (London: Routledge and Kegan Paul 1955); Herbert Read, *The Tenth Muse: Essays in Criticism* (London: Routledge and Kegan Paul 1957).

12 Robertson Davies, 'The Individual and the Mass,' *Sat. Night* 73:11 (24 May 1958), 26–8.

13 Cameron, 36.

14 Ibid. 41.

15 Robertson Davies, 'Toward a Long Perspective,' *Sat. Night* 68:20 (21 February 1953), 30.

16 C.G. Jung, 'The Phenomenology of the Spirit in Fairy Tales,' *The Archetypes and the Collective Unconscious*, CW 9(i):400:217.

17 Sigmund Freud, 'Creative Writers and Day-Dreaming,' *The Complete Psychological Works of Sigmund Freud*, ed. James Strachey (London: The Hogarth Press and the Institute of Psycho-Analysis 1959), 9: 143–53.

18 Robertson Davies, 'Irregular and Wild,' *Sat. Night* 56:23 (15 February 1941), 18.

19 Robertson Davies, 'Literature's Twin Sister,' *Sat. Night* 70:34 (25 June 1955), 34.

20 Robertson Davies, 'The Clouded Target,' *Sat. Night* 71:2 (31 March 1956), 15.

21 C.G. Jung, 'On the Relation of Analytical Psychology to Poetry,' *The Spirit in Man, Art, and Literature*, CW 15:129:82.

22 Sigmund Freud, *An Autobiographical Study* (London: Hogarth Press 1936), 118–19.

23 For Jung, the terms *transcendent* and *transcendence* have specific meaning. Joseph Henderson offers the simplest explanation of the Jungian concept in discussing the 'symbols of transcendence': 'these symbols ... point to man's

need for liberation from any state of being that is too immature, too fixed
or final ... they concern man's release from – or transcendence of – any
confining pattern ... as he moves towards a superior or more mature stage
in his development ... They provide the means by which the contents of the
unconscious can enter the conscious mind, and they also are themselves
an active expression of those contents' ('Ancient Myths and Modern Man,'
Man and His Symbols [London: Aldus Books 1964], 149–50). Jung
himself emphasizes that 'the spirit [or transcendent personality] is alive only
when it is an adventure eternally renewed ... but once it is fixed it has long
ceased to be' (Jung to Vetter, 8 April 1932, *Letters*, 2 vols. [London: Routledge and Kegan Paul 1973], 1 [1906–50]: 90–2). It is in the Jungian
sense that I use the term throughout.

24 Davies, 'The Clouded Target.'
25 Robertson Davies, 'A Kind of Magic,' *Sat. Night* 73:9 (26 April 1958), 25.
26 C.G. Jung, 'The Transformation of Libido,' *Symbols of Transformation*,
   CW 5:221:156.
27 Jones, *The Last Phase*, 405.
28 Robertson Davies, 'Are We Really Fascinating?' *Sat. Night* 56:39 (7 June
   1941), 18.
29 Paul Huson, *The Devil's Picture Book* (New York: G.P. Putnam 1971), 79.
30 Robertson Davies, 'The Ballet, Ladies and Gentlemen, Is for You,' *Sat.
   Night* 57:1 (13 September 1941), 5. As literary editor in his earlier period
   with the magazine, Davies wrote occasional theatre criticism, including
   not only drama but ballet and opera as well.
31 Jolande Jacobi, *The Psychology of C.G. Jung*, rev. ed. (London: Routledge
   and Kegan Paul 1968), 80.
32 Robertson Davies, 'The Romantic Temperament,' *Sat. Night* 71:7 (9 June
   1957), 22.
33 Sigmund Freud, 'Creative Writers and Day Dreaming,' 153.
34 Moreover, what poets and other artists say about the creative process (which,
   although it may not be the final word, must at least be taken into account)
   does not agree with Freud's reductive description. In fact, their evidence in
   general is so far from any resemblance to Freud's account that it would
   seem likely that a writer of Davies' sensibility would appreciate a description
   of the creative process by someone more involved in it than Freud. On the
   other hand, Jung's account of the genesis of 'Seven Sermons to the Dead'
   (MDR 189–91) clearly demonstrates an experience similar to accounts of
   the creative process by painters, poets, and others (see, for example, the
   accounts in *The Creative Process*, ed. Brewster Ghiselin [Berkeley: University of California Press 1952]).
35 Davies to Monk, 9 January 1976.
36 Northrop Frye, 'The Search for Acceptable Words,' *Spiritus Mundi: Essays on*

Literature, Myth, and Society (Bloomington and London: Indiana University Press 1976), 10.

37 It should further be evident that because they are archetypes common to all humankind, their presence is not dependent on Davies' knowledge of or feeling for Jung (although perhaps strengthened by it.)

38 Jacobi, *The Psychology of C.G. Jung*, 40.

39 See M. Esther Harding, *The I and the Not-I: A Study in the Development of Consciousness* (Princeton: Princeton University Press 1965), 9–12.

40 Ibid. 14–15.

41 Georg Christoph Lichtenberg, cited in Søren Kierkegaard, *Stages on Life's Way*, trans. Walter Lowrie (Princeton: Princeton University Press 1940), 26.

42 Robertson Davies, *Shakespeare's Boy Actors* (London: J.M. Dent 1939).

43 Strictly speaking, the persona is not an archetype because it does not lie in the unconscious but is the interface between the ego and the external world.

44 Robertson Davies [Samuel Marchbanks], 'The Double Life of Robertson Davies,' *Liberty* (April 1954), 18–19, 53–8; reprinted in *Canadian Anthology*, ed. C.F. Klinck and R.E. Watters, rev. ed. (Toronto: Gage 1966), 393–400. All subsequent references are to *Canadian Anthology*.

45 Robertson Davies, *Eros at Breakfast*, in *Four Favorite Plays* (Toronto: Clarke, Irwin 1949); *General Confession*, in *Hunting Stuart and Other Plays* (Toronto: new press 1972); *Question Time* (Toronto: Macmillan 1975).

46 Robertson Davies, *Tempest-Tost* (Toronto: Clarke, Irwin 1951); *Leaven of Malice* (Toronto: Clarke, Irwin 1954); *A Mixture of Frailties* (Toronto: Macmillan 1958).

47 Robertson Davies, *Fifth Business* (Toronto: Macmillan 1970).

48 Ibid. 213.

49 Robertson Davies, *The Manticore* (Toronto: Macmillan 1972).

50 Jung to Gilbert, 2 January 1929, *Letters*, 1: 56–7.

51 C.G. Jung, 'Psychology and Religion,' *Psychology and Religion: West and East*, CW 11:66:40.

52 Robertson Davies, *World of Wonders* (Toronto: Macmillan 1975).

53 CBC 'Ideas' (25 February 1977).

54 Davies to Monk, 9 January 1976.

55 Frye, 'The Search for Acceptable Words,' 11.

CHAPTER TWO

1 Davies [Marchbanks], 'The Double Life of Robertson Davies,' 396.

2 Jacobi, *The Psychology of C.G. Jung*, 26–7.

3 Davies, *Shakespeare for Young Players* (Toronto: Clarke, Irwin 1942), 14–15.

4 C.G. Jung *Psychological Types*, cw 6:801:465.
5 C.G. Jung, 'The Relations between the Ego and the Unconscious,' *Two Essays on Analytical Psychology*, cw 7:246:158.
6 Jacobi, *The Psychology of C.G. Jung*, 28.
7 The complete chronological development of Samuel Marchbanks from 1940 to 1953 can properly be traced only in the original newspaper columns for, although three volumes of extracts (*The Diary of Samuel Marchbanks* [Toronto: Clarke, Irwin 1947]; *The Table-Talk of Samuel Marchbanks*, [Toronto: Clarke, Irwin 1949]; and *Samuel Marchbanks' Almanack*, [Toronto: McClelland and Stewart 1967] were published, they were considerably edited and rearranged out of the chronological sequence. Because of the relative inaccessibility of the *Peterborough Examiner* for the period, I have used the *Kingston Whig Standard* as my source, the material having appeared simultaneously in both (or at most a week later in the Kingston paper) for both were owned by the Davies family. All quotations from the columns and all references to their dates, therefore, refer to the *Kingston Whig Standard*, abbreviated to kws. A column with the byline Samuel Marchbanks first appeared on Thursday, 1 August 1940. At first the column was titled 'Cap and Bells' and appeared on three days each week (Tuesday, Thursday, and Saturday); later (starting Wednesday, 25 November 1942) the column appeared only twice a week, on Wednesday and Saturday. The last column to appear under the original title was on Saturday, 16 August 1940. From the following Tuesday (19 August 1940), the column was headed according to its topic, for example, "The Cult of Exercise" (19 August 1940), 'Britain's Food Problem' (21 August 1940), and 'Psychic Research in Winnipeg' (19 November 1942). Most of the columns were book reviews, and they continued twice-weekly until late in 1943. The column for Saturday, 13 November 1943, however, was headed 'About Keeping a Diary,' and established a diary format of seven paragraphs, one for each day of the week (beginning on Sunday). The diary appeared on Saturdays only and the Wednesday column remained a book review, appearing for the last time on 15 May 1943. At first the diary entries were dated, for example, the first entry in 'About Keeping a Diary' is dated 'Sunday Oct. 24th;' later the dates were dropped and only the day of the week given. The diary was headed according to the major topic of the week, such as 'Diary of a Minority Opinion' (29 April 1944), 'Diary of a Recluse' (20 November 1943), 'Diary of a Year's End' (8 August 1944), 'Diary of a Measly Man' (10 March 1945), and 'Diary of a Rusty Magician' (7 March 1945). A topic was often used on more than one day, and one day's entry frequently contained more than one topic. The diary breaks off in June 1949, apparently for the summer (although there is no statement to this effect). At the

beginning of September 1949 a Samuel Marchbanks column reappeared headed 'The Marchbanks Correspondence' (3 September 1949). Each weekly column consisted of a number of letters from or to a wide variety of correspondents and on a wide variety of topics; the fictional correspondents are given names appropriate to the subject of the letters: Adam Mulligrub is a landscape gardener (17 June 1950), Hugo Mahlstick is a painter (25 November 1950), and Raymond Cataplasm is a doctor (3 September 1949). This format continued until the end of 1950. The first column of 1951 returned to the diary, beginning with 'Diary of New Year's Irresolution' (6 January 1951), and the diary format continued until the end of June, when 'Diary of a Moving Experience' was followed by an editorial note that 'The Marchbanks Diary will be discontinued during the summer' (30 June 1951). The break, however, lasted until September 1952, although during this interval occasional book reviews appeared in 'Bibliomania' over the initials RD (e.g., 'The Wanderings of Mother Goose' on 7 November 1951, 4). When the diary column did resume it was under the title of 'The Journal of Samuel Marchbanks,' instead of under a different title for each instalment. In the summer of the following year the instalment for 30 May was followed by an editorial note that 'This will be the last "Marchbanks" column for the Summer months.' The diary was not resumed again.

8 Davies, 'Cap and Bells,' KWS, Thursday, 1 August 1940, 4.

9 Ibid. 15 March 1944, 3 January 1945, and 13 June 1945, respectively.

10 I do not mean to suggest that there is no personality in the reviews – on the contrary, they give a clear impression of the reviewer, but the reviewer is Davies, not Samuel Marchbanks.

11 Robertson Davies, 'The Bookshelf,' *Sat. Night* 56:13 (7 December 1940), 28.

12 Ibid. 57:14, 13 December 1941, 32. The relationship between Dr Amyas Pilgarlic and the Amyas Pilgarlic of the later Marchbanks correspondence is not clear, but the repetition of the name is probably without significance.

13 Eleanor Roosevelt's *My Day* column was syndicated in approximately 135 newspapers in the United States, and appeared daily between 30 December 1935 and 11 September 1940; *Diary of a Nobody* by George and Weedon Grossmith had been published in Bristol in 1892.

14 Robertson Davies [Samuel Marchbanks], 'About Keeping a Diary,' KWS, 13 November 1943, 4. Quotations from particular instalments will from here on be identified by date only, placed in parentheses at the end of the quotation.

15 Robertson Davies, 'The Urge to Confession,' *Sat. Night* 69:14 (9 January 1954), 13.

16 Gordon Roper, Introduction to *Samuel Marchbanks' Almanack*, New Canadian Library Edition (Toronto: McClelland and Stewart 1968), ix.

17 The reference is to South African twin girls who had undergone a sex-change operation the previous year (1947).

18 There is a perceptible difference between a pseudonym adopted for convenience (such as 'Junius' of the Junius Letters) and the creation of a fictitious self (William Sharp writing as 'Fiona Macleod'). Davies exploits the reader's uncertainty about which alternative he is employing in the use of Samuel Marchbanks.

19 Davies [Marchbanks], 'The Double Life of Robertson Davies,' 393.

20 Each of the first two of these terms has been the subject of a full-scale literary investigation. Ralph Tymms' *Doubles in Literary Psychology* (Cambridge: Bowes and Bowes 1949) is primarily a study of the phenomenon of the Doppel-gänger, a term he appears to reserve to describe the double figure in German romantic and post-romantic literature. Davies is certainly familiar with the German romantic writer E.T.A. Hoffmann, whom he recommends for Christmas reading ('A Classic at Christmas,' *Sat. Night* 70:12 [25 December 1954], 10). But it is clear that Samuel Marchbanks is not a Doppelgänger in the same sense as any of Hoffmann's characters for, according to Tymms, in German romantic works the author creates both the original and the duplicate, relating them either naturalistically, supernaturally, or psychologically. This may be true of 'The Double Life of Robertson Davies,' but is not of the diary itself. In *A Psychoanalytic Study of the Double in Literature:* (Detroit: Wayne State University Press 1970), Robert Rogers makes an extensive study of the literary pheomenon of doubling in terms of orthodox Freudianism. Like Tymms, Rogers includes as doubles only cases where original and duplicate are both created characters in the work, excluding from consideration any case where a single character is said or implied to be the author's double. (The third term, *alter ego*, used by the editors of *Canadian Anthology*, is popular, but it seems to have no specific definition, clinical or critical, and hence is too vague to be useful.)

21 E.T.A. Hoffmann, 'The Sandman,' in *Selected Writings of Hoffmann*, ed. and trans. Leonard J. Kent and Elizabeth C. Knight (Chicago: University of Chicago Press 1969), 1: *The Tales.*

22 Rogers, *The Double in Literature*, vii.

23 This at least is the view of Hugo McPherson: 'In parodying the synopsis of a French play, for example, Marchbanks gives the characters such names as Alphamet, Feenaminte, Flanalette, Clitore, Merde, and Vespasienne. This particular example is unfortunately juvenile; nevertheless Davies uses crude humour deliberately ...' 'The Mask of Satire,' *Canadian Literature*, 4 (Spring 1960), 20.

24 Jacobi, *The Psychology of C.G. Jung*, 110.

25 Ibid. 111.

26 This is true at least of good writers; it is not always true of bad writers or beginners (for example, an autobiography only thinly disguised as a first novel).

27 Jacobi, *The Psychology of C.G. Jung*, 60.

28 See Jacobi, *The Psychology of C.G. Jung*, 102–5.

29 Jacobi, *The Psychology of C.G. Jung*, 110.

30 Ibid. 109–10.

31 C.G. Jung, *Aion: Researches into the Phenomenology of the Spirit*, cw 9(ii):15:8.

32 Jacobi, *The Psychology of C.G. Jung*, 112.

33 Barbara Hannah, *Striving towards Wholeness* (London: Allen and Unwin 1972), 19.

34 Roper, Introduction to *Samuel Marchbanks' Almanack* xi.

35 Simon Paynter, review of *The Diary of Samuel Marchbanks* by Robertson Davies, *Canadian Forum* 27 (March 1948), 284.

36 Lucy van Gogh, 'Can Davies Be in Mortal Danger from Disembodied Marchbanks?' *Sat. Night* 63:15 (13 December 1947), 35.

37 Davies [Marchbanks], 'The Double Life of Robertson Davies,' 399–400.

38 Hannah, *Striving towards Wholeness*, 17.

39 Jacobi, *The Psychology of C.G. Jung*, 114.

40 Ibid. 109.

41 C.G. Jung, 'On the Psychology of the Unconscious,' *Two Essays on Analytical Psychology*, cw 7:92:61.

42 Jacobi, *The Psychology of C.G. Jung*, 114n.

43 Davies [Marchbanks], 'The Double Life of Robertson Davies,' 400.

CHAPTER THREE

1 A *psychologem* (or *psychologoumenon*) is 'an archetypal psychic structure,' according to Jung (cw 9(i):465:260; cw 10:716:378; cw 5:580:374); it can refer not only to a psychic anthropomorphic or theriomorphic figure but also to the pattern of activity associated with the figure.

2 A fourth class, consisting of forms of illusions which are voluntary and incorrigible, is obviously implied, but in the Salterton trilogy it is a class with no members. The concept of religious faith is considered as a possible member of this fourth class, however, in the discussion of *Fifth Business*.

3 Robertson Davies, 'Midsummer Night's Dream,' in *The Stratford Scene 1958–1968*, ed. Peter Raby (Toronto: Clarke, Irwin 1968), 180.

4 Cf. C.G. Jung: 'The achievement of a synthesis of conscious and unconscious contents, and the conscious realization of the archetype's effects upon the conscious contents, represents the climax of a concentrated spiritual and psychic effort, in so far as this is undertaken consciously and of set pur-

pose. That is to say, the synthesis can also be prepared in advance and brought to a certain point ... unconsciously, whereupon it irrupts into consciousness of its own volition and confronts the latter with the formidable task of assimilating the contents that have burst in upon it, yet without damaging the viability of the two systems ... Classical examples of this process are Paul's conversion and the Trinity vision of Nicholas of Flüe' (cw 8:413:210–11).

5 McPherson, 'The Mask of Satire,' 22.

6 Martin, *Experiment in Depth*, 165.

7 Jacobi, *The Psychology of C.G. Jung*, 21.

8 See C.G. Jung, *Psychological Types*, cw 6.

9 Jacobi, *The Psychology of C.G. Jung*, 12.

10 Ibid. 17.

11 Martin, *Experiment in Depth*, 81–2.

12 At this point personal identity can be understood in Jungian terms; Ridley comes close to confusing persona and ego for his theory implies that a persona can be chosen which will alter the underlying ego.

13 Martin, *Experiment in Depth*, 72–3.

14 This is certainly true, for example, of Hector Mackilwraith, whose close relationship with his mother is emphasized. Hector, however, goes through this stage of his personal development very smoothly; his problem starts later.

15 Prospero, the king and magician, is clearly an archetypal figure: the magus, or wise old man, described by Jung as 'a wise magician, who goes back in direct line to the figure of the medicine man in primitive society. He is ... an immortal daemon that pierces the chaotic darknesses of brute life with the light of meaning. He is the enlightener, the master and teacher, a psychopomp' (cw 9(i):77:36–7). He adds that 'like all archetypes it has a positive and a negative aspect.' As the inverted image of the character he plays, Vambrace clearly represents the negative aspect of the magus.

16 This distinction is interesting for it is not, as might at first be expected, a distinction between love and death, because *love* would be the literal trans-lation of εpωs, and *death* the literal translation of θανατos. Davies' use of these particular terms may stem from his reading of Freud, who used eros to symbolize the life-force and thanatos the death-instinct (cf. Jones, *Freud: Life and Work*, 3: 294–5).

17 Jessie Fothergill, *The First Violin* (London 1877).

18 Robertson Davies, *Feast of Stephen* (Toronto: McClelland and Stewart 1970), 11.

19 C.G. Jung, 'Commentary on "The Secret of the Golden Flower,"' *Alchemical Studies*, cw 13:18:15.

20 Edward F. Edinger, *Ego and Archetype: Individuation and the Religious Function of the Psyche* (New York: G.P. Putnam 1972), 3.
21 Ibid. 6–7.
22 Ibid. 38
23 Ivor H. Evans, *Brewer's Dictionary of Phrase and Fable*, rev. centenary ed. (London: Cassell 1970), 335.
24 Davies' use of the inner voice in this connection may owe something to Jung's discussion of the relation of the disembodied voice in dreams to the dreamer's self (CW 11:63–76:38–40).

CHAPTER FOUR

1 *Numinosum* is the term used by Jung in *Psychology and Religion* where he defines it as follows: 'Religion ... is a careful and scrupulous observation of what Rudolf Otto [in *The Idea of the Holy*] aptly termed the *numinosum*, that is, a dynamic agency or effect not caused by an arbitrary act of will. On the contrary, it seizes and controls the human subject, who is always rather its victim than its creator. The *numinosum* ... is an experience of the subject independent of his will ... either a quality belonging to a visible object or the influence of an invisible presence that causes a peculiar alteration of consciousness' (CW 11:6:7).
2 The process of canonization, by implication, would in Father Blazon's view merely confirm the fact that a number of individuals have all experienced similar psychic events in connection with the same person.
3 'In the pleroma all opposites are said to be balanced and therefore they cancel each other out ...' June Singer, *Boundaries of the Soul* (London: Gollancz 1973), 330.
4 Jacobi, *The Psychology of C.G. Jung*, 54.
5 Ibid.
6 The term 'spagiric' is borrowed from Hochheimer: 'Jung called his psychology "analytical" as well as "complex." He opposed his "synthetic," even "constructive," method to the "reductive" method of Freud, pointing out at the same time, however, that the two methods supplement each other. An attitude of "not only, but also" is therefore characteristic of his teaching. To identify any part of it, say its practical therapeutic aspect, as belonging to one or other of these opposite concepts would be an arbitrary oversimplification. The only concept which seems to me suitable is the peculiar conception known as "spagyric," which occurred in natural philosophy during Hellenism and the Renaissance in the teachings and practices of the Hermeticists and alchemists. "Spagyric," also written "spagiric" or "ars spagyrica" ... means the equivalent of "analysis-synthesis" ... If one surveys

Jung's life work, revolving as it does with increasing intensity around the
psychological and psychotherapeutic contents of alchemical themes and
problems, the concept "spagiric" thrusts itself forward as the fitting designa-
tion for his labours.' Wolf Hochheimer, *The Psychotherapy of C.G. Jung* (New
York: Putnam 1969), 18–19.

7 Jacobi, *The Psychology of C.G. Jung*, 54.

8 A comparison of *Fifth Business* with Hermann Hesse's *Der Steppenwolf* (Berlin:
Fischer 1927), trans. Basil Creighton (London: Martin Secker 1929), will
make this clear. In the latter, the fantastic elements in the status and
experience of the eponymous hero are so effective, in contrast to the mundane setting of the introductory narrative, that they lift the novel entirely
into the transcendent mode; as a result, the reader is left suspended without
any way of relating his reading to his own experience.

9 Jacobi, *The Psychology of C.G. Jung*, 1.

10 This reflects the human incapacity for apprehending the *numinosum* directly,
and leads to the construction of a metaphoric form of illusion (faith) to act as
an intermediary.

11 The phrase is used by W.F. Hall in his review of *Fifth Business*, 'The Real and
the Marvellous,' *Canadian Literature*, 49 (Summer 1971), 80–1.

12 C.G. Jung, 'The Autonomy of the Unconscious,' cw 11.

13 The noun *psychography* is used here to refer to a narrative of the events of a
psychic life, as distinct from *biography*, which should perhaps be reserved for
the narrative of the physical and intellectual events of a life.

14 '*Active imagination* is the term Jung uses to describe a process by which the
individual enters consciously into the happening of a phantasy and takes
part in its development. He reacts to the phantasy situation while allowing
complete autonomy to the phantasy images. In this way a setting face to
face ... of the conscious and the unconscious is brought about, so that an
effective interchange between them takes place.' M. Esther Harding, *Journey into Self* (New York: Longmans Green 1956), 3n.

15 *Vitzlipützli* denotes, according to Basler's definition, 'Stammesgott (aus Huit-
zilopöchtli) der Azteken; Schreckgestalt, Kinderschreck; volksm. auch:
Teufel.' *Der Gross Duden: Rechtschreibung der deutschen Sprache und der
Fremdworter*, ed. Otto Basler (Leipzig: Bibliographisches Institut AG, elfte,
neubearbeitete und erweitete Auflage, 1934). According to C.G. Vaillant in
Aztecs of Mexico, rev. ed. (Harmondsworth: Penguin 1962), 187, of the
principal members of the Aztec Pantheon, Huitzilopochtli was 'Hummingbird Wizard, War and Sun God, chief god of Tenochitlan.' For an excel-
lent study see F.L. Radford, 'Heinrich Heine, the Virgin, and the
Hummingbird: *Fifth Business* – a novel and its subconscious,' in *English
Studies in Canada* 4:1 (Spring 1978), 95–110.

16 C.G. Jung, 'A Psychological Approach to the Dogma of the Trinity,' *Psychology and Religion: West and East* (CW 11:291:197).

17 Tom Harpur, 'Author Says Messiah Could Be a Woman,' *Toronto Star*, 16 February 1974.

18 Ibid.

19 Ibid.

20 C.G. Jung, 'Answer to Job,' *Psychology and Religion: West and East* (CW 11:696:434).

21 Harpur: 'Messiah ... a Woman.'

22 According to legend, the devil once appeared in the form of a beautiful woman to St Dunstan who immediately seized the devil's nose in his goldsmith's tongs and refused to let go until the devil promised never to tempt him again.

23 Harpur: 'Messiah ... a Woman.'

24 Thomas Overskou, *Den Danske Skueplads i dens Historie*, 7 vols. (Copenhagen 1854–76).

25 Jacobi, *The Psychology of C.G. Jung*, 135.

26 C.G. Jung, 'The Psychology of Eastern Meditation,' *Psychology and Religion: West and East* (CW 11:945:573).

27 C.G. Jung, 'Concerning Mandala Symbolism,' in *The Archetypes and the Collective Unconscious* (CW 9(i):713:387).

28 Jacobi explains this point further: 'It would be quite mistaken to regard all the mandalas as "pictures" of completed individuation, i.e., the successful union of all the pairs of psychic opposites. For the most part the mandalas produced in the course of analysis are only preliminary sketches, more or less successful steps towards ultimate perfection and wholeness ... In principle mandalas can appear during the whole individuation process, and it would be a mistake to interpret their appearance as an indication of a particularly advanced stage of development. In line with the psychic trend towards self-regulation, they will always appear when a "disorder" in the realm of consciousness calls for them as compensating factors. The mandalas with their mathematical structures are pictures, as it were, of the "primal order of the total psyche," and their purpose is to transform chaos into cosmos. For these figures not only express order, they also bring it about' (*The Psychology of C.G. Jung*, 138–9).

29 'Besides the tetradic figures (and multiples of four), there are also triadic and pentadic ones, though these are much rarer. They should be regarded as "disturbed" totality pictures' (CW 9 (i):646:361).

30 Jung: 'These four constitute a half-immanent and half-transcendent quaternity, an archetype which I have called the *marriage quaternio*' (CW 9(ii):42:22). Hannah explains this quaternity further as 'consisting of two pairs, one of

which usually represents the real man and woman, the other the animus and anima in projected form, although sometimes both pairs are real. This is an age-old social pattern which one can trace back to the "cross-cousin marriage" of the primitives' (*Striving towards Wholeness*, 76).

31 Patrick White: *Voss* (New York: The Viking Press 1957) and *Riders in the Chariot* (New York: The Viking Press 1961). I have discussed this in more detail in 'Beating the Bush: the mandala and national psychic unity in *Riders in the Chariot* and *Fifth Business*,' *English Studies in Canada*, 5:3 (Fall 1979), 344–54.

32 This does not contradict the brazen head's remarks, because 'he was killed by the usual cabal' does not necessarily imply that the only function of the cabal is to kill; in describing fifth business, Liesl says only that he may 'be the cause of someone's death if that is part of the plot' (FB 267). The 'cabal' is the cast of an individual's life-drama, and the end of the drama is the end of his life.

33 Boy can be said to 'keep' the stone in the sense of being the person responsible for bringing it into Ramsay's life and for removing it.

34 In Ramsay's psyche, Leola is a representative figure for the anima archetype. There is a long series of inimical and/or inadequate women in his life with whom he is not able to establish good relationships (although he learns enough of himself and of them to make this a conscious avoidance, rather than a repeated failure), and it is not until he meets Liesl that he is able to establish a stable and rewarding relationship with a woman.

35 Cited in Hannah, *Striving towards Wholeness*, 96.

36 C.G. Jung, *Letters*, 2:611.

CHAPTER FIVE

1 Geoffrey James, 'Mystic of Massey College,' *Time*, 21 May 1973, 9; Gordon Jocelyn, review of *The Manticore* by Robertson Davies, *Canadian Forum*, 52 (February 1973), 44–5

2 Earlier, Dr von Haller has been encouraging David to understand his shadow; here she tells him that he is not to understand but to feel. The contradiction is only apparent because there is a distinction implied between understanding experientially (through feeling) and understanding cognitively (through thinking), a distinction made clear in Dr von Haller's illustrative distinction between the theologian and the martyr (M 91).

3 Bacon, so the legend runs, having made the head, left his servant to call him when it spoke. After a long wait, the head announced, 'Time is.' The servant did not think it was worth calling his master for two words, and did nothing. Some time later the head added, 'Time was.' Still the servant did

nothing. After another long pause, the head said, 'Time's past,' and exploded into small pieces.

4 According to David's two accounts of the incident (M 2, 53), the sound of someone (whom we know to be Ramsay) collapsing into one of the theatre boxes came *after* the question, but *before* the head started to answer. Ramsay's own account leaves the timing ambiguous (FB 313). If David is right, then we may legitimately assume that it was the question which shocked Ramsay into a heart attack, not the answer.

5 'The German word for symbol is *Sinnbild*, a compound which strikingly denotes the two realms of which the symbol partakes: the *Sinn*, or meaning, pertains to the conscious, rational sphere, the *Bild*, or image, belongs to the irrational sphere, the unconscious' (Jacobi, *The Psychology of C.G. Jung*, 96).

6 Had it existed, the original brazen head would have been made not of brass as we know it, but of bronze. Originally, the words *brass* and *brazen* denoted an alloy of copper and tin, but in the eighteenth century the words *brass* and *brazen* were reserved for the 'new' alloy of copper and zinc, and the Italian word *bronze* was borrowed to rename the older alloy. 'The physical goal of alchemy was gold, the panacea, the elixir of life; the spiritual one was the rebirth of the (spiritual) light from the darkness of Physis: healing self-knowledge and the deliverance of the pneumatic body from the corruption of the flesh.' C.G. Jung, *Mysterium Coniunctionis: an Inquiry into the Separation and Synthesis of Psychic Opposites in Alchemy*, CW 14:104:90.

7 The Greek δεισιδαιμονία is given in the revised edition of Liddell and Scott's *Lexikon* (Oxford: Clarendon Press 1940) as 'fear of the gods.'

8 C.G. Jung, 'Transformation Symbolism in the Mass.' *Psychology and Religion: West and East*, CW 11:365–6:240. The disembodied human head serving as an oracle occurs in an interesting modern adaptation in C.S. Lewis's novel *That Hideous Strength* (London: John Lane 1945).

9 Distinguished women students and associates of Jung include Marie-Louise von Franz, Aniela Jaffé (the editor of *Memories, Dreams, Reflections*), Jolande Jacobi (who prepared the standard textbook introduction to his theories), M. Esther Harding, Barbara Hannah, and June K. Singer (all analysts and authors of works on Jungian psychology).

10 C.G. Jung, 'Analytical Psychology and Education,' *The Development of Personality* CW 17:195:105. See also 'Principles of Practical Psychotherapy,' *The Practice of Psychotherapy* CW 16.

11 Jacobi, *The Psychology of C.G. Jung*, 104.

12 M. Esther Harding, *Journey into Self*, 56–7.

13 C.G. Jung, 'The Practical Use of Dream Analysis,' *The Practice of Psychotherapy* CW 16:304:142.

14 Harding, *Journey into Self*, 276.

15 'So in a depth analysis, when the inferior function begins to come up into consciousness and is allowed to come into play, it, too, will not behave as if it were the corresponding function in one whose superior function it is. In other words, when a thinking introvert ... acts from his feeling extraversion, his behaviour will not be superior, but will probably be rather ill-adapted and compulsive' (Harding, *Journey into Self*, 277).

16 Harding, *Journey into Self*, 281.

17 M.L. von Franz, 'The Process of Individuation,' *Man and His Symbols*, 164.

18 Jung to P.W. Martin, 20 August 1937, *Letters* I: 233–5.

19 Jung to K.C. Briggs, 4 July 1931, *Letters* 1: 83–4.

20 Harding, *Journey into Self*, 270.

21 Ibid. 281.

22 C.G. Jung, 'A Study in the Process of Individuation,' *The Archetypes and the Collective Unconscious*, CW 9(i):555:312.

23 Jacobi, *The Psychology of C.G. Jung*, 28.

24 Florence McCulloch, *Mediaeval Latin and French Bestiaries*, University of North Carolina Studies in the Romance Languages and Literatures, 33, rev. ed. (Chapel Hill, NC: The University of North Carolina Press 1962), 142–3.

25 Topsell, *Historie of Four-Footed Beastes* (1607), 442.

26 J.E. Cirlot, *A Dictionary of Symbols*, trans. J. Sage (New York: Philosophical Library 1962), 44.

27 Beryl Rowland, *Animals with Human Faces* (Knoxville, Tennessee: University of Tennessee Press 1973), 125.

28 1 Peter 5:8.

29 Harpur, 'Messiah ... a Woman.'

30 Harding, *Journey into Self*, 52.

31 Ibid. 4.

32 Ibid. 88.

33 The change of name is significant as a characteristic of the twice-born, but the choice of Naegeli for Liesl's original family name is not immediately apparent. There are several famous Naegelis in Swiss history.

34 von Franz, 'The Process of Individuation,' MHS, 211.

35 Joseph Campbell, *The Hero with a Thousand Faces* (Princeton: Princeton University Press, Bollingen paperbacks ed. 1972), 30.

36 Harding, *Journey into Self*, 63.

37 Joseph Campbell, 'Bios and Mythos,' *Psychoanalysis and Culture*, ed. G.B. Wilbur and W. Muensterberger (New York: International Universities Press 1951), 339.

38 Harding, *Journey into Self*, 52.

39 Campbell appears to be using the phrase 'the twice-born' as the translation of the Sanskrit *dvija*. The same phrase, however, also appears in Christian religious thought; it is cited by William James (*Varieties of Religious Experience*,

[London: Longmans, Green 1902], 80) as having first been used by Francis W. Newman in *The Soul: Its Sorrows and Aspirations* (2d ed., 1852). It is not clear whether Davies is alluding to one or the other or to both.

40 Campbell, 'Bios and Mythos,' 340.

41 I have argued for Davies' use of obviously factual archaeological material about the cave-bear cult caves in the Alps in 'Davies and the Drachenloch: a study of the archaeological background of *The Manticore,*' *Studies in Robertson Davies' Deptford Trilogy,* ed. Robert G. Lawrence and Samuel L. Macey, ELS monograph series 20 (Victoria: University of Victoria English Literary Studies 1980), 100–13.

42 Jacobi, *The Psychology of C.G. Jung,* 135.

43 Harding, *Journey into Self,* 277.

44 Martin, *Experiment in Depth,* 24.

45 Harding, *Journey into Self,* 156.

46 Cirlot, *Dictionary of Symbols,* 22, 310–11.

47 CW 9(ii):356:226. Jung implies that it is unlikely to be symbolized anthropomorphically, although von Franz implies in 'The Process of Individuation' (MHS 158–229) that this is quite common.

48 The bear as a symbol of the self also links the two themes of the pink stone in *Fifth Business* and the recurrence of excrement in *The Manticore.* Cirlot points out that, 'In alchemy, the bear corresponds to the *nigredo* of prime matter' (*Dictionary of Symbols,* 22) and according to Jung, 'Excrement in alchemy signifies the *prima materia*' (CW 5 352n). The *prima materia* is also symbolized by the *lapis philosophorum* which, however, is not only the beginning of the process but also the end, 'the prima and ultima materia' (CW 13:421:319). In addition, von Franz points out that 'the Self is symbolized with special frequency in the form of a stone, precious or otherwise' and that 'in many dreams the nuclear center, the Self, also appears as a crystal' ('The Process of Individuation,' MHS 208–9). David abandons his hold on the pink stone which symbolized his father's soul (by handing it over to Ramsay who throws it away), and symbolically produces the prima materia from which he must work his own soul (by defecating in terror at his encounter with the bear-spirit).

49 Jung to Gilbert, 2 January 1929, *Letters* 1: 56–7.

CHAPTER SIX

1 Goethe, *Faust* (Part I), trans. Philip Wayne (Harmondsworth: Penguin 1949), 43.

2 Jung to Gilbert, *Letters* 1: 56–7.

3 P.W. Martin, *Experiment in Depth,* 99.

4 Martin notes, for example, that the sybil represents 'the deep creative purpose of earth and of time' (101), and that 'death-and-rebirth is as naturally the province of the *Magna Mater* as the great work is the province of the Wise Old Man' (*Experiment in Depth*, 102).

5 Martin, *Experiment in Depth*, 100.

6 It is hard not to think that Liesl (or Davies in the persona of Liesl) is being somewhat disingenuous, however, when we are told that, although everybody in the beast-legend is afraid of the wolf, he is 'not such a bad fellow, really' (ww 331). Ysegrim (Isegrim) the wolf is certainly bloodthirsty, but the only apparent reason for his being 'not such a bad fellow' is that he is not very bright: some of his potential victims escape by being cleverer than he is.

7 C.G. Jung, 'Psychotherapists or the Clergy,' *Psychology and Religion: West and East*, CW 11:523:341.

8 Robertson Davies, 'Ham and Tongue,' *One Half of Robertson Davies* (Toronto: Macmillan 1977), 17.

9 On Lord Raglan's scale of 22 points, the gospel narrative of the life of Christ would score at least 18. See Lord Raglan, *The Hero: A Study in Tradition, Myth and Drama* (London: Methuen 1936), 179–80.

10 P.M. Palmer and R.P. More include the whole of the *Ulmer Puppenspiel* as representing the earliest form of the puppet play of Faust. In this, Vizibuzli is the second of the three devils to introduce himself to Faust, saying 'Ich bin ein fliegender Geist and heisze Vizibuzli, der Liebesteufel.' *The Sources of the Faust Tradition: From Simon Magus to Lessing* (New York: Haskell House 1965), 261.

11 Palmer and More, *The Sources of the Faust Tradition*, 5.

12 Emma Jung and Marie-Louise von Franz, *The Grail Legend* (London: Hodder & Stoughton 1971), 355.

13 Davies, *Feast of Stephen*, 11.

14 The composition of the music for *The Golden Asse* illustrates the process: 'Where the music came from, not even Giles' most intimate associates – and this now meant Monica and Domdaniel – could guess, for as the work progressed he had grown increasingly freakish, his moods alternating between one of morose incivility and another of noisy hilarity. There was nothing of the serene wisdom of his music to be discerned in himself' (AMF 316). This clearly parallels Jung's description of the artist in this situation: 'The energy needed for [the growth of an autonomous complex] is naturally drawn from consciousness – unless the latter happens to identify with the complex. But where this does not occur, the drain of energy produces ... an *abaissement du niveau mental.* The intensity of conscious interests and activities gradually diminishes leading either to apathy – a condi-

tion very common with artists – or to a regressive development of the conscious functions, that is, they revert to an infantile and archaic level and
undergo something like a degeneration' (CW 15:123:79).

15 'The mythological hero, setting forth from his commonday hut or castle, is
lured, carried away, or else voluntarily proceeds, to the threshold of adventure. There he encounters a shadow presence that guards the passage.
The hero may defeat or conciliate this power and go alive into the kingdom
of the dark (brother battle, dragon battle; offering, charm), or be slain by
the opposition and descend in death (dismemberment, crucifixion). Beyond
the threshold, then, the hero journeys through a world of unfamiliar yet
strangely intimate forces, some of which severely threaten him (tests), some
of which give magical aid (helpers). When he arrives at the nadir of the
mythological round, he undergoes a supreme ordeal and gains his reward.
The triumph may be represented as the hero's sexual union with the
goddess-mother of the world (sacred marriage), his recognition by the
father-creator (father atonement), his own divinization (apotheosis), or again
– if the powers have remained unfriendly to him – his theft of the boon he
came to gain (bride-theft, fire-theft); intrinsically it is an expansion of
consciousness and therewith of being (illumination, transfiguration, freedom). The final work is that of the return. If the powers have blessed the
hero, he now sets forth under their protection (emissary); if not, he flees
and is pursued (transformation flight, obstacle flight). At the return
threshold the transcendental powers must remain behind; the hero
re-emerges from the kingdom of dread (return, resurrection). The
boon that he brings restores the world (elixir).' Joseph Campbell, *The
Hero with a Thousand Faces* 245–6.

16 For a discussion of this point and of the use of the term 'freak', see Leslie
Fiedler, 'The Fascination of Freaks,' *Psychology Today*, 11:3 (August 1977),
56–9, 80, 82; also Fiedler, *Freaks: Myths and Images of the Secret Self* (New
York: Simon and Schuster 1978).

17 Cameron, *Conversations with Canadian Novelists*, 44.

18 Davies made this claim in the course of a radio discussion on modern
theatre. CBC 'Ideas' (25 February 1977).

19 Campbell, *Hero with a Thousand Faces*, 19.

20 Ibid. 19n.

21 Anne Montagnes, 'Metaphor and Myth: the Deptford Trilogy of Robertson Davies,' *Sat. Night* 90:6 (November 1975), 73.

22 James Neufeld, 'Structural Unity in "The Deptford Trilogy": Robertson
Davies as egoist,' *Journal of Canadian Studies*, 12:1 (February 1977), 70.

23 Cameron, *Conversations with Canadian Novelists*, 38.

24 In describing Sir John Tresize's idea of theatre, Eisengrim talks about ro-

mance as a humanist mode: 'Romance is a mode of feeling that puts enormous
emphasis ... on individual experience. Tragedy puts something above
humanity; so does Comedy; Romance puts humanity first' (ww 194). But this
humanist definition does not preclude the idea that romance is a world of
the spirit — of the human spirit, however, rather than the divine or the
diabolic.

25 Northrop Frye, 'Spengler Revisited,' *Spiritus Mundi*, 191.

26 Oswald Spengler, *Der Untergang des Abendlandes* 2 vols. (1918, 1922), trans.
Charles Francis Atkinson, 2 vols. (New York: Knopf 1926, 1928), 2: 237.
All subsequent page references are to this edition and are given in paren-
theses in the text. Italicized words and phrases in quotations from
Spengler are in all cases italicized in the original text.

27 The concept of the dual universe is demonstrable, for example, in the
Odyssey, and to a very great extent in medieval treatments of the Grail legend.
In contemporary literature, it can be seen in the work of C.S. Lewis; in the
third novel of his science fiction trilogy it is presented as 'the haunting' of
'something we may call Britain ... by something we may call Logres,' the
manifestation in the earthly Britain of its 'heavenly,' Christian, and ideal
counterpart. Lewis also makes the point that 'Those who have forgotten
Logres sink into Britain,' losing their share of the spiritual reality. For
him the concept of the dual universe serves the ends of the Christianity
which he presents in fictional form in the trilogy, and thus it has a universal
application in the spiritual lives of individuals. See C.S. Lewis, *That Hideous Strength* (1946); reprint ed., New York: Macmillan 1968), 369, 372.

28 Cameron, *Conversations with Canadian Novelists*, 37.

29 Neufeld, 'Structural Unity in "The Deptford Trilogy,"' 72.

30 Robertson Davies, 'Phantasmagoria and Dream Grotto,' *One Half of Robertson Davies*, 208.

31 Robertson Davies, 'The Devil's Burning Throne,' *One Half of Robertson
Davies*, 199.

32 Ramsay comments that Lind's 'films possessed a weight of implication – in St
Paul's phrase, "the evidence of things not seen" – that was entirely his
own' (ww 169).

33 Davies, 'Phantasmagoria and Dream Grotto,' 208.

34 Robertson Davies, 'Ham and Tongue,' *One Half of Robertson Davies*, 17. The
single action in question is, of course, the throwing of the snowball with
the stone in it, which triggers the events that shape the lives of Boy Staunton
(who throws it), Ramsay (who successfully dodges it), and Paul Dempster/
Magnus Eisengrim (who is born prematurely because it strikes his mother).

35 Davies, 'Ham and Tongue,' 16.

36 Philip Toynbee, review of *The Wisdom of Words* by Geoffrey Wagner, *The Observer* (1 June 1969).

EPILOGUE

1 Robertson Davies, 'The Conscience of the Writer,' *One Half of Robertson Davies*, 131.
2 Robertson Davies, 'Ham and Tongue,' *One Half of Robertson Davies*, 16.
3 Ibid.

Index

action, unconscious 94, 95, 97, 132–4
active imagination 86, 195 n14
affinity 4, 5–21 passim, 42, 182
alienation 66–7, 71
alter ego 33, 192 n20
ambiguity 159, 160, 161
ambivalence: of archetypes 56; of Davies 20, 33, 105–46 passim, 148, 179; of delusion 77–9; of diary 29; of faith 76; of fantasy 77; of fifth business 99, 100, 104; of reality 74, 82; of Samuel Marchbanks 28, 33, 90; of shadow 39
analytic process (analysis) 40, 115, 117–18, 137; dialectic of 117; hero-journey and 135
analysis. *See* analytic process
anamnesis 118, 121, 127, 135, 145
anima 15, 45, 47, 49–52, 55, 101, 148, 150–1; celestial 59; demonic 56, 59; dream appearance of 50; as eros principle 144; fascination of 56; as guide to unconscious 125; as *ligamentum corporis et spiritus* 125; mother as bearer of 56; numinosity of 128; as projection 51, 52; as soul-image 49–50, 52, 122

animus 15, 56, 67, 68; as soul-image 50, 56; father as bearer of 57; demonic 57, 69, 70; celestial 70
archetypal process 15; individuation as 16; as infrastructure 17, 19; as superstructure 19
archetypes 4, 15; and creative process 16, 189 n37; as disembodied voices 71, 195 n24; as illusions 19; in individuation 44; as infrastructure 17; in psychologem 43; as 'specific illusions' 20; as 'subjectively known forms' 164, 180; as transcendent powers 44, 103; *see also* anima, animus, magus, self, shadow, sybil
art 61, 63, 125, 176
attitudinal habitus 49
autonomous complex 14, 16
axis, ego-self 66–7, 68, 69, 70, 71, 73

Bacon, Friar Roger 110, 112, 155, 198 n3
bear 106, 143–5
bear-cult 141, 200 n40
beauty 13, 47
belief, religious. *See* faith

208 Index

  composition of 112, 198 n5; shadow
  counterpart of 113–14, 115

Cameron, Donald 5, 163, 170
Campbell, Joseph 139, 140, 154, 159,
  203 n15
Case, Virginia 7
celestial (light): anima 57, 59; animus 70; magus 70; self 145
Cirlot, J.E. 132, 144, 201 n47
coincidence v, 138
coincidentia oppositorum 98, 143
common sense 135, 136, 142
conscious, the 111
contrasexual image 72; anima/animus
  as 15
creative process: and archetypes 16;
  as autonomous complex 14, 16;
  Jung's theory of 16; and *telos* 17;
  and unconscious content 37

daimon 156, 157
'dark brother' 41; *see also* shadow
day-dreaming 44, 52
Davies, Robertson: affinity for Jung 4,
  5–21 passim; editor of *Peterborough
  Examiner* 28; enthusiasm for stage
  22; literary editor of *Saturday Night*
  6, 188 n30; as a moralist 184; works:
– 'Cap and Bells' 26–7
– 'Conscience of the Writer, The' 182
– 'Devil's Burning Throne, The'
  173
– *Diary of Samuel Marchbanks, The*
  28, 39
– 'Double Life of Robertson Davies,
  The' 18, 26, 40, 42, 43, 189 n44
– *Eros at Breakfast* 18, 189 n45
– *Feast of Stephen* 61, 156, 194 n18
– *Fifth Business* 19, 41, 44, 73, 74–104,

  105, 106, 110, 115, 145, 147, 153,
  154, 155, 189 n47 n48
– *General Confession* 18, 189 n45
– 'Ham and Tongue' 154, 174, 184
– *Leaven of Malice* 18, 43, 44, 52–9,
  60, 72, 189 n46
– *Manticore, The* 3, 5, 14, 19–20, 41,
  105–46, 147, 148, 153, 154, 164,
  170, 179, 181, 183, 189 n49
– 'Midsummer Night's Dream' 45,
  193 n3
– *Mixture of Frailties, A* 18, 43, 44,
  57, 59–72, 73, 74, 75, 92, 156, 189
  n46, 202 n14
– *One Half of Robertson Davies* 154,
  172, 173, 174, 182, 184
– 'Phantasmagoria and Dream Grotto'
  172, 173
– *Question Time* 18, 189 n45
– reviews in *Saturday Night* 5–13 passim
– *Samuel Marchbanks' Almanack* 29,
  39
– *Shakespeare for Young Players* 22,
  189 n3
– *Shakespeare's Boy Actors* 6, 18, 22–6,
  41, 42, 43, 182, 189 n42
– *Table-Talk of Samuel Marchbanks,
  The* 39
– *Tempest-Tost* 18, 43, 44–52, 55,
  57, 59, 60, 72, 189 n46
– *World of Wonders* 4, 20, 147–81,
  183, 184, 189 n52
deception 63, 166

de Laszlo, Violet 8, 187 n11
delusion 17, 44, 75; ambivalence of
  77–9, dangerous 53; and insanity
  60; irony in 46; in projection 52
demonic (dark): anima 56, 59; animus 68; magus 59; self 134; sybil
  59; unconscious 113

devil 95, 97, 153, 156, 172; Liesl as
90; revised concept of 95
diary 28–9
Domdaniel 70
dominants of the collective unconscious. See archetypes
doppelgänger 33, 192 n20
double 33, 192 n20
dream(s) 86, 118; and myth 164,
183; symbolism in 118
dream interpretation 115, 118–20
duality 43, 72; of demonic and celestial 73; of fact and appearance
72; of good and evil 42, 75, 91, 148;
identity in 104; of life and anti-
life 73; in Magianism 169; of mundane and transcendental 52, 72,
73, 81; of physical and psychic 81;
of true and false identity 72, 73;
of universe 170

Edinger, Edward F. 66–7, 195 n20
ego 18, 67–71; as centre of consciousness 101; and animus 69; and
magus 70; and self 65–7; and
shadow 38, 39, 40, 101
egoism (of artist) 156, 157
ego source 59, 67
elements (of psyche) 19, 41
extraversion/introversion 49
eros 61, 92, 93, 144, 194 n16
evidence 112, 118
evil 42, 75, 91, 148, 163; psychological revision of 97, 174
excrement 143, 201 n47

faith 79; ambivalence of 76, 80; as
apprehension of numinosum 81;
illusion as 19, 75; insanity and 76;
metaphor in 80; psychology of
91
fantasy 17, 44, 45, 75; dramatic

45; harmless 45; as illusion 52; and
insanity 77; interpretative function
of 60; stage magic as 76, 77; in
role-playing 18
fantastic 29, 30
Faust 154, 155, 158, 159
feeling (function-type) 49, 63, 71,
136, 144, 153; association with
music 63
Fiedler, Leslie 160, 203 n16
fifth business 19, 87, 97, 98, 103;
ambivalence of 99, 100, 104; and
cabal 100; interpretation of 99–100
folk-lore 9–10
Fothergill, Jessie 61, 70, 194 n17
freak show 160
Freud, Sigmund 5, 6–7, 7–8, 9, 10,
12, 13, 14
friend, the 123–4
Frey-Rohn, Liliane 3, 186 n1
Frye, Northrop 14, 15, 168, 188 n36
functions, theory of 48–9, 71, 115,
120–1, 136, 153

Ghiselin, Brewster 188 n34
Goethe 10, 147
gold 39, 199 n5
golden head 112
good 92, 93; and evil 42, 75, 91, 148;
psychological revision of 91, 92,
94, 97, 101, 152, 174–5, 184
Grossmith, George 28, 191 n13
Grossmith, Weedon 28, 191 n13

Hall, W.F. 85, 196 n11
Hannah, Barbara 39, 40, 102, 199
n8
Harding, M. Esther 17, 117–18, 120,
121, 122, 123, 135, 136, 139, 140,
144, 199 n8 n14
Harpur, Tom 92, 93, 94, 95, 97, 132
Henderson, Joseph 12, 187 n23

hero, the 135, 147, 158, 164; mono-
  myth of 154; as mythologem 182
hero-journey 137, 138, 145, 159,
  163, 203 n15; and individuation
  136, 148; as mythologem 135
Hesse, Hermann 196 n8
Hochheimer, Wolf 83, 195 n6
Hoffmann, E.T.A. 33, 192 n21
Humphrey, Dr George 5
Huson, Paul 13, 188 n29

id 17, 36
identity 18, 19, 20, 27, 40, 43, 45, 51,
  52, 73, 105; alternative myths of
  20, 145; ambivalence of 33;
  archetypal 19; duality of 65–7;
  good and evil in 42; as illusion 20;
  persona in 26; and role 25; and
  second self 27; shadow in 40;
  synthesis in 41; unity 104
– personal 53–5, 72; analysis of
  53–7, 72–3; distinct from psychic
  53; as illusion 55; and mundane
  72; mythologem of 182; synthesis
  of 73
– psychic 43, 35, 51; analysis of 72–3;
  distinct from personal 53; transcendent 72
illusion 18, 19, 20, 40, 44, 51, 52, 59,
  73, 75; and ambivalence 43; as
  appearance 88; categories of 43–4,
  81; criteria for 43–4; dangerous
  43, 111; as deception 19, 43, 109;
  delusion as 18, 44, 75; and faith
  19; fantasy as 18, 44, 75; identity as
  18; innocent 77; and imagination
  23; insanity as 18, 44, 60, 75; as
  mask 43, 75, 81, 109; as metaphor
  75, 80, 81, 109; as mode of apprehension 80; negative 19, 43;
  as non-congruence 17; paradigm of

43–4, 74, 75, 81, 105, 109; paradox
  in 19, 109; as perception 19, 109;
  positive 19; and psychic identity
  65; psychology as 145; in Salterton
  trilogy 43; shift in concept of 19,
  75; and spirit 20; as superstructure
  17; in theatre and film 20, 162
– art of 149, 167; see also magic, stage
– dramatic 6, 18, 22–6; convention
  of 22
'illusions, specific' 20, 146, 147, 189
  n50
imagination 23, 84, 149
imago Dei 66, 184
individuation 15, 19, 44, 51, 55, 68,
  73, 74, 137, 143, 179, 180; anima
  in 45; animus in 58, as confrontation with transcendental powers
  47; hero journey and 136, 148,
  164; objectification of 165
infinity, the smaller 3, 182, 184
insanity 18, 53, 75, 76, 77
interface: of realities in psyche 72, 82,
  110; wonder as 177–8
inversion 41, 46
irony 46

Jones, Ernest 7, 12, 187 n6
Jacobi, Jolande 13, 15, 22, 26, 36–42
  passim, 48, 49, 82, 83, 85, 98, 116,
  126, 188 n31, 189 n38, 197 n28,
  199 n8
Jaffé, Aniela 186 n2, 199 n8
James, Geoffrey 105, 198 n1
Jocelyn, Gordon 105, 198 n1
Jung, Carl 7, 8, 9, 42; works:
– Aion 15, 38, 41, 42, 56, 95, 130–1,
  194 n15, 197 n30
– Alchemical Studies 201 n47
– 'Analytical Psychology and Educa-
  tion' 116

- 'Answer to Job' 94, 97
- *Archetypes and the Collective Unconscious, The* 99, 124, 125, 197 n29
- *Civilization in Transition* 96, 97
- 'Commentary on "The Secret of the Golden Flower"' 62
- *Collected Works* 3, 9, 185–6
- 'Concerning Mandala Symbolism' 98–9
- *Development of Personality, The* 116
- 'Good and Evil in Analytical Psychology' 96
- *Letters* I 20, 122, 145–6, 188 n23, 189 n50
- *Letters* II 103, 188 n23
- *Man and His Symbols* 119, 164, 201 n47
- *Memories, Dreams, Reflections* 3–4, 18, 50, 93, 94, 104, 116, 130, 137, 143, 182, 183, 188 n34
- *Mysterium Coniunctionis* 112, 199 n5
- 'Nature of the Psyche, On the' 45, 193 n4
- 'Phenomenology of the Spirit in Fairy-Tales, The' 124
- 'Practical Use of Dream Analysis, The' 119
- *Practice of Psychotherapy, The* 199 n9
- 'Psychological Approach to the Dogma of the Trinity, A' 91, 94, 96, 145, 152
- *Psychological Types* 25, 48, 49, 63
- *Psychology and Religion* 20, 36, 38, 42, 86, 91, 94, 95, 96, 97, 98, 111, 113, 114, 122, 145, 147, 152, 175, 183, 189 n51, 195 n24, 195 n1, 196 n12
- 'Psychology and Religion' 20, 36, 38, 42, 86, 94, 95, 97, 111, 113, 122, 147, 183, 195 n24, 196 n12
- 'Psychology of Eastern Meditation, The' 98
- 'Psychology of the Unconscious, On the' 41, 83
- 'Psychotherapists or the Clergy' 152
- 'Relation of Analytical Psychology to Poetry, On the' 11, 13, 14, 16, 187 n21, 202 n14
- 'Relations between the Ego and the Unconscious, The' 25, 26
- 'Role of the Unconscious, The' 97
- 'Seven Sermons to the Dead' 3–4, 182, 188 n34'
- *Spirit in Man, Art, and Literature, The* 11, 13, 14, 16, 187 n21, 202 n14
- 'Study in the Process of Education, A' 125
- *Structure and Dynamics of the Psyche, The* 138, 193 n4
- *Symbols of Transformation* 12, 125, 130, 131, 139, 143, 144, 183, 188 n26, 201 n47
- 'Synchronicity: an Acausal Connecting Principle' 138
- 'Transformation of Libido, The' 12, 188 n26
- 'Transformation Symbolism in the Mass' 114, 175
- *Two Essays on Analytical Psychology* 41, 56, 82
- *Undiscovered Self, The* 8, 14, 187 n10
Jung, Emma 156
Jungianism 3, 4, 147; as myth of human identity 20, 179

Kingston Whig Standard 190 n7
knowledge 89, 147, 181

laugh, Merlin's 156
Lewis, C.S. 199 n7, 204 n27

libido 68, 69, 70, 139, 143, 144
Lichtenberg, Georg Christoph 17, 189 n41
literature 10–12; as map of reality 183–4; as subjectively known form, 183
love 93, 101

McCulloch, Florence 128
McDougall, Curtis 6
McPherson, Hugo 6, 46
Magianism 148, 168–79; as myth of human identity 179; and romance 179
magic 12–13; stage 76, 77, 162–3
magus 15, 67, 101, 122, 125–6, 148, 149–50; celestial 70; demonic 59
mana 56, 70, 149, 150
mandala 97, 99, 103; in literature 99; marriage quaternio as 99; as symbol of totality 98, 99, 145
manticore, the 106, 124, 128–34, 135, 138, 143, 145
Marchbanks, Samuel 22, 26–42, 190 n7; ambivalence of 28, 32, 33; autonomy of 38; and human identity 26; mischief of 34; as satirist 35; as second self 26, 33; as shadow 18, 40
marriage quaternio 99, 197 n30
Martin, P.W. 8, 48, 51, 56, 122, 144, 150–1, 187 n11, 201 n4
marvellous, the 85
mask 22, 43, 75, 81, 103, 109
meaning 105, 109, 112
meaning-picture (Sinnbild) 143
memory 87, 88
Mephistopheles 155
meridian crisis 48, 49
Merlin 154, 155, 156, 159; demonic 156, 158; laugh of 156

metaphor 75, 80, 119
Montagnes, Anne 168, 203 n21
moral criterion 94
moral responsibility 174
moral valuation, differential 94, 95
mundane, the 45, 46, 52, 53, 61, 72, 81, 85
music 63, 65
myth 20, 180, 181; and dream 164, 183; and Jungian psychology 147, 148; as 'peculiarly necessary' 183; as subtext 179, 180; triple 181; as way of knowing 181
mythologem 135, 139, 182
mythos, Jungian theory as 20, 148

Neufeld, James 170
numinosum 79, 92, 93, 113; apprehension of 80, 81
numinous, sense of 136, 142

opposites: energetic potential of 83; fact and illusion as 86, good and evil as 41, 82, 83, 98, 109, 148; light and dark 86; in psyche 19, 41; psychic and physical as 82, 83, 98, 109; and psychic whole 43; relative values of 82; tension of 173; transcendent and mundane 109; truth and falsehood as 82, 83, 87, 88, 98, 109, 148, 176
Otto, Rudolph 79, 195 n1
Overskou, Thomas 98, 197 n24

Palmer, P.M. 155, 202 n10
paradox 19, 33, 41, 105, 148
Paynter, Simon 39, 193 n35
persona
– dramatic 22
– Jungian 18, 22–6, 41, 126–7, 148; fifth business as 103; and identity

26; malfunction of 26; and role 19, 25

Peterborough Examiner 28, 39, 190 n7

pleroma 82, 104, 195 n3

possession, demonic 13

Powys, John Cowper 10

primordial images. *See* archetypes

privatio boni 41

projection 51, 52, 118, 151; as delusion 52; withdrawal of 42, 51

psyche 41, 85; as interface 72, 86, 110

psychic process 110, 111

psychography 86, 88, 105, 195 n3

psychologem 43, 44, 51, 52, 55, 68, 72, 74, 193 n2

psychology 37, 91, 143, 147, 180; and common sense 135; and hero-journey 135; Jungian and Freudian 115–16

psychosis 69, 113

psychosymbolic patterns 74, 82, 83, 97, 183

Radford, F.L. 196 n15

Raglan, Lord 155, 202 n9

Read, Sir Herbert 8, 187 n11

reality 73, 74, 82, 85, 86, 102; ambivalence of 74; dual 86; inner 182–4; nature of 74, 75, 76, 82, 105; subjective and objective 105, 148; unmediated 75; validation of 81; as a variable 81

rites of passage 139

Rogers, Robert 192 n2

role 19; and identity 25; and Jungian persona 19, 25

role-playing 41; in analytic process 117; as defence of identity 60; as

mythologem 182; relation to insanity 60

romance 13–14, 145, 147, 148, 154; and Magianism 179; as myth 179

romance universe 165, 168; congruence of 165, 166, 170; dark and light of 167; as mode of feeling 204; unity of 165, 166, 168

Roper, Gordon 29, 39

Roosevelt, Eleanor 28, 191 n13

Rowland, Beryl 132

self 4, 15, 18, 19, 72, 147, 179; autonomous 74; bear as 145; demonic 132; and ego 65–7; as illusion 20; individuated 44; as mythologem 182; second 26, 27, 29; and unconscious 20; unique 183

– deception 63

– discovery 87

– knowledge 87, 88, 101; illusion in 77; and shadow 41; true 90

– possession 87, 88

– realization 121

– recognition 17, 19

shadow 15, 36, 41, 69, 122–3, 138, 148; ambivalence of 39, 90; autonomy of 38, 96; of brazen head 113–14, 115; as devil within 101; ego and 39, 40, 101, 152–3; energy of 38, 39; gold in 39; hostility to ego 95, 102, 152; in human identity 40; as moral problem 41, 95; projection of 37, 42; raising to consciousness of 38; resolution of 40; Samuel Marchbanks as 18, 36–7; as unexamined side of life 45; as wolf-brother 152

Singer, June 82, 195 n3

soul: Magian 182; perils of 113

spagiric 83, 195 n6
Spengler, Oswald 20, 148, 168–79
  passim
subtext 179
sybil 15, 67, 68, 122, 148, 150;
  demonic 59, 67
symbol 111; *coincidentia oppositorum*
  143; meaning-picture 143
synchronicity 138
synthesis 41; of ego and contrasexual element 72; in psyche 41, 43;
  of self 73; of spagiric whole 83; of
  transcendent and mundane 72, 86

telos 17
thanatos 61, 92
theatre 162
thinking (function-type) 48, 153
Topsell, Edward 129
Toynbee, Philip 181
transcendent 12, 19, 44; powers
  47, 84; and transcendence 12, 187
  n23; reality 45, 47, 52, 61, 64,
  65, 70, 72, 81, 84; world 53, 62

truth 88, 104; literal and psychological 80, 81; and meaning 105,
  109, 112; objective 177; poetic 11;
  variable 176
twice-born, the 58, 90, 140, 145, 200
  n38
Tymms, Ralph 192 n2

unconscious, the 37, 66, 86, 98, 101;
  demonic 113; hinterland of 183;
  'illimitable ... addition to personality'
  147; relation to conscious mind
  111

Vaillant, C.G. 196 n15
van Gogh, Lucy 40
von Franz, Marie-Louise 121, 138,
  199 n8, 201 n47

White, Patrick 99, 198 n31
wisdom 93, 102, 158
wolf: artist as 157–9, 175; shadow as
  152, 159
wonder 177